Designing for Newspapers and Magazines

SECOND EDITION

Chris Frost

LONDON AND NEW YORK

First published 2003
by Routledge

This edition published 2012
by Routledge
2 Park Square, Milton Park, Abingdon, Oxon OX14 4RN

Simultaneously published in the USA and Canada
by Routledge
711 Third Avenue, New York, NY 10017

Routledge is an imprint of the Taylor & Francis Group, an informa business

British Library Cataloguing in Publication Data
A catalogue record for this book is available from the British Library

Library of Congress Cataloging-in-Publication Data
Frost, Chris, 1950–
Designing for newspapers and magazines / Chris Frost. – 2nd ed.
p. cm. – (Media skills)
Includes bibliographical references and index.
1. Newspaper layout and typography. 2. Magazine design. 3. Newspaper publishing.
4. Periodicals–Publishing. I. Title.
Z253.3,F76 2012
686.2'252–dc23
2011019837

ISBN: 978–0–415–66653–4 (hbk)
ISBN: 978–0–415–66654–1 (pbk)
ISBN: 978–0–203–18108–9 (ebk)

Typeset in Goudy
by Keystroke, Station Road, Codsall, Wolverhampton

MIX
Paper from responsible sources
FSC
www.fsc.org
FSC® C004839

Printed and bound in Great Britain by the MPG Books Group

Designing for Newspapers and Magazines

A hugely beneficial introduction to students and professionals in print media and design, *Designing for Newspapers and Magazines* offers guidance on how to produce attractive publications and how to tailor them to their target audience using colour, text placement, typography and images.

Written by an experienced journalist and designer, the book details the elements of good design and provides instruction on how to get the most out of computers and computer-aided design.

The book examines a broad range of local and national publications, including the *Sun*, the *Daily Mail* and women's magazines, and explains the reasoning that underpins their design choices, including:

- how to set up a new publication
- planning an edition of a newspaper or magazine
- typography and working with text
- working with images and technical production
- designing pages and how to use colour
- design and journalism ethics
- a glossary of journalistic and design terms.

Frost shows here how a well-designed publication can be a powerful platform for good journalism. This text will be invaluable in the study of design and print media.

Chris Frost is head of journalism at Liverpool John Moores University. He has worked in journalism for 40 years as a reporter, sub-editor and editor. He is the author of *Media Ethics and Self-Regulation* and *Reporting for Journalists*.

Media Skills

EDITED BY: RICHARD KEEBLE, LINCOLN UNIVERSITY

The *Media Skills* series provides a concise and thorough introduction to a rapidly changing media landscape. Each book is written by media and journalism lecturers or experienced professionals and is a key resource for a particular industry. Offering helpful advice and information and using practical examples from print, broadcast and digital media, as well as discussing ethical and regulatory issues, *Media Skills* books are essential guides for students and media professionals.

English for Journalists, 3rd edition
Wynford Hicks

Writing for Journalists, 2nd edition
Wynford Hicks with Sally Adams, Harriett Gilbert and Tim Holmes

Ethics for Journalists, 2nd edition
Richard Keeble

Interviewing for Journalists, 2nd edition
Sally Adams, with Wynford Hicks

Researching for Television and Radio
Adèle Emm

Reporting for Journalists, 2nd edition
Chris Frost

Subediting for Journalists
Wynford Hicks and Tim Holmes

Writing for Broadcast Journalists, 2nd edition
Rick Thompson

Freelancing for Television and Radio
Leslie Mitchell

Programme Making for Radio
Jim Beaman

Magazine Production
Jason Whittaker

Production Management for Television
Leslie Mitchell

Feature Writing for Journalists
Sharon Wheeler

Interviewing for Radio, 2nd edition
Jim Beaman

Designing for Newspapers and Magazines, 2nd edition
Chris Frost

This book is dedicated to my family. Thanks to them for allowing me to use their pictures in various illustrations.

Contents

	List of figures	ix
1	Introduction	1
2	The history and function of design	5
3	Publication style	12
4	Production processes	23
5	Pre-planning and copy tasting	44
6	Designing pages	53
7	Master pages, templates and style sheets	79
8	Typography	83
9	Words in type	106
10	Using pictures	118
11	Using colour	137
12	Publishing ethics	145
13	Design masterclass	160
	Glossary	178
	Bibliography	185
	Index	187

Figures

5.1	A dummy	45
5.2	A contents listing	46
5.3	A flat plan	47
6.1	A visual	56
6.2	A grid draft for a tabloid page	57
6.3	A page draft	59
6.4	An example draft first story	63
6.5	A draft lead	65
6.6	A draft final	67
6.7	A feature page	69
6.8	A strapline	73
6.9	A double-column intro	75
6.10	Double-column intro with secondary heading	75
6.11	A triple-column intro with standfirst	75
7.1	Style sheets	82
8.1	A font comparison	84
8.2	Paper colour is as important as ink	86
8.3	Metal type	87
8.4	Type and its parts	88
8.5	The variety of type size	89
8.6	Leading considered as a reporter's notebook	91
8.7	Leading can have a dramatic effect	93
8.8	Font styles	95
8.9	Using different fonts	97
8.10	Capitals versus lower-case letters	98
8.11	Different ways of ranging text	99
8.12	Different ways of breaking a long run of type	103
9.1	A cliché-headline generator	109
9.2	Headlines	111
9.3	Standfirsts	114

9.4 Byline styles 115
9.5 Caption styles 117
10.1 a Changing a picture's shape (i) 123
10.1 b Changing a picture's shape (ii) 124
10.2 Cropping 126
10.3 Editing pictures 127
10.4 Cutting away background in a picture 128
10.5 Using a sports picture 129
10.6 Scaling a picture 132
10.7 Using different filters 134
10.8 A graphic using photographs to add information 135
10.9 A picture graphic 136
12.1 Editing a picture can alter its meaning 151
12.2 Ethics of altering a picture 151
12.3 A picture pixellated to hide identity 153
13.1 A tabloid front page: *Daily Mail*, 11 October 2002 161
13.2 A tabloid news page: the *Sun*, 26 April 2011 164
13.3 A fashion page in a women's magazine: *Glamour*, October 2002 166
13.4 A tabloid local newspaper page: the *Gazette* (Blackpool), 2 April 2011 168
13.5 A feature spread in a women's magazine: *Woman & Home*, April 2011 170
13.6 A tabloid picture page: *Daily Mirror*, 11 October 2002 172
13.7 A magazine news page: *Computer Shopper*, November 2002 174
13.8 A large-circulation male-interest magazine: *Stuff*, March 2011 176

1
Introduction

Newspapers and magazines are a potent mix of text and image designed to grab the reader's attention and hold it, making the experience of reading the news easy and enjoyable and, more importantly for some, tempting readers to carry on shelling out a reasonable amount of precious cash to pay for it.

A magazine front cover or a newspaper front page is there solely to invite the reader to buy, to tempt him or her into picking up the publication and becoming engrossed in its content. The aim of the inside is to continue that experience by offering information, education and entertainment.

The aim of this book is to look at how this is done, both from the point of view of the student who seeks to know about publications and their ability to hold onto readership day after day, and from that of the student or practitioner who wants to become a newspaper or magazine editor or designer and needs to know how this ambition is to be achieved.

Designing publications is part craft and part art. The craft of producing good publications that will attract readers can be taught, but it has to be said that, as with many other things, talent is important and either one has the talent to produce good publication design or one hasn't. However, with or without talent, anyone can learn how to put together a sound and attractive publication with a bit of effort and practice. Average weekly papers, and particularly small newsletters and specialist publications, are often at the very basic end of the design spectrum. There is usually only a small staff and these are often writers rather than designers.

Putting a publication together is a delicate process. It is not possible to lay down fixed rules: first do this, then that. The good designer knows what is right and what is wrong, but often finds it very difficult to explain why this is the case.

Publication design involves a number of differing elements: headlines, body text, pictures, graphics, typefaces, white space and the technical limitations of the production process must all be thought about while following a publication's style and the fashion of the time – for the final element of any design is fashion. It is important to try new things, to keep a design fresh, but not so new that the publication appears too bizarre, repulsing potential readers. Too traditional and the publication will appear old-fashioned, but too new and it will appear quirky and unappealing to many readers.

Because explaining design is difficult, this book tends to aim at technique. I start the next chapter by looking at the function of design and how it can help sell the publication and help the reader use the product.

Chapter 3 looks at publication style. All publications are designed to follow a certain style to help build identity. A number of decisions are taken when a publication is first set up so that it has a particular look that will be easy to recognise, giving the publication a character all of its own. This also applies to specialist sections within a newspaper or magazine. The weekend leisure pull-out or a spring wedding special, for instance, might have very different styles as compared with the rest of the publication. This chapter examines these style choices and discusses the process and the likely decisions made.

Chapter 4 looks at the production process: printing. Printing has been with us for more than 500 years, but it has limitations. There are things we can't do with printing, and designers need to be aware of what these are. These limitations involve things such as the size of publication, the frequency of publication and the speed at which we can publish. The Internet, for instance (in theory at least), allows us to produce thousands of pages and publish them instantly, updating them as often as we like. Moreover, the publication can be of any size. This is not an opportunity we have with printed material, but there are other advantages: newspapers and magazines are still the easiest media to access on the train or bus. If the good designer is aware of the printing process and how it works, a better-quality product can be achieved.

Chapter 5 looks at the pre-planning process a designer needs to go through in order to set up an *edition* of a publication. How many pages will be needed, what will go on those pages and how are those decisions made?

Once the edition is planned, then the designer can look at individual pages and how they are best presented to give the reader the best experience. Designing pages involves making life easier for the reader, allowing him or her to find all the material on the page easily, making the task of reading the material as easy and as enjoyable as possible. A light entertainment, coffee-break magazine should have easy-to-read pages with small snippets of information, easily tracked so that the reader feels he or she has had an entertaining experience. A serious broadsheet should also make it easy for the reader to find and read a serious column on, say, the financial plight of Aids victims in Uganda, but this time there should be plenty of solid information presented in a way that minimises the difficulty of the task of reading thousands of heart-rending words.

After looking at structuring individual pages, in Chapter 7 I turn to discussing templates and style sheets. Most computer systems these days try to ease the designer's task by allowing the development of templates, which produce standardised pages and style sheets that pre-select the shapes, fonts and sizes required for that publication. These can make life a lot easier and so you should be aware of the part they can play in production. Some publications have so taken to templates that there is little real design to be done.

Typography is the subject of Chapter 8. Type is the primary tool of a publication designer. What font you use, how it looks and how you use it will radically alter the look of a publication and will also vary the reader's experience. Choose the right font and the right size and the reading experience is effortless; make a bad choice and readers may well give up without even realising why they found it such a strain.

After we have looked at type in Chapter 8, Chapter 9 discusses it as a display device, showing how we can use type as part of the design to draw readers into the page and keep them there.

The other vital element in any publication is the images, whether these are photographs or graphics, or a mixture of the two. Pictures are a vital ingredient in telling any story and also help to form the style of a publication, whether they are the page three girls of the *Sun*, the more serious-minded photographs of the *Guardian* or the traditionally posed interiors of *Hello!* Chapter 10 looks at choosing pictures, at how you should crop them to suit the purpose for which they were chosen and how to go about scaling them to fit into the space available.

Colour has become very important to all publications over the past 30 years and is discussed in Chapter 11. Magazines have been using full colour for nearly 40 years, but newspapers have only really been using extensive colour since the late 1980s, following its introduction onto Fleet Street with the now defunct *Today*. Although at the time, some of the more traditional papers resisted introducing colour onto their pages, there is now hardly a newspaper in the land that does not use some colour, and using it to maximum advantage has become an important element of design.

Chapter 12 looks at some of the ethical dilemmas of publishing and concentrates very specifically on the ethical dilemmas of design and editing, ignoring the more general ethical difficulties of journalism such as truth-telling, invading personal privacy and protecting people's reputations. As well as discussing copyright, it also looks at the issues of taste and decency. How far can a publication go in producing material that might offend a reader? Is it legitimate to publish photographs of dead bodies or nudes, for instance?

Chapter 13 attempts to address the deficiency of the previous chapters, which have all been largely about technique. This chapter analyses pages from newspapers and magazines to see how designers have tackled particular problems and found solutions or produced particularly attractive designs. It is an attempt at a master class where you will be invited to study the pages outlined in detail and be guided through what has been done to make those pages a success. Please try to examine these examples, as well as pages in every newspaper and magazine you come across from now on, in order to see how good design is both unobtrusive but vital in giving the reader an entertaining and effortless reading experience. Some of the limits of publishing that I have spoken of apply to this book, and I'm afraid we were unable to use colour. This is a limitation when considering the design examples in this chapter. I have attempted to overcome these by loading colour images of these pages onto a companion website, www.chrisfrost.me.uk

At the end of the book you will find a glossary of technical terms, and when a term in the glossary is used in the book, it will appear in italics to remind you that its meaning is explained in the glossary. There is also a bibliography which contains additional reading, together with one or two websites that are particularly useful.

2
The history and function of design

Before considering how to do something, it is always worth thinking about why we do it. In this case, before deciding what makes a good design and how to go about achieving it, it is well worth considering why we spend the time, effort and expense required to produce good design.

The purpose of good design

Newspapers and magazines are carefully designed in order to present the journalism they contain in the clearest and most attractive way to the reader; the purpose of good design is to sell the journalism to the reader and make the act of consuming it as easy as possible.

Good design, whether for newspapers, cars or electric toasters, makes the product as easy to use as possible. A toaster might look very sleek, modern and easy to clean if it had the slots for the bread placed underneath, but having to juggle with a hot toaster in order to get the toast out would not make the design attractive to its users. I bought a new kettle recently, but although the model we favoured was by far the best-looking, it did not have a measure to show the amount of water it contained. Consequently, we would have had to remove the lid and look inside before each use – a serious waste of time – and so the kettle was discarded as being too much like hard work.

Similarly, we might be smitten by the look of a 1950s chrome-plated classic car, but we would be unlikely to exchange it for our reliable, comfortable, easy-to-run modern hatchback, at least on a day-to-day basis. Good design can include looking attractive and fashionable, but it must also mean convenient, easy to understand and helpful to the user. In addition, all newspapers and magazines have to sell themselves; the majority of sales are made on the news-stands, where the competition is fierce, with row upon row of publications. Your publication needs to be able grab the attention of your target readers and make them realise they cannot possibly afford to ignore this issue.

Newspaper design history

Newspapers and magazine design, like most things, is heavily affected by the available technology. Electrical goods of the 1930s and 1940s were angular in design because their cases had to be made of wood. Modern electrical goods, moulded from plastic, can be almost any shape the designer requires, and so the shapes are often much rounder, with a lot of detail. That said, of course, provided the container is essentially box-shaped to hold the parts and prevent users from touching dangerous electrical terminals, it can be any shape, and nowadays many designers have gone 'retro', copying the squarer shapes of earlier years and using wood or metal rather than plastic. Fashion also has a very definite part to play in design. In addition, the designer needs to take into consideration that the item will be stored somewhere, and so, for instance, a flat base may be essential to prevent the item rolling off tables or shelves.

Newspapers have been around since the early days of printing. A hundred years ago, copy used to be run in single columns until the story ended. Another would then follow on immediately. Single-column headings would run in *decks*, the only indication of the strength of the story being the number of decks. The headlines were usually straightforward:

THE WAR IN THE CRIMEA

Troops advance

A dispatch from our correspondent

The technology at this stage made it difficult to produce a more sophisticated design, nor was there a need to. The people reading newspapers were from the middle classes and were anxious for news of domestic and world affairs. There was little need to entice them to buy a paper. In any case, before the invention of radio there was very little to entertain a person at home once the domestic duties had been completed. Some people played musical instruments; others read. Newspapers were a cheap and convenient method of providing information and entertainment.

The First World War saw increased competition and the move into more elaborate display with the introduction of regular multi-column headings and banners in the *Express*. Most newspapers followed suit and started to use double-column headings, at least occasionally. Lower case was sometimes used but type sizes were still small in comparison with today, rarely larger than 36pt (Hutt 1967: 36). Newspapers also standardised on seven columns with measures of 14 or 13½ ems (an em is a standard measure of width, with 6 ems to the inch; see Chapter 8 for a more detailed explanation).

The transfer of the printing and publishing of the *Daily Herald* to Odhams was accomplished in 1929 after much soul-searching by its owner, the Trades Union Congress, and the subsequent publication of the Odhams *Herald* in March 1930 was 'a technical sensation' (Hutt 1967: 38). At last a newspaper had been produced that was designed with strong headlines, clear shapes and a bold outlook. Still very much a paper of its time as viewed from today, for the period it was a revelation.

In 1933, Arthur Christiansen was appointed editor of the *Express*. Christiansen is seen by many observers as the most influential Fleet Street editor of all time and is certainly the most important in terms of design. Christiansen's choice of type and his move to more modern styles of headline writing turned the *Express* into the biggest-selling daily paper of its time. In 1934, Harry G. Bartholomew turned the *Mirror* and the *Sunday Pictorial* into tabloids with big, bold sans serif headings and large (for the time) picture spreads. The *Mirror*'s circulation rocketed, overtaking that of the *Express*, turning it into Britain's biggest selling daily newspaper – a position it held well into the 1980s, when it was overtaken by the *Sun*. The *Mirror* averaged sales of between 4.5 and 5.2 million throughout the 1950s and 1960s (Smith 1974: 97). This early *Mirror* was produced with four 15-em columns and it was not until the Second World War that the paper took up the seven 9-em columns that were the norm until very recently.

The *Daily Mail* was the next paper to radically change the way papers were designed. Editor Mike Randall and his production editor Leslie Sellers took a new approach in the mid-1960s, with Randall seeking to free the *Mail* from the 'old restrictive orthodoxy', while Sellers introduced a streamlined new style with lower-case centralised splashes and new, easier-to-read typefaces: Century Schoolbook for headings and Jubilee for the body text. At this stage the *Mail* was still a *broadsheet*, but had a style that is still apparent in many a broadsheet provincial daily. Sellers may not have invented modern sub-editing, but he was certainly one of its biggest publicists, and his two books on sub-editing (see the bibliography) are still must-reads for all would-be sub-editors.

The next major change was technologically driven. Starting in the provinces in the 1970s, newspapers slowly moved over to *web-offset* production. This greatly improved the reproduction of photographs and type, and newspapers were able to use much bigger pictures and display headings. The move to computer setting freed these papers from the fixed column and they gradually started to make their columns wider and use more *bastard setting*. Magazines had been using web-offset for some time, mainly to allow them to introduce more colour. They also moved over to computer setting faster than newspapers.

'Single-keystroke' computer setting was a late introduction to the British publishing scene, but once introduced it quickly took over. Single-keystroke setting, often called direct input, meant that reporters could type their stories directly into the computer and sub-editors would then edit them on-screen. Under the traditional system, reporters had to type their stories on typewriters. The sub-editors then edited this 'hard copy' on paper before sending it to the composing room to be set by the compositors. Proofreaders then checked the copy against the edited original to remove errors inadvertently inserted into the text by the setters. The sub-editors then rechecked the work as it was placed onto pages on the *stone*.

Resistance to single keying came from the main printing union, the National Graphical Association (NGA) – the forerunner of today's Unite union – which feared that many of its compositor members would lose their livelihoods. It was the job of NGA members to re-enter material typed by members of the National Union of Journalists (NUJ) into the computer. The NGA had considerable power in the publishing industry because it operated closed shops and was not afraid to pull its members out on strike, preventing the publication in question from being printed. Because the NGA failed to reach agreement with publishers over the introduction of single keying, direct setting was not introduced into Britain until more than ten years after it came into use in the United States.

Eventually an agreement was reached between the NUJ (whose members would type and edit their stories directly into the new computer setting systems) and the NGA in 1986. Their 'direct entry' agreement allowed for the retraining of displaced NGA members as journalists in return for journalists being able to enter their stories directly into the computer system. The unions were then able to negotiate new technology agreements with the newspaper owners, and computers were introduced. Within five years of the direct entry agreement, you would have been hard pressed to find a magazine or newspaper that was not directly set on computer.

This combination of direct setting and web-offset printing was soon followed by computer systems capable of making up pages on-screen, so that all the setting and design work could be done on-screen, with the plates for the press being produced directly from a plate-making machine attached to the computer. Today, even photographs are now digitally produced, allowing them to be sent over telephone networks and inserted directly onto computer-set pages.

This new direct-set technology allowed for considerable freedom of design as editors no longer had to work within the old restraints of the *hot-metal setting* machines (Linotypes) and the rigid columns they required. This new freedom was developed by the introduction of colour presses in the late 1980s. Driven by advertisers' demands, magazines had been printing in full colour since the mid-1970s. But the extra time the process involved meant that newspapers had not done more than use *spot colour*.

The newest presses allowed the use of full colour on several of the pages in the modern newspaper, including the front and back pages. This allowed newspapers to add colour to their designs, and the newspaper as we know it today started to roll off the press. Although many of the daily papers resisted its introduction, feeling that it would add nothing and indeed, in the case of some of the more serious broadsheets, would trivialise what they were offering, all national newspapers and most provincial ones were printing in full colour, on some pages at least, by the mid-1990s.

The importance of brand

The look, size and shape of a publication have an important impact on the way it is viewed by the reader. In an age when brand is all-important and designer labels determine which consumer items we buy, how the publication is marketed and its design are important considerations. The *Daily Star* is aimed at a youthful male market while the *Daily Mail* seeks a more sober, aspiring female audience: middle-class, middle-aged and middle England; *Cosmopolitan* is after a younger, less traditional but still female audience; while the *Oldie* aims for those seeking to relax in their autumn years. It doesn't take more than a quick scan of a newspaper or magazine to spot the audience it is seeking by considering the type of stories it is using, how it displays them and who advertises alongside them.

This brand image is as important for a publication as it is for any other product in today's retail-dominated lifestyle. In an age where many people describe their favourite leisure-time activity as shopping, publications need to be one of the things for which people shop.

The first job of any new production editor is to reconsider the publication's target audience and to assess whether its audience identifies with the brand presented.

Designers and subs

Newspaper and magazine designers come from several different sorts of backgrounds. Generally, provincial newspaper designers are journalists. They are sub-editors with sufficient seniority and experience to design and manage individual pages, while the chief sub-editor or production editor will design and manage the edition as a whole. In magazines and national newspapers, journalists control what goes onto each page and manage the entire edition, but it is often a graphic designer who will actually design the page and put it together on-screen. Magazine pages usually have more complex designs than newspaper pages and integrate graphics, photographs and text more closely. Although newspapers often have quite sophisticated designs in supplements and feature pages, the news pages are simpler, more modular and more likely to be produced to a standardised template. This is because speed is the most important factor for news pages, and the opportunities for sophisticated design are limited, while the journalistic decision-making is paramount.

In any publication the production team is led by the production editor or chief sub-editor. This executive answers directly to the editor for the way the publication looks. The editor, news editor, chief photographer and chief sub-editor meet regularly, every day on a daily newspaper, to discuss what is to go in the publication and how it should look. This gives the chief sub the chance to discuss with the other executives what stories are being considered, how significant they are for the target audience, how much copy there is likely to be and whether there are suitable pictures.

For instance, a newspaper news conference might hear that there has been a big house blaze overnight. The news editor would inform the conference that a reporter is writing up a basic report on the fire and the two dead and three injured involved. Other reporters have been instructed to:

- get a condition report on the family who lived in the house;
- track down relatives of the family for information about them and to get pictures;
- talk to neighbours to find out in detail what happened.

The chief photographer will report on the pictures obtained at the scene and any other photographs available. There might be a picture of one of the family members concerned in the newspaper's library, for instance.

The editor might then decide to make the story the front page splash, with further reports and pictures going inside the paper. It will then be the chief sub's job to ensure that those pages contain the appropriate copy and pictures.

The editor might also decide to instruct the features editor to assign a reporter to find out more for the next day's edition as there have been several fires in that area in the past few months, with one previous death. Is it coincidence or is something else going on?

In smaller weekly papers or magazines, the team might be smaller, with one person doing several of the jobs outlined above, but the basic process would be the same. Even on a magazine so small that there is only an editor, that person will need to go through the same process of considering what is available, what more is needed and how everything can be put together to make a suitable experience for the reader.

For a large magazine, however, it would be the art editor and his or her team who would be responsible for designing the pages, drawing together the text, pictures and graphics into an attractive package.

3
Publication style

When a publication is first set up, a lot of design decisions need to be made that will set the style for the publication. Once a publication is up and running, it is important that it continues to present a familiar face to its audience and that it has a clear identity that will suit its target audience. Readers should be able to recognise a publication on the news-stands easily and identify with it.

There is often an aspirational nature to a publication's style. People don't read *Vogue* because they are cool, hip, trendsetting style-leaders, but because they would like to be thought of or feel they could become cool, hip, trendsetting style-leaders who mix easily with the stars at fashionable parties. If they feel they are (or want to be) young, cool, hip and up with the latest fashions, then that is the image the publication should present. If, by contrast, the target audience of a publication includes people who are comfortable with their lives, who like things to stay the same and are conservative, at least by nature if not politics, then again this is what the publication should reflect. The modern publication needs to be up-to-the-minute while still maintaining an identifiable style. The traditional publication needs to appear unchanging and classic, without being boring and dull; even those who want to relax in comfort with their slippers on want to read something that will interest them!

The trick is done by thinking carefully about how the publication will look from issue to issue and how the design will allow the publication to have a distinctive identity without always appearing the same. It's a trick all successful publications achieve. The *Daily Mail* is good at it; get hold of a couple of copies produced several weeks apart and see how there is a clear identity that a reader can easily spot on the news-stand, without each issue appearing to be an identikit of the other. *Daily Mail* readers tend to be traditionalists, likely to be establishment oriented, royalist, middle-class, middle England. They are more likely to be female, middle-aged and family oriented. See Figure 13.1, which shows a *Daily Mail* front page with its traditional style of headline font, bold use of pictures and a clear modular structure.

Although this book is aimed at journalists working on established newspapers and magazines, where the house style will already have been decided, you may well be called upon to start a new publication, perhaps for a company that wants to circulate an internal newsletter among its staff, or a highly specialised newsletter for a society or business. I have tried to bear that in mind while writing this chapter.

Target audience

The first consideration when designing any publication is the audience at which it is aimed. The whole style of the publication will vary depending on who is to read it and why.

A consumer magazine aimed at entertaining young women with fashion, celebrity gossip and beauty tips while they relax will be entirely different from a business-to-business magazine aiming to provide detailed product information on office machines to a busy purchasing officer in a large company.

You need to think carefully about the target audience and its needs. There is often a temptation to say that one is producing a publication that will be read by everybody, but this is never true. There will always be a target audience. This could be based on geography, demographics, interest, work, school or college. Even a local weekly newspaper that is aimed at the whole community is only bought by a certain sector, or at least a certain sector for certain purposes. There is not enough space here for an in-depth discussion of who buys and reads newspapers, but a quick look at the local newspaper will show up certain distinct markets. Readers buy the newspaper because they:

- are interested in the local community (including looking at births, marriages and deaths);
- are looking for a new job;
- want to buy a house or a car;
- follow local sport;
- are looking for rented accommodation or have some other interest in the small ads;
- want to know about local events, news and 'what's on';
- want to keep up with local gossip;
- had their attention caught by an interesting-looking local story on the front page;
- find the paper an interesting read that helps them to relax at home.

Although each of these groups will buy the newspaper, not all of them are likely to be affected by the design. Those seeking jobs, cars, houses, and so on are likely to buy the paper regardless of design, although specialist inserts on cars, property or jobs are now pretty standard for most local papers as they try to maximise their income from the advertising that supports these inserts. Those readers with a serious interest in their local community probably have the paper on order at their local newsagent and would only cancel the paper if the standard had become atrocious, and maybe not even then.

The only groups likely to base their decision to buy on the design of the paper are those in the last two categories listed above. However, those who buy for the ads are likely to stop buying once their demands have been met, and again good design and an interesting read may mean they will stick with the paper. So, the design does not need to aim at everybody, only those likely to buy the paper on impulse from a newsagent, news-stand or those latest and most important news sellers, the local fuel filling station or supermarket.

Usage

Another consideration to bear in mind when designing a publication from scratch is what will happen to the publication once the reader has bought it. The reader will take it from the shelf (or the letterbox if it's a subscription) and flick through it. What happens then?

We need to consider how the reader will read the publication, when they will read it and what they will do with it once they've finished reading it.

How the reader will read the publication depends on what it is. A newspaper is read fairly soon after it is bought. You don't buy a newspaper to read a week later (although you might keep the occasional article or supplement in order to read later or to show to someone else). Newspapers, whether bought at a shop or delivered, are read while commuting, on a break from work, or at home in the evening, often while watching television. Once they are read, they might be passed on to someone else or they are thrown in the bin to be recycled as packaging or kitty litter.

They therefore need to be cheap and easy to recycle (so that throwing them away is acceptable), and they do not need to be stored. Storing large-sized publications such as newspapers is not as easy as storing small-sized ones (A5). However, larger sizes (A2 or A3) do not require sophisticated (and expensive) binding.

Tabloids are generally preferred by readers because they do not require the arm stretch of a gorilla to read them. While this is not the main reason that tabloids are more popular, it is certainly one of them. However, since tabloids limit how much can be written on one story and since requiring readers to turn pages to follow stories is a bad idea, those papers that carry more in-depth journalism prefer a *broadsheet* format, or at least a larger page format.

Since even tabloid-sized newspapers are fairly large in area, we have to understand that storage of such newspapers is not easy, which is one reason why libraries go to the trouble and expense of putting them on microfilm.

Newspapers are cheap because of the production methods they are able to use. Relatively cheap newsprint (i.e. paper) is used and it is printed on in a way that limits expensive technical processes. If newspapers had to be trimmed more carefully, cut, folded and bound, they would be much more expensive and would probably not be economically viable.

Consumer and business magazines, on the other hand, are very different. The typical monthly magazine is designed to be kept for at least a month. It is not expected that you would read it in an hour or so and then get rid of it. It is designed to be read over several sessions. This means that you will need to store the magazine somewhere – on a coffee table, in a magazine rack or down the side of the sofa. Either way, the publication needs to be more robust than a newspaper. The paper needs to be more robust and better able to stand up to a lot of handling. There might be a light card cover to help stiffen and protect the contents. Better-quality bonded paper means the quality of printing can be much higher than that of newspapers, allowing for better presentation of pictures. Magazines are usually fully printed in colour, which requires a very white paper for maximum effectiveness. They also need to be relatively easy to store, while still being as cheap as possible. This means that a much thicker, higher quality of white paper is used that is bonded (laminated with a plastic) to keep the ink in place and to repel sticky fingers, coffee and other accidents of everyday life. Magazines are normally of A4 size, because this balances the cost of dealing with a large number of pages with ease of storage. However, a number of magazines now publish in smaller sizes, closer to A5. This allows them to fit more easily into bookshelves, handbags or pockets. It is interesting to note this new storage imperative started with women's magazines to allow for storage in a handbag, but was quickly followed by some of the men's magazines, although in this case one presumes that handbag storage is not the main reason. Many of these magazines still publish additionally in A4 format, allowing readers to choose the format they prefer. Although fashion and gossip magazines are likely to be recycled within a few days, the point about some consumer magazines is that the reader may want to keep them – often for years. Keen hobbyists will find there are several magazines to support them these days, whether they are keen on collecting teddy bears, fishing or surfing the Internet. All carry reviews and how-to-do-it-style articles, and the hobbyist may well want to keep these on his or her shelf. An A4 or A5 sort of size is ideal for this kind of storage. Of course, book publishers tend to stick with a size near to A5 because bookshelves, whether in a library or at home, are designed for that sort of size. Book-size publications are easy to handle and to store. Books stand upright easily without collapsing under their own weight and they are easy to carry about. Occasionally a book is published that is larger than A4 size, but this is fairly rare and is usually limited to books containing pictures that need to be of a certain size.

Ultimately it is always budget that limits the main features of a publication. Additional money is spent on higher quality for magazines only because publishers know that without it the magazine would not sell well. A publication's design always needs to consider the budget and whether the spending can be justified by the potential sales.

Colour

One of the first things to affect budget is colour. Printing in a single colour is always cheapest. Usually black ink on white paper is used, although that isn't necessarily the case. Ink comes in a huge range of shades. Paper similarly comes in a number of shades. However, white paper and black ink are by far the cheapest and are certainly the easiest to read. If cost transcends any other consideration, then print black on white.

If the budget is tight but not that tight, then it is worth considering coloured paper or coloured ink. Usually this is best considered if you wish to use two colours of ink (*spot colour*). This will allow you to print the main text in black but put the occasional headline, caption or other piece of text in a different colour. This is relatively cheap, much cheaper than *process colour* (full photographic-style representative colour). Once you go past two colours of ink, however, it's often just as cheap to go for full colour.

Paper

The type of paper can vary enormously, as can its cost. Visit the sales room of a new luxury housing estate and pick up a sales brochure. No nasty newsprint here. The brochure is likely to be printed in full colour on high-quality art paper of the sort artists use for watercolours. Thick and stiff, it might be separated from the next page by a light page of tracing paper – all highly luxurious and very expensive. The builder has spent a lot on printing, knowing that the only way to sell luxury homes is with luxury brochures. Penny-pinching here would be a waste of money, as it would suggest to the potential buyer that corners might well have been cut on their luxury home as well. The satirical magazine *Private Eye*, on the other hand, can use cheap newsprint for its fortnightly publication because its readers not only are not concerned with paper quality but would actually be suspicious of such a magazine were it printed in full colour and on high-quality paper; they would accuse it of having sold out. They like the slightly anarchic anti-establishment look of the magazine, and it has remained unchanged for years.

Pagination

The number of pages and the balance between editorial content and advertising is another budgetary consideration. Pages cost money to produce and so need to be supported by the income produced by advertising as well as by sales. The calculation of ad rates and percentages of adverts to editorial content is really outside the scope of this book, but journalists certainly need to be aware of the impact of income on pagination. A free newspaper that relies solely on advertising for income can have as little as 20 per cent of its space devoted to editorial. Even a paid-for newspaper or magazine may have as little as one-third of its overall space devoted to editorial, as this helps reduce the cover price, which might otherwise deter readers.

Technical data

Once basic decisions have been taken about the way a publication should look – its size, style and shape – more detailed decisions have to be made about how each page will look.

The size of the margins, *headers* and *footers*, artwork and the number of columns used will all affect the publication's appearance and how the reader will react to it. Try going into a large newsagent's and looking at all the different publications: newspapers, consumer magazines, specialist weeklies, and so on. Look quickly at the size and style and then see how each page is presented. All will differ from each other, but all will have been chosen to look as they do to be as attractive as possible to their potential readers.

Margins

Most newspapers are obliged to have margins around the page as part of the printing process. The machines that print newspapers are designed to run a large number of copies very quickly. Margins allow for there to be a certain amount of leeway about exactly where the fold and the centre margins go and where the edges of the pages are cut.

Magazines these days are not normally run off at such speed as newspapers and are printed in much higher quality, in terms of both colour and the quality of paper. Magazines therefore can be 'bled' so that the ink runs over the edge of the notional page size, leaving it flush with the edge of the page after the magazines have been trimmed by an enormous and powerful guillotine during the production process.

Newspapers normally want to keep the waste of space for margins to a minimum, so these are normally set very narrow, as is the space between columns, called the *gutter*.

Page structure

The next decision to be made is about the structure of the page. Should it be run into columns? If so, how many, and should the column widths be rigidly adhered to? There are two main considerations here. The first is the legibility of the print and the difference column width makes to the speed of reading. The second concerns the effect the number of columns has on the reader in terms of design.

Research suggests (Tinker and Paterson, cited in Tinker 1963: 78) that a 10pt solid (unspaced) line of type is read most easily if it is between 19 picas (8.045cm) and 32 picas (13.55cm) wide (pica-ems are a measurement for type – see Chapter 8 for a full description). Type with more space between the lines becomes easier to read. However, in another study it was found that 8pt type set solid (without too much space between the lines) was best read in lines of between 13 picas and 25 picas (ibid.). It seems that the smaller the type, the narrower the column can be. Using the examples given by Tinker, we can see (not too surprisingly) that we read best if there are at least 8 words per line and no more than 19 words per line. Since newspapers traditionally have narrower columns and are often read in less than ideal conditions (all Tinker's experiments were carried out in ideal conditions), then a narrower column width might be acceptable. Being jogged around on a commuter train is likely to make a reader lose his or her place more easily; a narrow column should make it easier to find the place again.

Most normal newspaper columns of 8 pica-ems in a tabloid and 10–11 pica-ems for a broadsheet are too narrow to allow readers to make maximum use of their peripheral vision (ibid.: 80) even when the type is set in 8pt (a normal size for newspapers). Many modern newspapers have increased their column widths in recent years to cope with this problem. Computer setting and modern methods have made this much easier to do. The tradition of narrow columns still exists, however, and many editors stick to seven or eight columns because that is the way newspapers are 'supposed to look'. Many have changed, though, particularly with the move to smaller papers. The *Guardian* is now a large-sized tabloid and runs its text across five columns, although these are quite wide.

Many newspapers vary the number of columns between pages so that feature pages may have wider columns than news pages. This is because features are usually longer than news and it makes sense to sacrifice the busy, active look of narrow columns for a more leisurely and straightforward read for a longer feature piece.

It is also possible to move away from the traditional, rigid approach which demands that news pages should have a particular number of columns to a freer approach that allows the number of columns to be varied from page to page or even within a page. This is easy to do nowadays with modern production methods. Today, many newspapers will vary the number of columns down a page depending on what stories and pictures they want to use. This is known as *bastard setting*. I'm not sure whether this is because it used to be hard to do or because it was seen as something improper; however, it is widely practised these days and newspapers tend to look the better for it.

Magazines have never been as tightly structured as newspapers. Again the width of columns is open to debate, but magazines tend to use bastard setting as a norm. There might be a vague feeling that there should be three or four columns per page and over-narrow or over-wide columns should be avoided, at least for any length of text, but otherwise magazine design is pretty free these days.

The only other consideration, when it comes to columns, is whether there should be an even or odd number. In practical terms it probably makes little difference, but having an even number can lead to the temptation of making pages that are too symmetrical and risk breaking the page into a number of subsections. Sometimes, of course, this may be the effect that's wanted, but generally a page is designed to present the reader with an entire shape, and an odd number of columns is often easier to work with.

It is also worth mentioning at this point that facing pages should really be designed as pairs. Often (in newspapers at least) this is not done, unless the pages are a *spread* specifically designed to work as a pair. However, where possible it is wise to design facing pages together (deadlines often mean this is not possible). Research from the Poynter Institute (Garcia and Stark 1991: 30) shows that that is how the reader deals with them, whether we design them individually or not.

House style

House style is an important element to think about when designing a new publication.

If you are producing the work for a corporate customer, they may already have a house style, a certain font they always use, a colour or colours that always appear on their documents. If you are dealing with a customer who has never produced such work, you will need to discuss with them what fonts, colours and logos they intend to use throughout the publication.

The importance of a house style cannot be overstated. Think how often you have identified the source of material just by the way it looks. The way a publication looks tells the world about the company that produced it. Showing that you are lively and go-ahead, or honest and reliable, can be done via the type used to produce the publication, the paper colour and the colours used for the text. Virgin's brash, go-ahead image is underlined by its use of bright red and its distinctive script, signature-style logo. The Beatles will always be identified, even by people who were not born until 20 years after they disbanded, by the distinctive serif font caps used for their name.

The first selection you need to make is a choice of colour. This can be fixed in your desktop publishing software to ensure that you always produce material to the house style. Fonts also need to be chosen and loaded onto the publication. A font can say a lot about a customer and should be chosen with care.

Logos are also important, and if a customer has not yet got a logo, they should be guided to a suitable graphic designer. If they already have a logo, get a copy to scan into their publications.

Type

Just as there is a house style for colours and fonts, there is also a house style for the way you use the text. What font should you use? Should it run justified or ragged left? Do you use bold? What is the headline style?

Most newspapers and magazines tend to call in specialist consultants when it comes to setting up the designs (or redesigns) of newspapers and magazines. They will balance the technical requirements of a newspaper's font against the design requirements.

Some of the elements they will consider are the legibility of the type. They will want to be sure readers can read it easily. They will check that it prints well and looks good after printing. Provided the font performs well in these technical areas, the designer will then want to know that it presents the style of image the publication wants. There are thousands of fonts, and it is difficult when looking at many of them to really spot the difference in the way they look, but the font will change the way people view that particular publication and reinforce the general image the newspaper seeks to present. That is particularly true of the chosen headline font, which thrusts its way into people's view, but even the body type carries an image, because even though it is a lot more subtle, there is far more of it.

There are also purely commercial considerations. A font might carry the right image and be highly legible, but if it takes 20 per cent more space to carry the same number of words, then that might not be acceptable. Readers like to believe they are getting value for money and they are more likely to read a magazine that carries more on its pages, provided everything else is equal.

Graphics and photographs

Even graphics and photographs are run in a house style. This may be to have a black line border around each picture, or it could be to fade out the edges. There will also need to be some consideration of size of pictures and perhaps the number of pictures per page.

Titlepiece

You also need to consider the *titlepiece* for a publication. This is the publication's name and is a crucial piece of the marketing jigsaw. The titlepiece is the presentation of the brand name and a lot of effort is given to consideration of this design – although the story goes that the *Sun*'s famous and simple logo was designed by Rupert Murdoch on the back of a napkin over dinner shortly after taking over the ailing broadsheet that was soon to become Britain's brightest and brashest tabloid. The *Sun*'s logo sums up everything the *Sun* represents: simple, straightforward, uncluttered and easy to read; brash, bright and very definitely in your face.

Unusually for the time, it was also set in the top left-hand quadrant of the page, allowing the right-hand to be used for *puffs* or *blurbs*, the pitches newspapers use to draw readers inside.

The *Daily Telegraph*'s titlepiece is also an ideal brand mark, recognisable well before the word becomes readable. Its use of an Old English-style font, set across most of the width of the page, is very traditional and classic, drawing on all the virtues the *Telegraph* seeks to represent.

Headers and footers

Every page of a publication carries the title of the publication, a page number and a date. Publications also need to decide how to present this information. Subtle with a small font? Large, with a border? The choices are varied, and again these *headers* and *footers* will be designed by the consultant who sets up the publication design. These days, they are usually built into the page templates produced for use on the computer system, often Apple Macs using QuarkXPress or Adobe InDesign.

Imprint

Last but not least, you need to ensure that the imprint is included somewhere in the publication. The imprint says who printed and published the document, and this is a legal requirement. Often it is put on the back page in very small type, but some publications make a virtue of it by putting it in a column that includes staff names and job titles. A magazine will usually list the staff and give phone numbers and contact email addresses. Many newspapers are also starting to follow this pattern, realising that it is a good way to get readers to send in stories or make contact if something newsworthy is happening. Newspapers usually list the news desk, sports desk and advertising team with numbers and emails.

Colours

The colours to be used in a publication also help to build the publication's image and brand. Coca-Cola's bright red is a central component of its image, and in a similar way various publications use particular colours to identify themselves. Using full colour for adverts and editorials might seem to suggest that there should be no limit to the colours used, and this would be true as regards the content; however, on the masthead, imprint and regular logos and page headings, careful use of colour can make a distinctive addition to the brand. In some newspapers not every page is set in colour, and so you need to be aware that colour might not run throughout. In magazines these days it is normal for all pages to be in colour; however, there are plenty of small-publication magazines or newsletters that use a limited amount of colour or rely more heavily on *spot colour* (see Chapter 4), and here specific colours can be used to give an identity.

4 Production processes

Design is largely about working with the technology available to you. Print is a fixed, two-dimensional medium with opportunities for colour dependent on budget. Most of this is visual, and we aim publications at the sense of sight. Touch, smell and taste could be considered, but the technology is expensive and probably not worth it for most publications – although from time to time some magazines do carry adverts from scent manufacturers who think it worth the money to produce scented adverts. It would also be technically possible to produce print with taste or texture, and even sound (birthday cards, for instance, are now available with small sound devices that cheer or jeer as you open the card), although whether it would be worth the expense for a newspaper is doubtful. It is much easier to put such material on the website if it is important. Magic pictures that move, such as those in the Harry Potter stories, are yet to grace newspapers, although the *Press Gazette* did publish a 3D picture in summer 2002 and provided readers with the special glasses to view it. To us as designers, then, the technology of print and what we can do with it is very important and so we need to know what is available so we can work out how to get the best from it.

Printing technology

Making the most of print technology (as with all technology) is about balancing what is possible at the present stage of development with cost. Newspapers are produced at the cheaper, throwaway end of the market using cheap paper, cheap binding methods and limited colour reproduction. Magazines tend to be higher up the expense range, with good-quality paper and full colour throughout. The time taken to do something is also a cost. Since experiments and new ideas always take up more time than established practice, the gains have to be carefully weighed against the cost.

The good publication designer should always consider ways of being imaginative and creative, while remaining within budget. Usually, of course, the basic structure of a publication is already predesigned and you are obliged to work within the production limits, but that doesn't mean that you can't try out new things from time to time. Just because your publication is of a certain size or style, does that mean you are stuck with it? Someone was the first to go with the gatefold or the pop-up book or scratch'n'sniff.

Printing processes

Printing started in earnest around the 1450s. Although wood blocks had long been used to reproduce copies of drawings and even type, the process was difficult and expensive. It was easier to get someone to copy the books by hand, and while the Church had monks employed solely at copying, the educated classes had to employ scribes to do the copying for them. Gutenberg's invention of movable type and an ink suitable to use with it brought together several technologies to launch printing as we know it.

History of printing technology

The origins of print are difficult to determine, as a number of ideas and processes needed to come together in order for it to be possible. Just as the computer could not be invented before electricity was discovered and tamed, so printing could not be considered until all the necessary elements came together in the same place at the same time.

The Chinese were significantly instrumental in the development of printing. They had invented paper by AD 105, replacing vellum and skins for the production of documents, thereby reducing their cost and so increasing their availability. The Romans invented inscribed lettering, with the generally accepted date of AD 114 for the inscription at the base of Trajan's Column in Rome. The design of type lettering as opposed to script was an important development towards printing, as it allowed a standardised alphabet to be reproduced.

Printing was developed during the first millennium AD. The legendary date of its inception is AD 594, although the oldest extant publication is the Diamond Sutra, which bears the statement that it was printed on 11 May 868 (AD) by Wang Chieh. This was done with carved wood blocks.

Movable type was the next thing that had to be invented before printing could develop significantly, although even this was not enough in itself. Movable type was invented in China around 1040, but because it was of complicated Chinese ideographs, it did not take off. It was made from clay, baked hard.

Movable copper type was cast in Korea in the early fifteenth century, but it was Johannes Gensfleisch zur Laden, known as Gutenberg (born c.1399, died 1468), who is credited with making the first press to use movable type. He also invented an ink suitable for use with the new metal type.

Several of Gutenberg's works still survive. The Gutenberg Bible (the 42-line Bible) was published in Mainz, probably by Gutenberg and his two associates Johann Fust and Peter Schöffer. It was probably begun in 1453 and completed in 1455. Printing in those days was not fast. The three associates fell out when Fust and Schöffer sued Gutenberg for the money they had lent him to set up his press. As is so often the case with inventors, Gutenberg died poor.

The press changed little over the next 300 years, with the initial inventions being consolidated 'in a predominately conservative way' (Steinberg 1955: 18). It says much of Gutenberg's achievement that while others improved on his ability as a printer, they did little to improve on the effectiveness of his press. Gutenberg could have walked into a press of 1720 and not only felt at home, but started work without problems.

Within 15 years of Gutenberg's death, presses had been set up in every country of western Christendom. Newspapers started during the 1600s, with the first daily newspaper starting in England in 1702 as the *Daily Courant*.

As printing became more widespread, the need for some standardisation became accepted. Fournier le Jeune had proposed a unit of measurement for print as early as 1737 but it was Didot who introduced the point system in 1775, which was adopted throughout France and later in Germany. The system related the body size of the type to the then legal measurement the *pied du roi*, the size of the royal foot. A different system is used in the United States and Britain today.

At the start of the nineteenth century, the trade started growing, fed by demand for more reading material from a public that was becoming more educated.

In 1798, mechanical methods of paper production were introduced. Paper costs plummeted by a quarter or even a third. Nicolas-Louis Robert invented a machine for making a continuous sheet of paper on an endless wire web. The patents were bought by the Fourdrinier brothers in 1804 and they developed it to make the first papermaking machines (Twyman 1970: 49).

Stereotyping was invented at the turn of the century and the patent was bought in Britain by Lord Stanhope. Stereotyping allowed far more copies to be made more cheaply. Type is set into a frame known as a *forme*. Before stereotyping was invented, the paper was to be printed was pressed onto the type which eventually became too worn or damaged to be used and the forme would need to be reset. By taking a plaster or papier mâché cast of the forme of type and then casting a new forme from this, reprints could be made without resetting.

Stanhope improved the press in 1804, exchanging the traditional wooden bed for an iron one and adapting the lever mechanism to allow the printing of a large forme in one pull instead of the old two pulls (Twyman 1970: 51).

These developments were quickly followed by steam-powered presses, patented by Friedrich Koenig in 1810 (ibid.). No longer would manpower be the driving force behind the press. A technological evolution was taking place which was to revolutionise the press.

In 1812, Koenig built his first cylinder printing machine to take advantage of the reels of paper now available from the newly invented papermaking machines. The forme was still a flat bed but a cylinder now ran the paper over it. Its worth was soon appreciated when *The Times* adopted it in 1814. The print run improved from 300 sheets an hour to 1,100.

The four-cylinder press, invented by Augustus Applegath and Edward Cowper some 14 years later, raised printing speeds to 4,000 copies per hour for *The Times* (ibid.).

It was Edward Cowper who had the idea of curving stereotype plates in order to fasten them to a cylinder. This beginning of the rotary press was significant, but its time was yet to come. Cylinder presses, with the paper being pulled across the forme before being pressed and then driven on and cut free from the web, were still seen as the way ahead, for financial reasons.

Rowland Hill patented a rotary press in 1835 but its advantages were nullified by the necessity of printing the duty-paid stamp onto each newspaper. Newspapers of the time were still obliged to pay stamp duty as a method of taxation, and the authorities would not allow this to be stamped onto a continuous web of paper.

The *Philadelphia Ledger* introduced a rotary press shortly after this, although this machine did not use stereotypes. Formes of type were affixed to a horizontal central cylinder by means of tapering column rules.

In 1863, William Bullock patented his rotary self-feeding and self-perfecting press (able to print on both sides of the paper simultaneously) (ibid.: 55) for use with curved stereos cast from a papier mâché impression of the original (a *flong*). This was built in 1865 and installed in *The Times* in 1866; it was capable of printing 12,000 sections an hour. A folding mechanism was added in 1868. By 1939 *The Times* was printing a 32-page paper at a rate of 40,000 copies an hour.

The year 1879 saw the introduction of a patent 'auxiliary printing mechanism for late news'. This printing device allowed late news to be added to the front or back page without stopping the press. It meant that newspapers could carry the latest news even as they were being printed, although the amount of space available was limited to about a half-column. This system was widely used by newspapers until very recently, when the introduction of *web-offset litho* machines made its use impossible. It is interesting to note that Twitter now admirably fulfils this ability to add to the news with short, snappy updates.

All this change throughout the nineteenth century brought in dramatic social changes. Rather than threatening jobs and wages, as had been feared, the increase in printing found a ready market in the newly educated. The growth of literacy meant that printers started making their money through printing larger runs. Before this, the money had been made in the composition rather than the printing, because after printing a few thousand copies the forme would need to be reset, as the type would be worn away. Stereos ensured the ability to cast new formes, and high-speed presses meant long runs could be contemplated. Type casting had also come under the scrutiny of the inventor.

The first typecasting machine was invented in 1805 in the United States by William Wing but it was eventually abandoned. Another machine was invented by Anthony Francis Berte, where a mould would be pressed against an aperture in the metal pot and hot metal squirted through under pressure. Many more variations were invented over the subsequent years and were received with mixed reactions.

Attempts to introduce typecasting machinery in Britain in 1823 met with a hostile reception from the embryonic trade unions, although a similar machine invented in the United States by Dr William Church improved the number of letters cast from 3,000–7,000 a day to 12,000–20,000. Other composing machines were invented by Robert Hattersley (1866) and Charles Kastenbein (1869). Hattersley's machine was used by the UK provincial press until 1891 and Kastenbein's at *The Times* until 1908 (Steinberg 1955: 196). Both machines needed manual justification and distribution of the type. This was so expensive that juvenile labour was used, a practice opposed by the London Society of Compositors, forerunner of today's Unite union. Only the non-union *Times* was prepared to oppose the union and used children to set type.

Ottmar Merganthaler invented the Linotype machine, which was installed in the *New York Tribune* in 1886 (ibid.). It was quickly taken up elsewhere, and nearly all newspapers in the twentieth century used the machines until computer setting allowed them to be retired in the 1980s and 1990s. Doubtless many newspapers are still produced by this method in places where investment in computers is too expensive and labour is cheap.

The Linotype works by bringing together pieces of suitably engraved brass in a line at the command of the operator's keyboard. These are automatically spaced, and this brass line is impressed on a line of lead-based metal hot enough to be sufficiently soft to produce a slug of type. The brass matrices are then returned to the channels of a magazine for reuse. Monotype machines developed a similar process in 1889 but each letter was cast separately, thereby allowing easier correction. The ability to cast shot up from 2,000 letters an hour to around 6,000.

In 1891 the *Birmingham Daily Gazette* used electricity to drive a single-roll press, becoming the first British paper to use electricity. In 1906, Washington I. Ludlow invented the Ludlow machine for casting large sizes of type. It was introduced in England in 1911.

In 1882 the first practicable photographic *halftone* process for *letterpress* printing was patented in Munich and was introduced into England two years later by the Meisenbach company. The use of photographs in publications was developed for printing by the invention of the cross-line screen that allowed halftone photography. This process allowed for the mechanical engraving of fine screen blocks and the printing of photographs in publications became financially possible.

With mechanical setting, photo-engraving, web-feeds and the power-driven self-perfecting rotary press, high-quality (in the production sense, at least) newspapers and magazines could be produced for a mass market of the newly literate, and the great newspaper days were born.

Until the nineteenth century, all printing had been relief printing: the image was made by pressing a raised inked original onto paper.

Lithography – a non-relief printing method – had been invented in 1798 by the Bavarian Aloys Senefelder, and this became more widely used later in the nineteenth century, particularly with the development of photography. It produced higher-quality images but was a much more difficult process.

Photogravure – another new method of printing – was invented around 1890, with the first successful prints being made in 1895. This was also a non-relief method but required detailed engraving of the plate, and so was difficult and expensive to set up. Once a plate had been engraved, however, it would print very long runs, making the cost per copy very low. This was to become the standard method of printing long runs of high-quality colour work for things such as stamps.

The first commercial development of *offset* lithography took place in 1904 and was followed in 1925 by the first tentative moves to *photocomposition* with the prototype of a machine called the Uhertype (Twyman 1970: 63), introduced by Edward Uher, a Hungarian engineer. This was developed in 1929 with the introduction in the United States of a photosetting machine with a claimed 7,000 letters an hour.

The year 1945 saw the first principles of Xerography and Xero-printing patented in the United States, quickly followed in 1946 by the installation of the first effective photosetter in the Government Printing Office in Washington. The Harris-Intertype Fotosetter was used to produce the first fully filmset book: *Handbook of Basic Microtechnique*.

In the same way that the turn of the nineteenth century was a period of almost frantic change in the world of newspaper publishing, so the 1960s, 1970s and 1980s saw a massive technological revolution for both magazines and newspapers. The early part of the twentieth century had been taken up with world wars, and any changes had been largely improvements on existing technology. Most newspapers were happy to use technology that had been largely unchanged since 1900. Fast rotary presses driven by electricity and supported by mechanical setting were adjusted with only such minor amendments as using plastic stereotypes rather than papier mâché.

The 1960s and 1970s now saw some rapid development. Photographic methods of typesetting, reproduction and printing led to vast improvements, and halftone lithography was developed to a commercially acceptable standard. The first *web-offset litho* presses were installed during the 1960s. Multiweb presses were introduced and speeds were reached that had previously been undreamed of.

Photocomposition was introduced during the late 1960s and 1970s, and by the end of the 1970s many provincial daily papers were producing photoset artwork that was then photographically converted into plates to be loaded onto either the new *web-offset* presses or converted into stereotypes for traditional relief printing. Magazines were also benefiting enormously from the development of presses capable of much more flexible design, high-quality pictures and colour. The increasing consumer power of the 1960s, 1970s and 1980s saw a huge increase in advertising budgets, and magazines were not slow to cash in with an increase in production that has continued largely unchecked to this day.

Direct input was introduced into publications in the United States during the late 1970s and early 1980s. This meant that the journalist's copy was no longer reset by a compositor into the traditional metal or photoset type but was set directly on computer by the reporter. Fears of job losses from the National Graphical Association (NGA) ensured that direct setting was not introduced in Britain at all until much later. The *Nottingham Evening Post* started using the method in the early 1980s but remained virtually alone until Eddy Shah introduced it at his Warrington plant in 1984. This was followed by the launch of *Today* in 1985 and the move to Wapping by Rupert Murdoch's papers in 1986.

Provincial newspapers began to get nervous because the old, compositor-run photosetting equipment was becoming unreliable and needed to be replaced.

No one wanted to buy the old-style equipment, even if it was available, yet the print unions were still strong enough at this stage to deter managements from introducing the new direct input technology by compulsion.

The NGA wanted its members to retain their jobs. Since money could only be saved by eliminating double keying, managements did not want to introduce the new technology yet keep all the printers and all the journalists in work. The National Union of Journalists (NUJ) saw the NGA's position as an attempt to turn printers into journalists and so put NUJ members' jobs at risk. In the end, both the NGA and the NUJ refused to work with the new equipment until it was decided who did what.

The Portsmouth News group tried to introduce the new technology against the wishes of the NUJ, sparking a strike during which NGA members set the paper, many of them working as sub-editors alongside Institute of Journalists reporters and subs. At the *Wolverhampton Express & Star* the NGA was locked out for refusing to work the new system, and NUJ members produced the papers using the new machines.

In 1986 the two unions forged an agreement on the introduction of new technology which spelled out who did what, and arranged for the retraining of NGA staff, who would be redeployed. They also worked out details of the negotiations that would take place with provincial managements.

Within six months of the deal, more than 25 provincial newspapers and newspaper groups, many of them dailies and many of them publishing a number of papers, had reached agreement with the unions and introduced direct input. Magazine publishers were also quick to move to the new technology.

Within two years there were very few publications, national or provincial, that were not printing using direct input, and I doubt that any publication in the United Kingdom now does not use direct-input *web-offset lithography*.

Because of the late switch to this new technology, many publications, especially magazines, went directly to full-page make-up on-screen. Most publications now use full-page make-up systems with journalists writing and designing on-screen and the finished result being output in the form of a plate ready to go straight onto the press.

Photographers have also joined the digital revolution, taking pictures with digital cameras that add speed and flexibility to their craft. Images can be sent from phones and edited directly on computer to be inserted directly in the publication, allowing news pictures to be virtually instant. Direct input has also allowed a good deal more flexibility in the siting of presses. Data links allow direct input information to be sent from anywhere to anywhere, allowing presses to be remote from the news desk. Journalists can now work in the centre of London or anywhere else and send the finished page electronically to a press situated outside London, where it is cheaper, and more convenient for transport. Pages can also be sent to a multitude of sites, allowing simultaneous printing in, say, London, Manchester, Bristol, Glasgow and Belfast, easing distribution and transport costs and difficulties. Many publications now have their editorial production offices and presses in cheap sites on industrial estates, with the more expensive 'front' offices in city centres staffed by only a handful of people.

Production processes

The good designer needs to know the basic operation of the key production processes he or she is likely to come into contact with, and the next section of this chapter will look at different processes, what they are and how they work.

Letterpress

Letterpress is the process of impressing an inked relief surface against paper. The type and any artwork in this relief process are usually made of metal, etched to stand proud from the bed of the forme (the metal 'page'). It is set in mirror fashion so that its impression will appear the correct way round after imprinting.

Although letterpress is no longer as popular as it once was, particularly in magazines, it is still one of the best and most efficient ways of printing small runs, cards and certain specialist non-colour runs. It provides a clear, crisp impression capable of extreme fidelity and consistency over long runs. It is not really capable of full colour, although it can produce spot colour, and of course the ink used can be any colour the printer wants.

The basic press for relief printing is the platen machine. In this machine the type is held in a *chase* (a rectangular metal frame) to make a flat *forme* which is brought against the *platen* (a metal plate) with the paper in between, in a more or less vertical position. Rollers spread ink over the type immediately before printing. These machines range from small hand-operated machines for proofing and specialist applications, to larger power-operated machines. They are all sheet fed, although the feeding can be done either by hand or automatically. All operate only mono colour, although this can be anything from black to fluorescent pink or a metallic finish.

Cylinder machines

Platen machines would have been recognisable to the inventors of print. They would have found cylinder machines, sometimes called flatbed machines, less obvious.

In these machines the forme still holds the flat relief printing surface but now this slides underneath a rotating cylinder which carries the sheet of paper into the press. These are capable of handling very large formes (66 inches × 46 inches), often with a number of pages which will later be guillotined to separate them.

Perfectors

Perfector machines use an elaboration of this principle to print on both sides. A cunning mechanical device grabs the sheet of paper coming off the plate cylinder and flips it so that the other side of the paper hits the second plate cylinder. Some machines have several units to allow additional colours to be added to build up two-, three- or four-colour images, while some allow the perfector to be turned off so that the second cylinder can be used to add an extra colour while printing on one side only.

Rotary machines

Rotary machines print from curved plates or stereos. In all the previous machines, the type was held in a chase to make a flat relief surface known as a *forme*. Now an impression is taken of that forme, known as a *flong*. This was originally made from papier mâché, but on later machines plastics were used. A process patented first in the early nineteenth century allowed this flong to be curved. A cast is made from this curved flong and this is loaded onto the printing cylinder of the rotary machine. Several pages will be loaded alongside each other and printed simultaneously. The paper is normally fed from a web between the impression cylinder and the plate cylinder, although there are some sheet-fed rotary presses. Curving the forme obviously distorts the print slightly, and specialist types were developed to cope with this. The rotary's big advantage is high speed.

Modern developments have improved the method by using plastic or rubber plates and, even more recently, photopolymer plates, allowing full advantage to be taken of modern photo reproduction in both plate-making and composition.

Lithography

Lithography has now overtaken letterpress as the main method of printing newspapers and magazines. It is probably possible to find a small weekly paper somewhere in the United Kingdom or United States still using letterpress, but there can't be many. Most have either re-equipped, or scrapped their expensive presses and subcontracted the printing to one of the large presses now available. Few weekly papers print more than 50,000 copies, and modern *web-offset* lithography presses can print that in under an hour, making it uneconomic for a small publisher to buy its own press. It would not be worth having a press that would cost £5 million and require a building and staff to print a magazine with a circulation of 200,000 once a month, since the printing can be done in a day.

The introduction of *lithography* was slow at first, as the high cost of re-equipping could not be seen to be justified, and although its principles were first espoused in 1798 by Aloys Senefelder and it flourished fairly quickly, it was not until the 1960s and 1970s that it became the dominant printing method in newspapers and magazines.

Lithography works on the principle that water and oil repel each other. A smoothed stone can be drawn on with a greasy crayon. If the stone is then wetted, the crayon will repel the water but the stone will remain wet. If the stone is then inked with a grease-based ink, the ink will adhere only to the area touched by the crayon. The ink can then be transferred to the paper by direct contact. This method was of most use for images such as pictures and graphics, which, until its invention, had been very difficult to produce with relief printing methods. However, the process did not really take off for newspapers until it became *offset*. Offset printing means that the image is taken from the plate onto a flexible rubbery surface known as a blanket, and it is this that prints onto the paper.

Stones are no longer used. Now a thin plate of aluminium is coated with a light-sensitive chemical. This allows the image to be transferred photographically to the plate, either by photographing an image of the page onto the plate or, more likely these days, by direct output from a plate-making machine connected to the computer setting system. Essentially it is the same as the black-and-white printer connected to your computer except it prints out onto aluminium sheets rather than paper. This plate is then treated so that the area to print will repel water and take up the ink. It is this direct link between photocomposition and the offset plate that has made offset printing so popular. Offset lithography is also popular because it makes it possible to produce full-colour output. However, although it is a much more sophisticated process than letterpress, it is nowhere near as robust. Because of the intense compression of the letterpress process, variations in paper, ink and plates were ironed out – literally.

In the offset process, very careful balances have to be made between the amount of water (damping) and the amount of ink. This can be upset by even a small increase in humidity or temperature. All the contact surfaces involved in the process are also critical. As the system is a transfer of image rather than an impression, as with letterpress, a slight variation can have disastrous effects.

Offset presses for publications are usually a rotary process. The thin, flexible aluminium plates are fixed around a cylinder and the paper is passed from a web between the blanket roller and the impression cylinder to pick up the image. Offset plates are thin and flexible and are easily wrapped around a cylinder without any noticeable distortion.

Some of the disadvantages of offset have been overcome by computer setting. Corrections used to be more difficult to make and plates were easily damaged. But now, new plates can be made from a corrected computer photo image within minutes, if not seconds. The advantages of using colour, and high-quality photo images, make offset ideal for printing newspapers and magazines.

To colour-print requires passing the paper through four different impressions, one for each of the colours used in the process, including black. Because each colour must print accurately over the others to produce a true colour image, the plates must be carefully aligned if registration is to be achieved. Difficult though this process is, the technique was impossible for relief printing because of the stresses set up by the process. The more subtle offset litho, however, allows good-quality images to be made in full colour.

With the high speeds used by modern web-offset machines, a number of problems come up of which journalists need to be aware. The technical difficulties of balancing ink and water mean that web-offset is very wasteful of paper, with up to 12 per cent wasted in running a press up to its full speed. A paper break means rethreading and rerunning up – a massive loss in time and in paper.

Presses are also inflexible with regard to the size of the final job. The size of the cylinder and the positioning of the folder cutter and other end-of-press features mean that most presses are designed to print only one length or 'cut off', giving any particular press fixed dimensions for its publications so that it is only able to print a broadsheet or tabloid to those dimensions.

Gravure

Gravure is the giant of printing. It is a complex process ideal for colour work that gives high-quality, consistent results but is suitable only for extremely long runs.

Gravure is an intaglio process – the reverse of relief. The print cylinders are engraved directly, with the areas that are not to be printed being etched away. The etched sections hold the ink, which is then transferred to the paper.

The depth of etching can be varied, and this is the clever bit. A very shallow pit will hold less ink and therefore produce a lighter tonal value than a deep pit. In this way, gradations of tone can be added. Both offset and letterpress put a consistent level of ink on the paper and are able to vary density of colour only by screening to build up a series of different-sized dots that will give the impression of tonal gradation. The surface of the gravure plate is engraved in a series of cells with a depth varying from 25 micrometres (thousandths of a millimetre) to 0.2 micrometres. The gaps between the cells are very small, and although when in action the printing cylinder is wiped clear of ink by a blade called the doctor blade, these microscopic lips have of necessity been inked slightly. This helps join up the gap between the cells, giving the impression of continuity.

Stamps are an excellent example of the quality of work that can be accomplished with gravure. Gravure is also used for things like packaging, and can print on paper, card and film.

Composition

Composition is no longer the skilled process that it used to be. Most newspapers and magazines are produced using computer systems that allow journalists to write their stories at one end of the process, for sub-editors to edit and design the material and for finished plates to come out at the other end. There are very few places left where the composing room puts together the pages.

Web feed

Because much of the cost of offset is in paper, and offset is very wasteful on run-up, good feed systems and automatic reel changeover are vital. This is particularly important considering that a big press producing a 32-page paper requires at least four separate reels that inevitably all run out at different times.

Presses are loaded with two reels that run through a tensioner. As the paper is close to running out, the paper feed is laid close to a new reel, the end of which is coated with sticky tape. As the reel is close to ending, the paper feed is pressed against the tape, picking up the feed from the new reel; at the same time, the old paper feed is sliced. The tensioner ensures that variations in the feed during this process are ironed out. The newspapers with the stuck-together bits of paper are later jettisoned by a machine minder.

Post press

After the paper has been printed, it has to be collated, cut and folded. Several sheets are often split and always collated so that all the webs come together in the correct order. They are drawn together folded and then cut. In broadsheet papers they would be folded again. They are then stacked, bundled and bound together.

Photo reproduction

Because letterpress and offset litho are both continuous processes, they do not allow directly for tonal gradations; they can print only in 100 per cent ink density or zero ink density. Pictures and tones, therefore, can only be printed as *halftones*. The image will appear either in the ink colour or the paper colour. This will generally be black or white.

In order to represent the continuous range of tones in a photograph or to add shading and tonal variety, the picture is broken down into a series of dots. The larger the dot, the darker the tone will appear.

Traditionally, a photograph is re-photographed through a cross-line screen (usually as any reduction or enlargement required is made), but most pictures are now digital or are scanned in using a digitising scanner. The computer then converts the digital pixels of the photograph into pixels suitable for the print screening process that is automatically applied to the photograph before the plate is printed. Photographs can be screened with a different number of lines per linear centimetre (the raster). Different densities of lines allow for different effects. A 26-line screen (26 lines to the linear centimetre) is coarse and gives low-grade printing results suitable only for the poor quality of paper used in newspapers. Since poor-quality paper acts a little like tissue, blotting up the ink so that it spreads throughout the paper rather than leaving a clean, crisp image, a coarse screen is required to prevent the lines bleeding over each other and instead present a viewable image. A 60-line per linear centimetre screen on the other hand would produce good results on coated stock that prevents the ink from being soaked into the paper and leaves a clean crisp imprint. The finest-detailed work might require 150 lines per linear centimetre. A daily newspaper typically uses a raster of 31.5 lines per linear centimetre or 80 lines per inch (80lpi). Sometimes the lines are measured in inches and a screen will be expressed as 75lpi. This is becoming more common because although Britain has been moving towards metric measurements, many computer-based printing machines are US-made, where imperial measurements are still the norm.

The angle at which the raster lines are presented is also important. The screen is normally put at 45° to the perpendicular for mono work. In two-colour work the main colour will be at 45° while the lighter colour will be at 75°. In four-colour work, black will be at 45°, magenta at 15°, cyan at 75° and yellow at 90° (ibid.). This angling means that the raster is less obvious when printing pictures with up and across lines such as are often found in pictures of buildings or human-made structures.

Output

Once the picture has been edited, cropped, sized, etc., we will need to output it and convert the pixels used to represent the picture digitally in the computer to pixels suitable for the printing process. In order to output a black-and-white halftone print from the computer, either separately or as part of a page, we need to convert the intermediate greys into patterns of dots. However, the image setter, like the printer you use with your computer, can only produce one size of dot. Since the number of halftones capable of being reproduced depends on the number of dots per inch (dpi) the output device is capable of delivering, then provided sufficient information is scanned in, the computer clumps together a number of these dots available in its output to form the screen patterns. Thus, an image setter outputting at 1,200dpi on a halftone whose screen has been set to 200 lines per inch will be using a block of 6 × 6 dots to make up each raster dot. However, this cell size will give a maximum of only 36 grey scales. Since the human eye can see at least 64 shades, and can certainly tell the difference between a 64-shade and a 256-shade halftone, we would normally want to increase the number of shades from 36 to anything from the acceptable 64 shades up to a perfect 256 shades. This would require a bigger cell of output dots to allow more variation in the raster dot. We can calculate the number of dots in the screen cell by dividing the image setter resolution in lines per inch by the raster. If the setter can reproduce 2,400 dots per inch and we want a raster of 120lpi, then we have a grid of 10 × 10 dots to make our output raster dot, giving us 100 shades of grey – not perfect, but certainly giving a reasonable image. A 4,800dpi image setter would allow a grid of 20 × 20, or 400 grey scales. This is more than enough and would allow the potential for a 16 × 16 grid to give 256 shades and up to 150 raster lines.

Since the number of dots in the cell directly relates to the number of grey scales, we can use this to calculate the best screen setting by squaring the number of dots in the raster cell (Kammermeier and Kammermeier 1992: 72):

Screen cell	Grey scale
4 × 4	16
6 × 6	36
8 × 8	64
16 × 16	256

We can calculate the number of grey shades by dividing the square of the printed dots per inch (the maximum output of the printer) by the square of the raster. This means the number of grey scales is equal to $dpi^2/raster^2$. If you were to possess a printer capable of 2,400 dots per inch and you screened at 120 lines per inch, then the number of halftones would be $2{,}400^2/120^2$. This works out at 5,760,000/14,400, which equals 400. This means we could reproduce up to 400 grey scales, but since it is extremely unlikely that we would have scanned in more than 256 grey scales, this information is not likely to be available to print out. This means that we could, if it was appropriate, reproduce with a smaller raster dot and more lines per inch.

The quality of the paper is also important. Newsprint, for instance, cannot handle a line image of 120. The ink soaks into the paper and spreads, making dots finer than 100 lines per inch pointless. Most newsprint screens are in the region of 70–90. Colour might use a finer screen. When it comes to producing colour, then four outputs are required to represent full colour. Each output is produced as described on pp. 41–43.

The calculations above will help us determine the resolution required to output the image.

Scanners

In order to output a photograph, we need to input it into the computer first. This can be done either by importing a digital photograph directly from the camera or by scanning the photograph. Direct input is becoming more common, with staff photographers and freelances using digital cameras as standard. However, often a picture will come from an outside source as a print, and this will need to be scanned in.

In computing terms, full colour is represented by the three primary colours. Each can have up to 256 tonal variations (the eye cannot detect more than 256 different shades). This gives a total of 16.7 million colours (256 × 256 × 256).

Each of the 256 tonal variations of a primary colour can be represented by an 8-bit number. All 16.7 million colours therefore require a 24-bit number – hence the expression '24-bit colour'. Modern colour scanners work at up to 48-bit depth. These allow for a greater number of shades to be scanned in. This is because the photograph will be darkened in the printing process. Making the picture lighter for publication means that many of the very light shades of grey will be removed and the darker greys are enhanced. If there are far more grey shades (up to 4,096 shades in a 36-bit scanner), then there are more dark greys to work with and the picture can still be 256 shades once the picture has been published.

When we come to input a picture into the computer (from whatever source), we need to decide on the resolution. The higher the resolution, the better the potential quality when outputting. However, scanning is very different from outputting. Scanners look at a very small area of the picture and render it as a dot (a pixel) by measuring the shade of the picture either in colour or black and white, depending on which you choose. The user can adjust the size of the area measured up to 2,400 dots per inch or even more. These scanned dots relate directly to the pixels on the computer screen. The modern PC screen usually displays 1,280 × 1,024 pixels. Some larger screens can show resolutions of 1,600 × 1,400 pixels or even greater. A picture scanned at 1,280 × 1,024 pixels will fill the screen whatever size it really is. In other words, if you instruct the scanner to scan at 100 dots per inch, then a 12.8-inch picture will be 1,280 dots wide and so will fill the screen. But a 2-inch picture scanned at a resolution of 600 dots per inch will also fill the screen. The result will depend on the software, of course, and a picture loaded into a desktop publishing package will appear in the size you have asked for because the software will copy the picture at the correct resolution for standard output at the size you have requested. The dots relate directly to the raster dot to be output by the image setter. Each raster dot output is intended to represent a shade of grey (for grey-scale pictures) or the shades of the four output colours for colour work.

When you are scanning in a picture, the temptation is to go for a very high resolution on the assumption that this will give the best results, but this is not necessarily true. If, for instance, you are scanning a black-and-white picture for a newspaper with a raster of 80 lines per inch (lpi), then your maximum output will be 80lpi. In other words, your output device will be trying to represent one out of 256 different shades of grey per one-eightieth of an inch. But your scanner can represent 256 different shades of grey as a colour, not a shade. It will only convert it to a half-screen dot to represent a shade when it is output. Thus, provided you don't want to enlarge the picture much on outputting, you can scan at a resolution of 80 dots per inch, as these will be capable of representing one of the 256 shades of grey every eightieth of an inch. There is no point in giving a higher resolution, because that is the resolution you are going to print at. The only reason for a higher scanning resolution is if you intend to enlarge the picture. Assuming you knew you wanted to make the picture twice as large, then you should scan it in at 160 dots per inch (dpi), so that when you output at twice the size, you will be able to do so with a raster of 80lpi.

We should remember that as we adjust the size of our picture in the computer, the amount of information scanned in remains constant. The computer merely juggles the information to give the impression of size change. A picture scanned at 100dpi and then reduced to 25 per cent of its original size now has only 25 pixels representing an inch on the screen, but it is in fact 400dpi. Similarly, if the picture were increased to 400 per cent, it would have only 25dpi and the pixels would appear to be four times as big. When pictures are enlarged, the pixels can often become so big that the picture appears to be made up of a number of square shapes. If the computer did not juggle the information received, then we would not be able to alter the picture later. If you have ever reduced the size of an image in Photoshop, saved the result and then tried to re-enlarge it to its original size, you will have seen that the computer struggled to enlarge it because the extra information needed to enlarge the picture had been ditched.

There is also the problem of file size. The higher the scan resolution, the larger the file: the processing time will be longer and the computer system is more likely to fail in attempts to print.

The following chart shows approximate file sizes for an 8 inch × 6 inch 256-grey-scale picture (8-bit):

Scan res (dpi)	*File size*
100	480kb
200	2Mb
400	8Mb
800	31Mb

You will notice that as the scan resolution is doubled, the file size is quadrupled. This is because the scan resolution is only linear while the file size represents area.

Since scanning at too high a resolution does not improve quality, but does make for very large files with consequent storage and processing problems, it is best to scan the picture at the right size to start with. If you know by how much you need the picture enlarged, then this should be taken into account, but if the picture will be used at about the same size or smaller, the scan resolution should be 1.4 times the raster dot size:

$$\text{Scan resolution} = \text{raster resolution} \times 1.4$$

If the picture is to be substantially altered, then the following equation can be used (Kammermeier and Kammermeier 1992: 83):

$$\text{Scan resolution} = \frac{\text{desired size}}{\text{raster resolution} \times 1.4 \times \text{original size}}$$

Colour print process

So far I have talked largely about grey scale: black-and-white printing. But much work nowadays, especially in magazines, is in colour.

Spot colour

Some newspapers still use spot colour printing. This is where the work is printed in one colour – usually black on white paper – and then another colour is printed on top of that. The second colour is known as a *spot colour*. It allows for emphasis on mastheads, advertiser titles and elsewhere. It was widely used on letterpress as a way of adding emphasis.

In spot colour the inks can be of any colour you like. The hue, saturation and value can all be adjusted by the printer using a different colour of ink in the same way that you can buy different shades of paint from a DIY store.

However, with spot colour, once that colour is chosen for a page or block of pages, you are stuck with it and it must be used for the whole page. Hence, spot colours in newspapers tend to be easy primaries. This is particularly true when the newspaper is being printed by contract printers, who may not be keen to clean out the spot colour unit to change from their usual red to orange just for you.

The tabloid nationals are often called red tops by virtue of the spot colour they use. Now that most presses are capable of producing full colour, spot colour is not so widely used. The other problem with spot colour is the impossibility of getting accurate register. In spot colour the press prints one colour and then the other. The process of registration – ensuring that the two colours are overlaid exactly in the same place – is difficult and expensive. Spot colour can only really be used on areas where it doesn't matter if the colours slip slightly.

Process colour

Process colour is more flexible although more expensive. Full colour allows the reproduction of all shades of colour.

Our eyes see the primary colours of red, green and blue, and TV sets use light guns of these colours to make up the range of realistic colours we see on our screens. A lot of red and a little green and no blue gives you a vivid red/orange. But if you tried this with coloured pens on a piece of paper, all you would get is a nasty muddy brown. Printing uses a subtractive method – the complete opposite of the additive method outlined above, the one used on your TV and computer screens. It uses the secondary colours to make up the colours we eventually see. Secondary colours are the complementary colours to the three primary colours. The complementary to green is magenta, the complementary to blue is yellow and the complementary to red is cyan.

When all these secondary colours are present, they print black; when all are absent they print white (provided you are using white paper). Add yellow and blue together and you will get the primary colour green.

For printing, the secondary colours of cyan, magenta and yellow are usually combined with black. This is because of deficiencies in ink. Although, theoretically, combining the secondaries should give black, in fact the best possible outcome is a muddy brown. The addition of black ink allows the printer to produce pure black and to alter the value of the colours from full black to white. Black is represented by the letter K to give the CMYK system.

The colours are separated out in the computer to produce four separations. The computer examines the picture and produces four different plates, one with all the values of cyan present in the picture, one with all the values of magenta, one with all the values of yellow and one with all the blacks. The four separate plates are loaded onto the press and printed one on top of the other using cyan, magenta, yellow and black ink on the appropriate plate to produce a colour reproduction. The black plate also carries the type, rather than have that reproduced on all four plates, unless some type is in colour. Each plate is printed in register. That is, they print precisely on top of each other. If they miss by even a small amount, the picture will look blurry and odd. A slight cast of one colour will appear around the left-hand outline of everything and a cast of another colour around the right-hand outline. Massive improvements have been made in colour reproduction over the past few years as presses become more capable and as equipment improves. The poor quality of colour images common 20 years ago is now rare.

If you want a tone patch of a certain colour, you can mark the page with the percentages of each colour or the Pantone number and the printer will arrange for the colour separation to include the information.

Pantone is a system for identifying shades of colour that gives every shade a number. Editors can choose a shade from a catalogue and give the printer the code. Pantone colour 150U, for instance, would be mixed with saturations of 0 per cent cyan, 31 per cent magenta, 60 per cent yellow and 0 per cent black to give a light orange. The editor could also simply give the colour percentages, but unless the editor has a viewer with the shades in it, that might not mean very much. In this way the saturation and lightness of each colour can be adjusted, and this varies how they will mix to provide the final shades.

5
Pre-planning and copy tasting

Producing a new *edition* of any publication requires you to go through a number of planning stages. These usually start with the advertising. Advertising is a key ingredient of any publication produced in the western, capitalist tradition. Whether we journalists like it or not, it is advertising that generally brings in the bulk of income to pay the bills and make a profit, allowing the company to continue in business. There are a few publications that can exist on subscription and sales income alone, but these tend to be very expensive and very specialist. Mainstream publications rely on advertising for a large part of their income.

Because of the importance of advertising space, the first thing to do when planning an edition is to see how many adverts there are and where they will be placed, as this will influence the size of the publication and determine what you can put on each page.

Someone in the advertising sales department will normally be responsible for planning the placement of advertising. They will usually discuss a draft with the editor or production editor. Some adjustments might be made because there are too many ads on one page, or because a special feature is going on certain pages and room needs to be made or particular advertisers excluded. Sometimes the advertising department will ask that specific advertisers go on a particular page alongside certain stories or features, and this might pose an ethical dilemma for the editor. It might be fine for a TV rental firm or video hire shop to advertise on the TV listings page of a newspaper, but it would be less acceptable to allow an advert from a local company to sit on the page containing a story about their winning a Queen's Award for Enterprise. After the discussion, the editor will be left with a firm decision as to how many pages the edition will include and what space will be available to the editorial department on each page.

Deciding on copy allocation

Once an edition has been agreed upon, the editor will want to draw up a page plan that allows him or her to decide what will go on each page and determine the structure of the edition. A lot of these decisions might be standardised – newspapers often carry the sports section at the back, for instance – but the editor will still need to consider things. During the World Cup or Olympic Games, for instance, a newspaper might decide to move sport to the front rather than run it at the back – a fairly radical move, but one that should be considered. There's nothing worse than doing something just because that's how you've always done it. On the other hand, there's no point in changing something for the sake of it. Readers come to expect certain things in certain places and get cross if they can't find them. Many newspapers now put the TV listings near the centre of the paper to make it easy for people to find them; magazines have index pages at the front and regular spots (such as advice columns aunts or the stars) in regular spaces, often towards the back, as their popularity means that readers will find them, leaving the earlier pages for features.

The page plan can be made on the computer or on paper. Newspapers have traditionally used dummies – mock-ups of the newspaper produced by folding A4 sheets of paper to represent the paper (see Figure 5.1) – or a listing (see

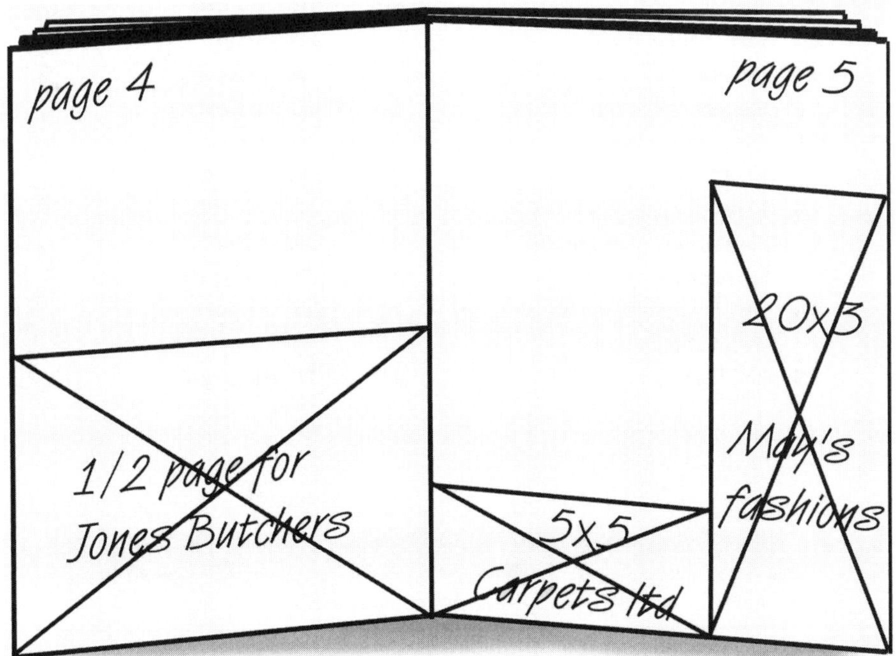

Figure 5.1 A dummy shows where the adverts go in a mock-up of the publication.

Figure 5.2). These don't work as well for large publications, and magazines have tended to use a flat plan (see Figure 5.3).

These days, though, the planning is usually done on computer, with the software used to design the publication presenting the pages with ad spaces marked on them. The editor can present the pages on screen in a flatplan format and move them around to different positions as required.

Once a final decision is taken about the plan, then it's possible to print it out, allowing the editor to take it to planning meetings and editorial conferences. It can also be used in discussion with designers, subs and other staff.

23/10/06 Nevermore Gazette

1	News	36	Sport
2	International news	35	Sport
3	News	34	Sport
4	Weddings	33	Sport
5	News	32	classified
6	News	31	classified
7	News	30	classified
8	Full page ad	29	classified
9	News	28	classified
10	Readers' letters	27	classified
11	Full page ad	26	classified
12	Features	25	classified
13	Features – fashion	24	classified
14	Features – fashion	23	classified
15	Entertainment	22	Wedding pics
16	Entertainment/what's on	21	Ad feature
17	Travel/leisure	20	Personal finance
18	TV listings	19	TV listings

Figure 5.2 A contents listing: a quick guide to what is where. Also shows which pages will be alongside each other on the press. For instance, pages 1 and 36 will print together, as will pages 18 and 19. If they are printed by a colour unit, they will all have colour.

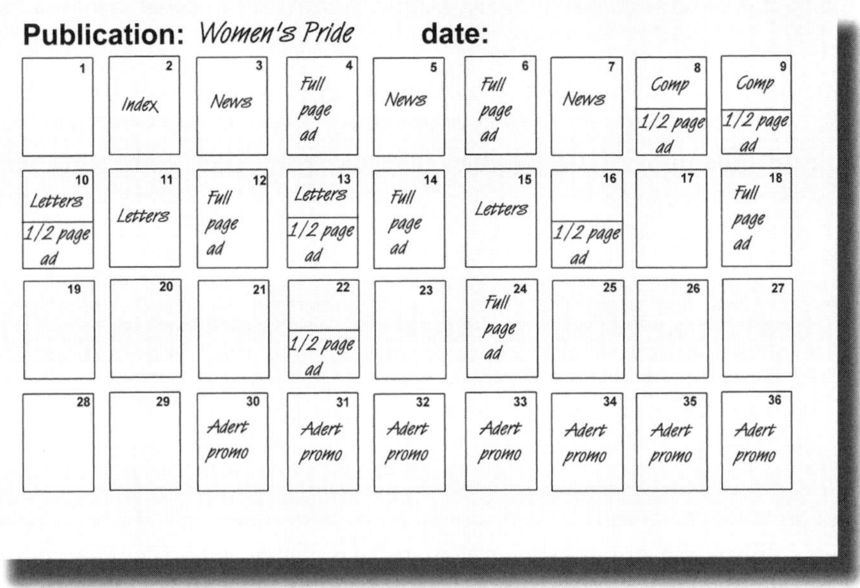

Figure 5.3 A flat plan: useful for large publications as it allows you to see all the pages at once.

Selecting pages

The editor will decide what goes where on the basis of need and tradition. Magazines tend to use early pages for indexes and advertising, while newspapers tend to use the first seven pages exclusively for the latest news.

Left versus right pages

One of the big debates in newspaper and to a lesser extent magazine design is the left page versus right page dilemma. Some editors believe that readers will tend to look at the right-hand page first because as they open the paper, this will be the first page they see. This is somewhat debatable, for one or two reasons. Readers are trained by practice to look at the top left-hand corner of any reading matter as this is where we are used to starting with books. You don't open a book and look automatically at the right-hand page; you tend to look at the left-hand page. The Poynter Institute's eye tracking research (Garcia and Stark 1991) shows that readers look at facing pages as a whole and do not distinguish between them. On the other hand, Garcia also points out that large picture or display areas on a page will draw the reader and inevitably they will see the right-hand page first and any graphic, picture or display area it contains. They might, therefore, be attracted to reading this first.

Kress and Van Leeuwen (1996: 186) believe that the right and left pages of magazines have a particular information value. They call this 'the Given' and 'the New'. The right-hand page offers new information key to the story while the left-hand page gives what is already known. They see the left as leading into the right: moving from the Given to the New.

> Looking at what is placed on the left and what is placed on the right in other kinds of visuals confirms this generalization: when pictures or layouts make significant use of the horizontal axis, positioning some of their elements left, and other, different ones right of the centre (which does not, of course, happen in every composition) the elements placed on the left are presented as Given, the elements placed on the right as New.
>
> (Kress and Van Leeuwen 1996: 186)

Kress and Van Leeuwen do not, however, suggest that this applies to newspapers – only to magazines, where the material is placed on two pages straddling the horizontal axis.

Whatever the actual readership habits, editors by and large still believe that the right-hand pages (odd-numbered pages) are of more importance. For this reason, adverts are kept off the first few right-hand pages if possible. Almost always, the first full-page advert you will find in a newspaper will be on a left-hand page, in an attempt to give editorial dominance. You will rarely find adverts that fill both facing pages, although this primarily reflects the advertiser's need to keep the reader reading editorial material alongside an advert.

Adverts are also kept to a minimum on right-hand pages for the same reason. It may well be the case (given the large page size of the average newspaper) that as the reader turns the page, if the first thing they saw was an advert, they might well continue until they found editorial matter. But if Garcia's argument is true, then readers deal with left and right pages as a whole and might be attracted anywhere on those two pages. They certainly do not treat the left and right page as separate entities to be read differently (Garcia and Stark 1991). It is important to remember that it might be better to plan and design the pages as an entity rather than deal with them separately. You will see in the plan (Figures 5.1 and 5.2) that it follows a traditional viewpoint, putting pages such as readers' letters and weddings on the left-hand pages opposite news pages. It is assumed in the traditional view that regular features that have a strong reader interest such as letters, weddings, horoscopes and agony aunts can be placed anywhere and that readers will seek them out. News on the other hand needs to attract fickle readers and draw them in, and requires all the assistance that editorial expertise can give.

Spreads

Spreads allow a designer to go to town on an idea. A *spread* is the use of facing pages to work on a single feature or news item tying the left and right page together. It needs to be remembered when working for newspapers that the technology of the press means that there will be a gutter (margins) between the two pages and that this can make it difficult to join the two together. Headlines and pictures cannot easily be run over the two pages as there will be a 3- to 4-centimetre gap between the two pages. The exception to this is the centre spread. The centre pages are printed as one piece on the press. The average press, whether printing tabloid or broadsheet, prints several pages on the same piece of paper and then splits them before gathering the pages together and folding them into a newspaper. This means that many pages are printed alongside each other, allowing the designer to print across the fold. Looking at the page listing illustrated in Figure 5.2 shows us which pages are printed together. The front and back, for instance, are printed alongside each other. Indeed, on most presses for a tabloid paper, the front, back and two centre pages are printed alongside each other, with the inside front, inside back and inside centres printed on the opposite side. The front and back are then cut off and the pages gathered and folded to make a newspaper.

This is important to understand because it allows us to decide on colour use as well as when we can print a spread across two pages. Most newspaper presses only have two or three colour units so that colour can only be printed on two or three blocks of pages that are printed together. So, for instance, the front, back and centre pages might be printed in colour, because they are printed alongside each other, but the inside back and front might not be, because they do not have a colour unit. The publication listing helps us to decide which pages have colour because we know that pages listed opposite each other will be printed together and so will have colour if colour is available on that unit.

This is important, because it allows us to decide which pages should go where. For instance, readers' letters probably do not need colour, whereas the wedding pictures page might well look better with colour. We would ensure that letters go on a page without colour while wedding pictures go on a page with colour.

The front and back pages of a newspaper normally have colour, which means the inside centre also has colour. Of course, magazines usually print in colour on all their pages, but, as with newspapers, if their inside centre pages are printed together, it is possible to print across both pages without the need to leave a margin to allow for the fold or binding. Headlines, graphics and photographs can span the two without problems. For this reason, most editors avoid wasting the centre pages on things such as TV listings or adverts; they'd rather use the space for a more interesting and expansive feature or news story. Fashion is often placed across this centre spread as it allows more attractive designs and colour than is possible elsewhere in a magazine. This also helps explain newspapers' enthusiasm for 'supplements'. Newspapers will often have a TV or entertainment supplement inserted in the newspaper. This method enables the editor to use a two-page spread, but deeper in the paper. Persuading readers that they should remove the 4- or 8- (or even 12- or 16-) page supplement means that there is then an additional two-page spread on what are in reality two inside pages.

Of course, all this is less of a problem in a magazine: colour is available on all pages, and there is no gutter to worry about because pages are bled to the edge. However, it is not possible to spread printing across two pages that are not printed alongside each other as there is bound to be a small mismatch, so even magazines welcome the centre pages and the ability these bring to spread across two pages. There is also more of a break between editorial pages in magazines because full-page adverts are more prevalent, as the pages are smaller than a newspaper. In advertising, although having what advertisers call *solus* position (the only ad on a page) is important, so is the actual size. Having a half-page ad in an A4 magazine means a smaller ad than a half-page in a tabloid. Therefore, big advertisers will normally seek a full-page advert in a magazine, and they would prefer this to be facing editorial material so that the reader will pause to read it and therefore (the theory goes) read the ad. For this reason, it is more usual to have only a one-page advertisement in a magazine so that it faces a page of editorial.

What should go where?

General decisions about where in the publication things should go will depend on the publication, its style, content and readership. Most newspapers and magazines that carry news prefer to have this near the start of the publication. Newspapers have news from the front page on. There is no particular reason for this other than tradition and the view that a strong front-page story will help to sell a newspaper. Magazines rely on a front cover that attempts to sell the full content and so do not put news on the front page. Some newspapers are now moving closer to this form of selling by putting short takes of their news items on the front together with *puffs* for key features, sport and entertainment.

Because the first few pages carry the latest news, their deadlines are normally as late as possible. This ensures that news pages are the last to be finished, so that the news is the freshest part of the publication. Deadlines are set to allow the flow of copy and the production of the paper to follow an orderly pattern. Some pages have to be designed and produced first, and it makes sense for these to be feature pages that can be prepared well in advance, leaving the news pages to be produced last.

In a typical evening paper the features and entertainments pages are normally produced the afternoon before. Many of the news pages will also be *overnights*: pages produced well before the final deadline. Often only the front and back page and possibly one or two specially dedicated *live pages* will be left to be filled the following morning with stories gathered in the past evening or morning of publication. Right-hand pages feature strongly in these live pages and it is likely that pages 3 and 5 will be the last to be designed before page 1.

Copy tasting

Once the various pages have been agreed upon, the editor, production editor or chief sub has to decide how the copy is allocated to the pages. In larger offices the pages might be divided up so that for a newspaper all the features pages are allocated to the features editor, sports pages to the sports editor and news pages to the chief sub-editor. On a really big newspaper even the news pages might be split between the foreign, home and other news desks. A magazine might split the pages between news, features and specialist pages that are a standard feature of that publication. Copy is then *tasted*: looked at to decide how and where it should be used. All the stories or features that are available will be considered by the appropriate editor and a decision made about where to use them and in what form.

When it comes to news, this is quite a complex process. A really good story might be difficult to use because there is so little information early on in its development; and while it might be entirely newsworthy, it might be difficult to fit such a small amount of copy onto the page and give it a suitable display. Another story might be tedious, but require a considerable amount of material to make it worth using. An example of the first scenario could be an announcement by the police that they have arrested the prime minister for treason. A big story, of that there is no doubt, and it is one that needs to appear on the front page of a newspaper. But the law prevents newspapers from reporting much detail following the arrest of someone for a crime and, legally at least, there is little that the newspaper can report. The page might end up comprising a huge picture of the prime minister, enormous headlines and 150 words of copy.

Another example could be the 11 September terrorist attacks. Every newspaper wanted to run copy on the first few pages, including the front page, as their readers would be looking for full coverage of such a horrific event. Yet early on there was little new or unexpected to be reported that hadn't already appeared on TV. There was a lot of material, but it was difficult for newspapers to match the drama of the TV pictures, and finding something dramatic or new in terms of meaning or analysis was very difficult. As time went on, of course, all this changed, but in the very early stages no one knew in sufficient detail what was really happening as reports were difficult to obtain.

It could also be that there are six good stories that could all be used on the front page, but all have at least two good pictures and 800 words of copy. There would not be enough room to fit this news feast on the front page. Discussions then have to take place about which stories are moved inside. Copy tasting is about selecting the right stories to run and then putting them on the right page with other stories to make balanced and interesting pages that the reader will enjoy reading.

Copy style

When the paper or magazine is first designed, the designer will not just decide about fonts and artwork, but also have some ideas of how different pages will look. This could be fixed by producing a series of templates that can be used for different pages. I discuss templates in more depth in Chapter 7, but essentially templates are ways of producing page layouts that can be lifted into the computer from central storage, allowing the sub to fill in the spaces: a headline here of a certain size, some copy there and a picture over here. Some newspapers are now even using templates to allow reporters to file a story direct to the page without the need for it to be edited. They are told where the story is going and then need to write it to fit and produce a headline as well. If we ignore the dangers of unedited copy going direct into a newspaper, we can say that these template productions remove the need for detailed design skills but can also lead to very samey-looking pages.

Even if templates are not used, the designer will still want to lay down a house style: rules about the way pages should look. This might have rules such as: no more than two lines of heading if the lead heading is across more than four columns, no reverse headings above the fold (the halfway point on a newspaper where it is folded; this usually only applies to the front page, as people can read the inside only if the paper is unfolded). Pictures should always be above or below the fold, never across it. The style might be very detailed, giving little latitude for *byline* styles, intros, captions, caption placement, picture styles, whether you can *pierce* pictures, and so on. This style needs to be followed as far as possible.

6
Designing pages

Once copy, pictures and graphics have been allocated to a page or pages, someone is going to have to do the design; to decide on the amount and type of display and how the page or pages will be structured. Many of these decisions are taken by the editor, production editor or chief sub-editor. These executives will have already discussed in conference which material will be used on the page and approximately how it should be handled: is the material to share the page with other stories or features? Will there be a significant number of pictures or graphics? To some extent this will be determined by the type of publication: a tabloid newspaper or fashion magazine will want to go big on the pictures, a quality newspaper or political magazine will concentrate more heavily on the text. These decisions are important both because they will determine how the publication sells with the reader and because even at this display level there are ethical decisions to be taken about the material. Giving a weak news story major splash treatment is to oversell it. The reader is likely to end up confused; the display suggested the story was important and it turns out that it wasn't. There is an area of science called false alarm theory which shows that constant false alarms reduce a person's trust in an alarm system. There is no reason to suppose this does not apply to newspapers and magazines as well, and so if we keep saying that something is a great story and it turns out not to be, readers will end up not trusting the newspaper and will therefore probably take another. So what could we do instead? Well, we could offer them value for money. Give plenty of stories and pictures on that page – all interesting but none of them heart-stopping. Many magazines do this with their news pages. None of the news is startling; it is all about an area of interest: new products, manufacturing changes, latest techniques or inventions, handy tips or gossip. All of it is of interest to the target group, and a couple of busy pages filled with small items and pictures can give a lot of information and reader satisfaction.

On a newspaper, the daily conference of newsroom executives may have decided the lead, and possibly the main picture story. Other stories on the page will be selected by the chief sub, probably in some sort of order. The chief sub will then brief the designer, explaining how the copy should be handled. The chief sub may well offer far more copy than can be fitted on the page and so it is then up to the designer to decide on the amount of copy required and the amount of display material. Sub-editors can then be instructed about the length of copy required for each page.

The traditional method

Although most newspapers and magazines are made up on computer desktop publishing systems such as QuarkXPress or Adobe InDesign, it is still worth discussing the traditional method of designing pages because the traditional ways often have something to teach us.

When pages were still made up by compositors, either in metal in the composing room or with photocomposition on light tables, journalists and designers had to produce a draft of the way the page should look. This had to be very detailed to ensure that the person who actually had to follow that plan to put the page together could not make a mistake about what was expected. It would show where the copy was to go, it would detail the headlines and give their sizes and it would mark up where the pictures should go and their sizes. Often this detailed draft would be preceded by a rough visualisation of the page, particularly if the page was complicated or was a busy feature page (news is often easier to design, as there is just a series of news 'blocks' or 'modules' to be put together). Producing a rough visualisation is still a good idea even in the days of computer design. The page visualisation is extremely useful in helping to grasp scale and to provoke ideas. Original ideas in design, as in writing, are paramount. Original pages that work and stay in house style (approximately, at least) are what set apart good publications from ordinary ones.

In my experience, beginners, whether students or practitioners, find the idea of a visual difficult. I always insist that students produce a visual first, but often they try to avoid this and go straight onto the computer. I think they are hoping that their nervousness at being faced by a pristine piece of paper which they have to turn into a page of a publication will vanish on the computer and that it will magically do the work for them. Certainly their first stumbling attempts do appear to look more professional on the computer; they're bound to! However, it can take them an hour to lay in their first couple of stories on the computer and then when they find the design doesn't work, they have to scrap it and start again. Producing a visual – once you have some experience – takes only a few moments. If the plan doesn't work, it can be thrown away and a new attempt made, building on what was learned from the failed attempt. In this way a visual can save you an awful lot of time and effort, helping to get some perspective and balance on a page within minutes, speeding up the whole process of producing a well-balanced page.

The visual can be produced on a piece of scrap paper (see Figure 6.1). This does not need to be very big and is only intended to work out the main elements of the page and give a rough idea of fit and scale. These visuals not only will help you to work out how the page will come together but should spark off ideas that will make the page more attractive and interesting.

In the traditional office, the visual would have been replaced by an accurate representation of how the page should look when it is finished, but in a computerised office this is not necessary, and when you are happy with the general feel of the visual, you can start laying out the frames on the page in the computer.

Whether you are doing a visual for a traditional office or a computerised office always check that you have the right adverts for the page, that they are the right size and that they have been drawn to the right size. There are few things worse than designing a page only to find that you have drawn in an ad as three columns when it had clearly been requested as four columns. Once you are sure you have all the ads and any other items such as *mastheads* and *blurbs* in the right place, you can start drawing – using pencil!

The visual is there entirely to help you get clear in your mind how the page should look. Although any old scrap of paper can be used, it's probably better to use a piece of A4 so that it is similar in proportions to the page you will be designing. Using a piece of paper smaller than the final page means that you will be working on a scaled-down version, and this can be a bit confusing at first. The smaller size of the visual makes the page look different to the finished item. This is something you will need to get used to, as you will often work on the page on computer at about this size. Very few screens are able to show you the whole of a tabloid page at full size. You must either see only a section of the page or switch to full-page view, which will reduce the scale of the page to as little as 25 per cent. However, if you find it very difficult to cope with the difference in scale, there is nothing to stop you using a piece of A3 paper, which will be very similar in size to tabloid or, when turned to landscape, the same as two pages of many magazines side by side, allowing you to work on the design for two pages at once, as will be required for many magazines.

Some places still use pre-printed pro-formas for visuals. These have grids on them to show the columns and scaled-down depth in centimetres (see Figure 6.2). These grids can be particularly useful in your early days as you start to get the hang of scale on a visual (see Figure 6.1). You might want to photocopy the grid shown in Figure 6.2 to use for yourself when you practise producing visuals.

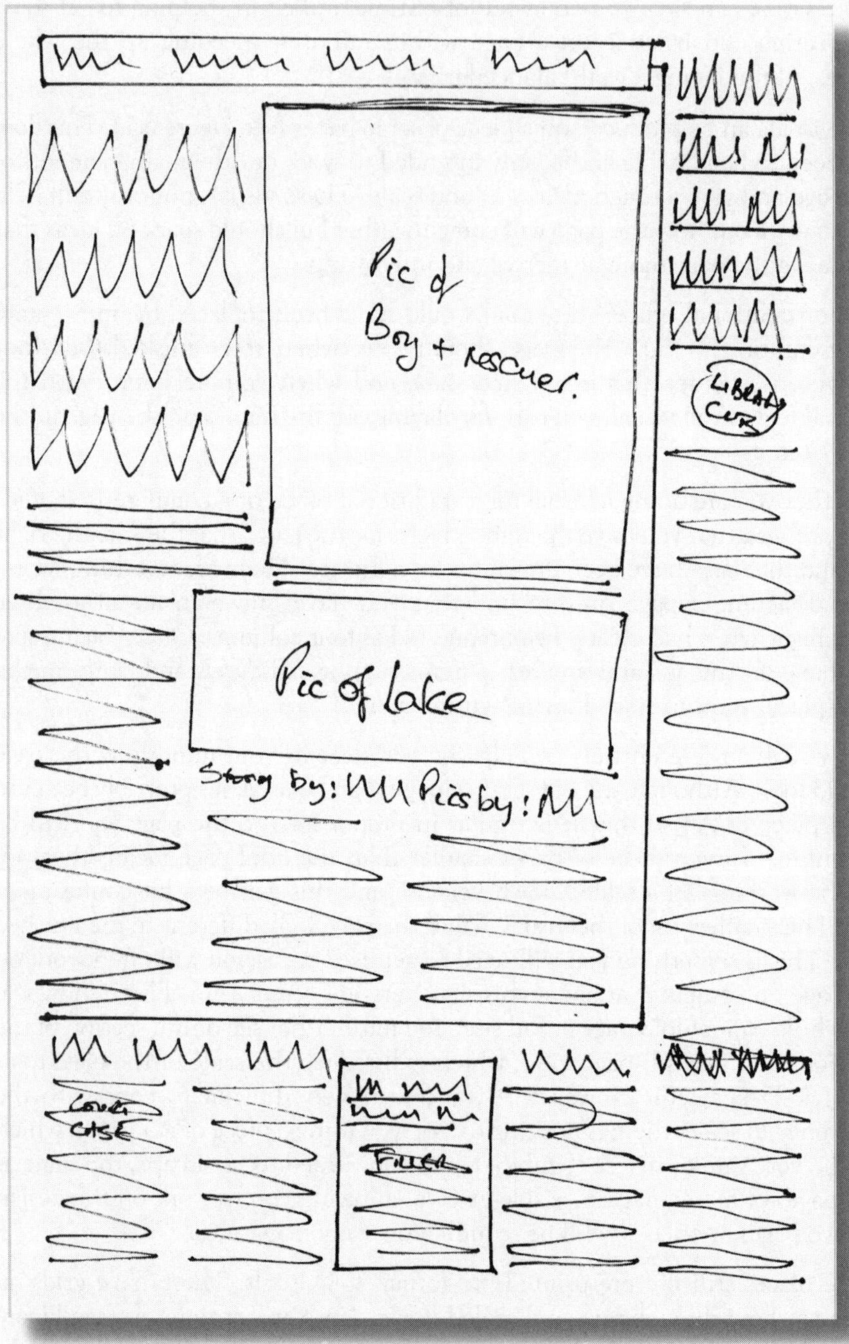

Figure 6.1 A visual: a quick sketch to try ideas, see how the page might look and get a sense of scale.

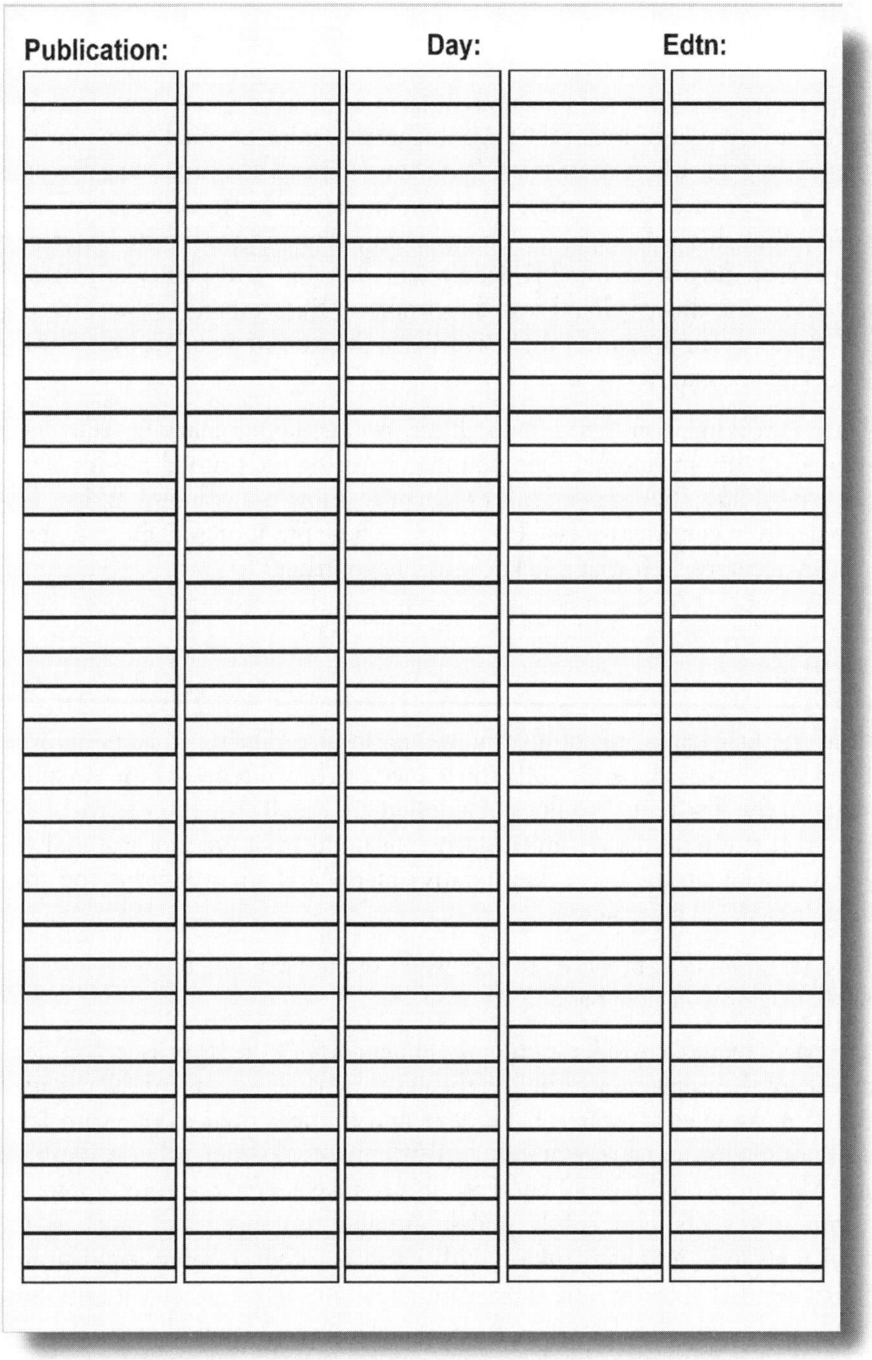

Publication: Day: Edtn:

Figure 6.2 A grid draft for a tabloid page (38cm usable depth) and seven columns. Allows the designer to draft accurate pages.

It would be worth enlarging it when you photocopy. If you prefer, you can draw up your own, using your DTP package.

A page draft (see Figure 6.3) is different from a visual in that a draft should be an accurate representation of the page you are designing to enable someone else to make the page up. A draft is used when a compositor is producing the page either on computer or in traditional hot metal or photocomposition. It is unlikely that this will happen in many publications in the United States or Europe, including the United Kingdom, but there are still plenty of places in the world using this tried and tested technology. Remember: if something can be read the wrong way on a draft, it will be. Make sure you label everything clearly and accurately.

If you are working in an office that still uses non-computer make-up, not a very likely possibility in Europe, then you may be using pre-printed pro-formas to draw your draft. These have grids on them to show the columns and scaled-down depth in centimetres (see Figure 6.2). These pro-formas make it easier to make an accurate draft that you know will fit together.

First steps

Just as the first few words of a story are the most agonising to come up with while you debate how best to sully the framed bright whiteness of the computer screen, so the first tentative lines of a design are usually the most stressful and difficult. It can help if you run through your mind what types of material you have to display on the page, their relative merits and any weighting the chief sub has asked you give them.

There are different approaches to take when you are working on news stories as against magazine or newspaper feature pages.

News pages require consideration of the immediacy of the story as well as decisions about the number of stories on the page and their placement. Newspapers need to make readers aware of the news and trumpet their stories with large headlines, pictures and a relatively unsubtle display, particularly on the front page. Magazines on the other hand are able to take a more measured approach, drawing in readers more subtly, and so are able to concentrate more on the actual text and pictures, working with them to produce more sophisticated approaches that suit the long time span readers are likely to allocate to them. Feature pages, whether for newspapers or magazines, are a more leisurely read. The text and pictures are likely to have around the same or a similar feel, and the weighting and design of the text, graphics and pictures is about aiding communication as well as selling the story. Even on front pages the difference

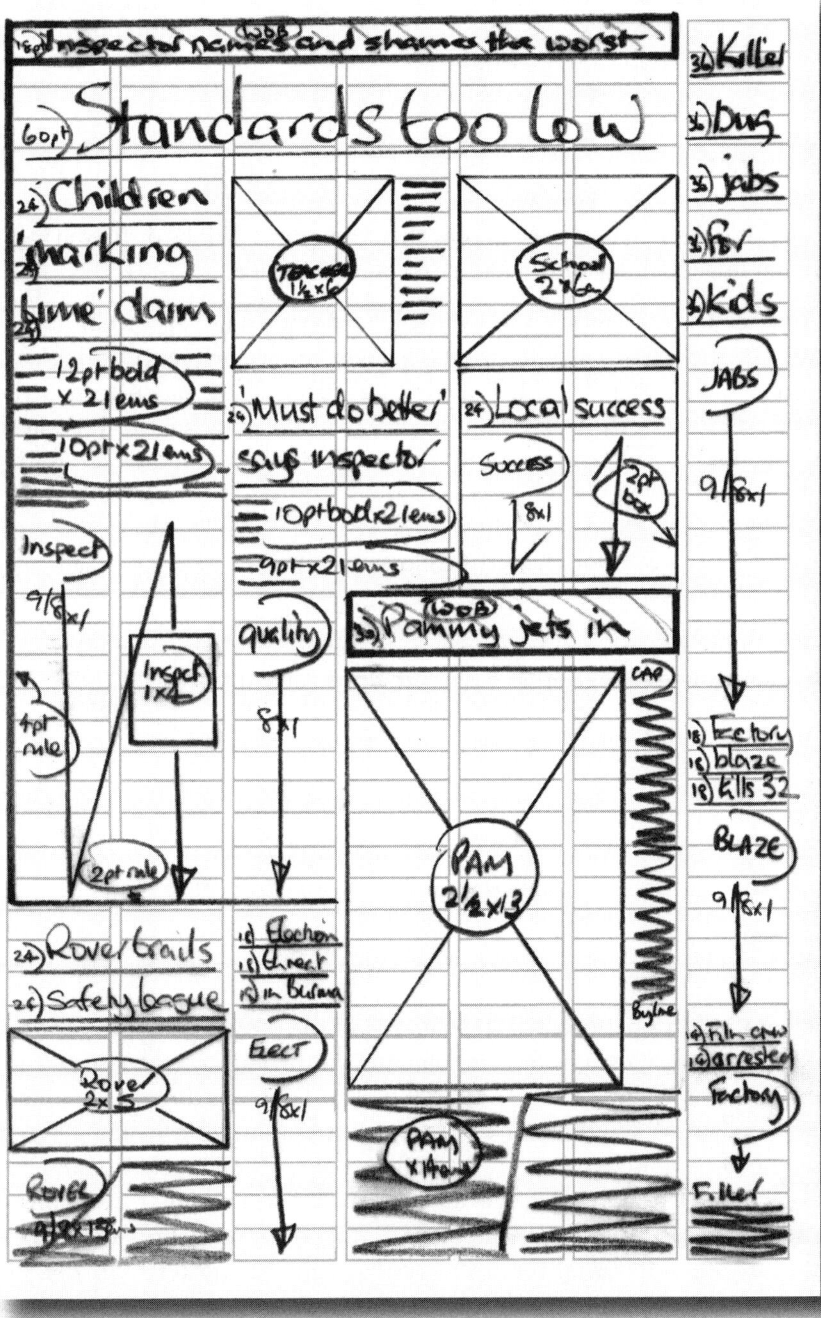

Figure 6.3 A page draft. Note that all the detail required is listed: headline, picture sizes, and so on.

between newspapers and magazines is obvious, with the newspaper screaming loud and clear why you need to buy it, but the magazine offering a much gentler introduction to what is on offer in it.

News stories

Newspaper designers need to plan how the news stories will be displayed to gain maximum impact along with maximum communication.

First you need to sort out what is available to you for that page, what has been allocated by the production editor, trying to get an idea of quantity and relative significance. Write yourself a list of what's available. How much copy is there and what are your instructions about its use? Does the copy have any pictures to illustrate it? If so, are they any good? Could you find some more pictures from the library?

Example 1 You have been given the following copy for a newspaper news page:

Story	*Length*	*Instructions*
Family home blaze – no deaths	26 cm	Lead story with pix
Council to change planning system	19 cm	Second lead, no pix
Presentation of safety award	7 cm	Presentation pic of 6 people
Road crash – non-fatal	15 cm	No pix
Assault case at court – man jailed	24 cm	Down-page story
Assorted fillers		

The length in Example 1 refers to the length of the copy if the type is set in the standard house style over a standard column width. The art of casting off is no longer an essential skill of the sub-editor. Before copy was directly set on computers, subs would get the stories on typewritten sheets from the reporters. These would be edited and then cast off: the sub would calculate how many words of copy there were and how much space this would fill at a certain type size. Accurate casting off was important, otherwise when the page was put together in the composing room, the story might be shorter than the space allotted, or, worse still, longer. Computers have made most of this work superfluous, because the sub can now see straight away if the story doesn't fit the space allocated. However, it can be much easier to design a page from scratch if you have a reasonable idea of how much space the story is likely to fill. All publications have standard styles and sizes of type. Typically, a newspaper's body type will be between 8pt and 9pt. Type in a magazine will tend to vary much more, depending on audience. For instance, magazines aimed at an over-50 audience among whom reading glasses are more prevalent might choose 10 or even 12pt as standard. A typical local newspaper I used as an example ran 133 words over 10 centimetres of one of its standard columns. This means that it typically fills each column centimetre with 13 words, and so we can quickly approximate how much space any story requires by dividing the number of words by 13. Of course, as I said, the computer will just place the story in and you can cut or adjust to leave space to fill as required, but it does make it easier to design a new page from scratch, as opposed to using a template, if you have a clear idea about how much space is required. So, for instance, our lead story will fill approximately 26 centimetres.

The instructions column in Example 1 above shows the instructions given by the chief sub to the designer. In this case, as the lead story and pictures are potentially good, you will want them to dominate the page. If the story had been weak, then the chief sub might have wanted to give other stories a more equal treatment.

It is not vital that the lead story be placed at the top of the page. This is a tradition that is upheld more by laziness than any other reason. What we are seeking to do is provide the reader with an *entry point* – a way of getting into the page. This entry point could be the heading for the story lead, but is more likely to be a picture. According to research carried out by the Poynter Institute in the United States, 'When the reader enters a page, attention is drawn to no predetermined position. Instead . . . the reader's attention focuses first on the dominant visual element' (Garcia and Stark 1991: 26).

This means that if we wish to draw the reader into the page at the bottom or in the middle, we can do so provided we offer the reader a suitable visual cue such as a large and dominant headline or picture, or a bright splash of colour. This is a technique that is often carried to extremes on the front of tabloids, which may have just a picture and a headline, with the copy carried on the following pages.

We traditionally read text from top left to bottom right, and some of this habit continues when we read newspapers, but we actually start to read at the entry point.

To return to our example, the lake rescue is the main story and there are no other stories for that page that can compete with it for newsworthiness, and so there is no reason to break from the tradition of taking the story to the top of the page. We also have some excellent pictures to go with the story and we can use these with the headline to provide a strong entry point to bring readers straight to the story we want them to read first, because we think it is the most significant.

When one is designing news pages, often the temptation is to run all the stories at similar prominence, but this rarely works well and merely offers flat and uninspiring pages that are difficult for the reader to navigate. If we can't decide which story is the most newsworthy and which the reader ought to look at first, we might as well give up design and run the stories one after another with only a few headings to separate them. By choosing one story to dominate the page and using the other stories to support that, we offer the reader a page that is attractive, logically structured and easy to navigate, offering entertainment, information and value for the cover price. That doesn't mean that we have to make all lead stories the same size, though. If a story is a big news item, we would give it more display than a lead that was not very interesting. Talking about using the same style of design and weight of lead heading day after day, revolutionary *Daily Mail* editor Mike Randall said, 'by slavish adherence to it you cannot avoid the false emphasis it gives . . . The whole system creates a straitjacket from which you cannot escape' (Hutt 1967: 46). Deciding on what leads a page and how big its display should be raises a number of important issues about the media and the way it presents news to people. The choice of story and its display can add considerable bias to the news, implying significance where there may be none and potentially hiding the important issues.

In the example I am using, the story is strong (a near-death rescue of a child is always good copy for a local paper; losing a child is about the worst disaster that can happen to someone) and there is no problem about making it dominate the page, but sometimes a story is not so strong. We still need to make such a lead dominate the page, but we can make other stories come close to that dominance by running the lead in the centre of the page or down one side, or even by putting it at the bottom of the page. That way we avoid the asymmetry of several similarly displayed stories on a page, without allowing the story we have chosen to lead the page to completely dominate the page when other stories are equally good. The other stories might not get the display, but they do get a good position. We need to develop a hierarchy on pages that assists readers and guides them through the material we are offering. In our example page, for instance, while the rescue is a strong story, the closure of a library is also strong, although nothing like as dramatic or full of human interest. A way of giving it prominence without its competing with the lead is to run it down the right-hand column. It will support the lead, but not compete. Being on the far right (assuming we are designing a right-hand page), it will catch the eye, but it will still be the lead that draws the reader in. Figure 6.4 shows the second lead in place, leaving a solid space across the centre for the lead, as envisaged in the visual. The story is run in single text with the *intro* 1 point larger than the body

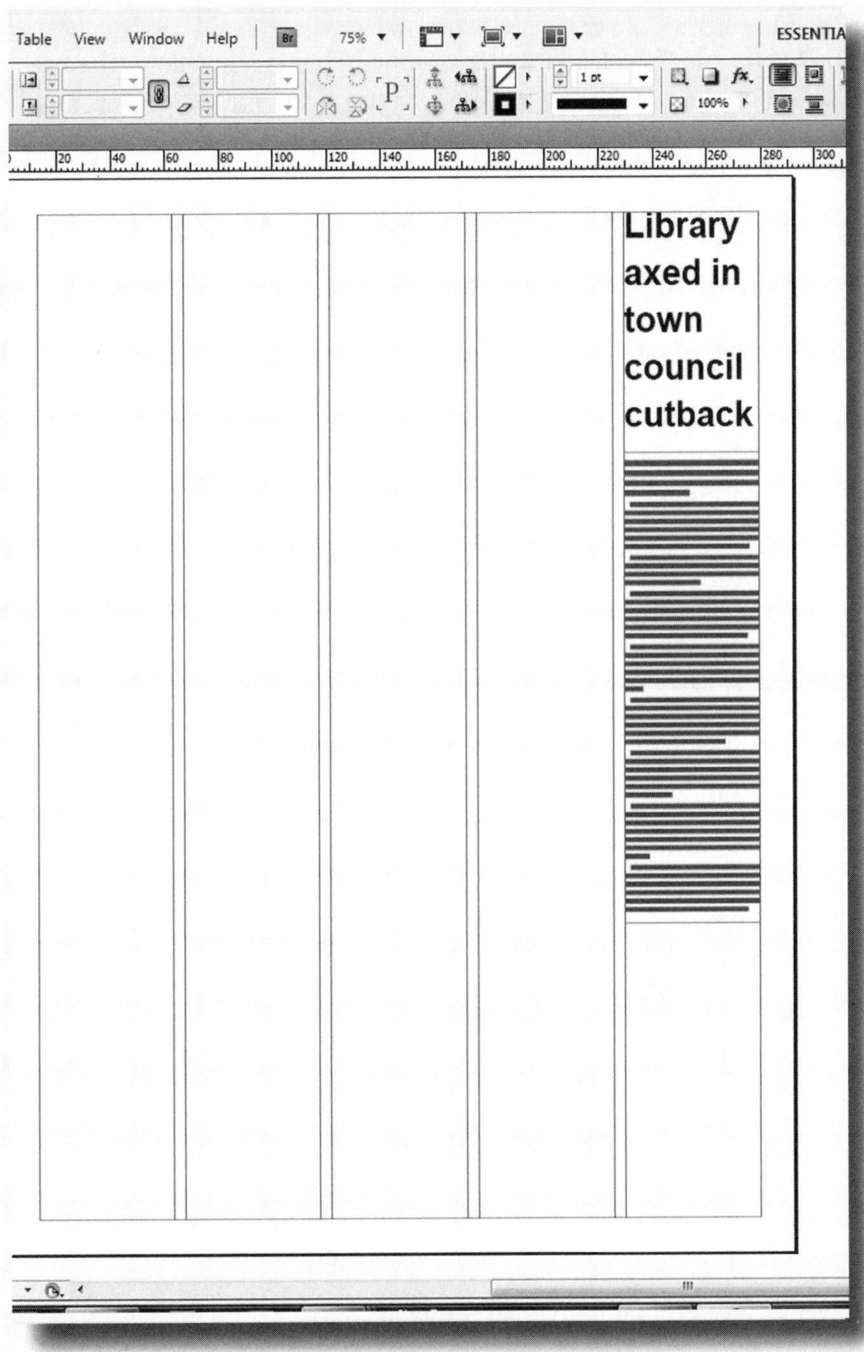

Figure 6.4 The first story is run into the page as identified by the visual.

type and in bold in order to give clear emphasis to the entry point. Also note how the first line of the intro par is not indented, while all subsequent paragraphs have a small indent to ease reading. This indent allows the eye to identify where it is on the page. The heading is in 36pt across five lengths, giving reasonable impact alongside the large space left for the lead. Although the text run is reasonably long, there is no crossheading. The text will be sitting alongside two large pictures and a crosshead would not aid the reader in tracking through the story; indeed, it would be more likely to confuse.

Now we have our start to the page, we need next to consider how much space to give to the lead story. It is going to run across all four remaining columns, but we need to decide how deep. This is a strong story: a child out enjoying himself thrust into danger but snatched from death at the last moment. Pictures of child and rescuer as well as the cold scene of the potential tragedy will add weight, so the bulk of the page is required for this story, as the visual shows. The pictures are central, drawing the reader in with a sound if relatively modest heading of 72pt running down the left and a *strapline* linking everything together at the top.

The text is run across several measures (see Figure 6.5). The *intro* follows straight after the headline across a wide measure, allowing emphasis to be provided with a large, bold font of 12pt. This is soon reduced to the more standard 8pt as the type goes into single column to sit alongside the picture. After the picture, and in order to hold it firmly in place and make it clear it is part of the story, the type expands again into a three-column measure across the four-column width of the paper. This slightly wider than normal measure improves readability and will also provide a clear distinction from the next story. The text and pictures are all indented on the right in order to allow the 3pt rule to be run from the reverse patch strapline down alongside the pictures and then along the base of the text, ruling the whole story away from the rest of the page. The rule is not essential, but it does give a little extra emphasis to the story. It would have been particularly useful if the lead had had additional copy such as a small *sidebar* piece about how to play safely on frozen lakes, as this would have helped tie all the copy and pictures together. In the end I decided not to insert the copy and picture *bylines*. Although they were on the visual, they did not look so good on the page and the picture of the lake is deeper than I had thought, so I left them out. Visuals are a useful guide, but that is all they are, a guide, and don't need to be followed slavishly. If something doesn't look as good as you had hoped once it is on the page, leave it out or change it.

The page is now well on the way to completion, but we still need to put in the court case and the road accident. The visual calls for these to be placed as double-column stories, one either side of the page, split by a single column of news in brief, and this should be easy to manage.

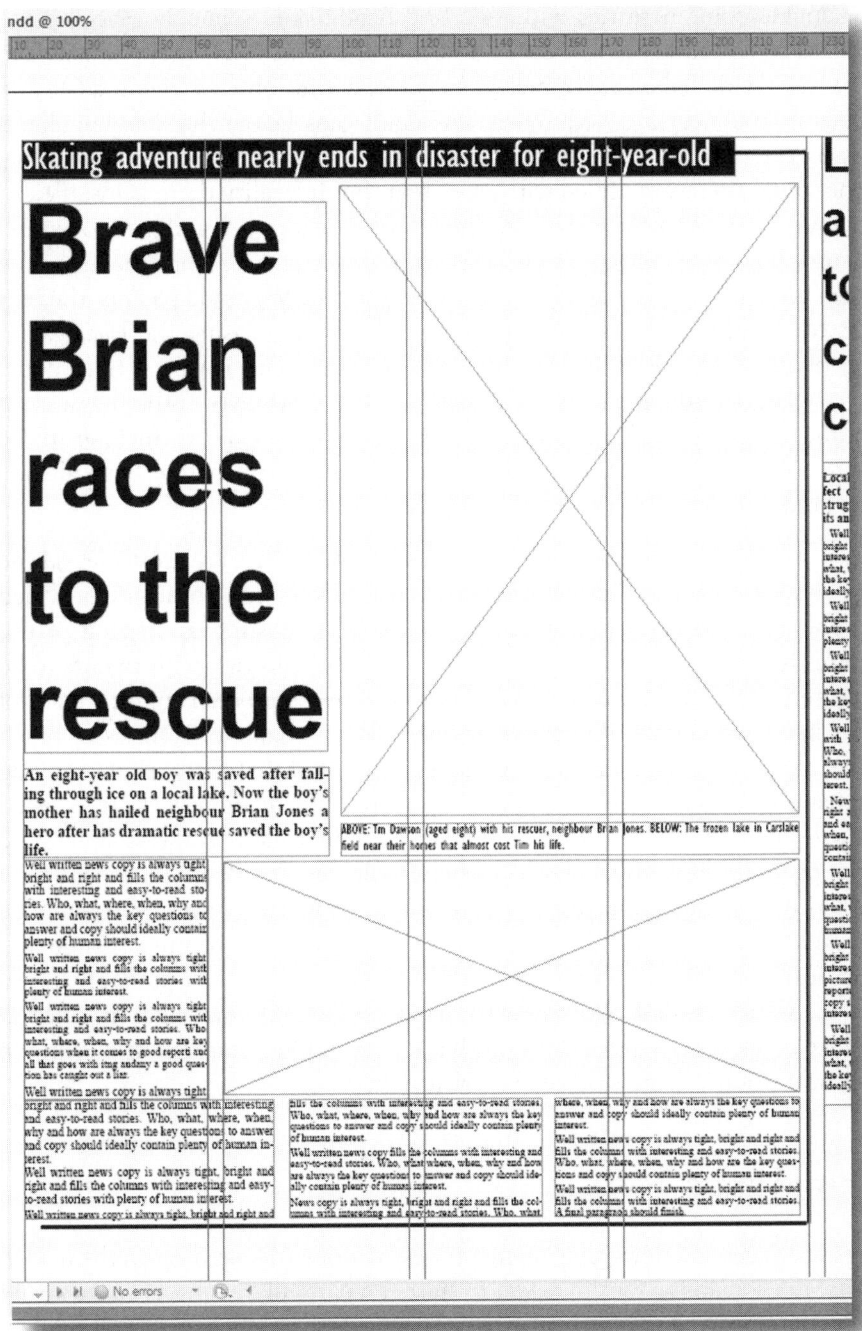

ndd @ 100%

Skating adventure nearly ends in disaster for eight-year-old

Brave Brian races to the rescue

An eight-year old boy was saved after falling through ice on a local lake. Now the boy's mother has hailed neighbour Brian Jones a hero after has dramatic rescue saved the boy's life.

Well written news copy is always tight bright and right and fills the columns with interesting and easy-to-read stories. Who, what, where, when, why and how are always the key questions to answer and copy should ideally contain plenty of human interest.

Well written news copy is always tight bright and right and fills the columns with interesting and easy-to-read stories with plenty of human interest.

Well written news copy is always tight bright and right and fills the columns with interesting and easy-to-read stories. Who what, where, when, why and how are key questions when it comes to good reporti and all that goes with itng andamy a good question has caught out a liar.

Well written news copy is always tight bright and right and fills the columns with interesting and easy-to-read stories. Who, what, where, when, why and how are always the key questions to answer and copy should ideally contain plenty of human interest.

Well written news copy is always tight, bright and right and fills the columns with interesting and easy-to-read stories with plenty of human interest.

Well written news copy is always tight, bright and right and fills the columns with interesting and easy-to-read stories. Who, what, where, when, why and how are always the key questions to answer and copy should ideally contain plenty of human interest.

Well written news copy fills the columns with interesting and easy-to-read stories. Who, what where, when, why and how are always the key questions to answer and copy should ideally contain plenty of human interest.

News copy is always tight, bright and right and fills the columns with interesting and easy-to-read stories. Who, what, where, when, why and how are always the key questions to answer and copy should ideally contain plenty of human interest.

Well written news copy is always tight, bright and right and fills the columns with interesting and easy-to-read stories. Who, what, where, when, why and how are the key questions and copy should contain plenty of human interest.

Well written news copy is always tight, bright and right and fills the columns with interesting and easy-to-read stories. A final paragraph should finish.

ABOVE: Tm Dawson (aged eight) with his rescuer, neighbour Brian Jones. BELOW: The frozen lake in Carslake field near their homes that almost cost Tim his life.

No errors

Figure 6.5 The lead is put in place with its pictures.

The double-column stories with two-line headings are quickly placed using standard style and the single column of nibs (news in brief) dropped between them to provide balance, symmetry and limit confusion (see Figure 6.6). The page is now almost finished. There are small gaps below the double-column story on the right and the second lead down the right-hand column. Of course, in the visual these were filled with story text, but in reality there is insufficient copy. We could of course go back to the reporter or copy sub and seek to extend the story, but there's little point in doing this as the reporter would have put the information there in the first place if it was worth it. We could pad out the text by putting extra space between paragraphs or by increasing the *leading*, but probably the best way is to put a filler in the space. This is what I have done; one is separated from the story above with a 2pt rule, while the other has a small heading. The sharp-eyed will note that the filler is the same as the filler in the centre column. Do ensure that you are not picking up fillers that have already been used. I've done it in order to make the point.

Take a good look at the page: the story count is fine – there are six stories on the page and two fillers, and it is lively and active. Good entry points are provided and there are strong pictures in the centre. The placing and sizing of the pictures is crucial but this was shown in the visual, allowing adjustments to be made very early on if needed. Because the visual was scribbled out on a piece of paper in only a couple of minutes, it only takes a couple of seconds to bin it before replacing it with a sketch that takes account of that discovery by moving or enlarging (or reducing) the size of the pictures. The amount of effort invested in the original draft is minimal, and in any case the time is not wasted, because it was possible to go on to produce a better version. But if you had spent time doing this on computer, laying in the text and sizing the pictures, you would be far less keen to change the page; there would have been too much time and effort invested, but an attempted redesign at this stage would probably fail to produce what's needed. Working with paper and pencil in the first instance to produce quick visuals makes sense and saves effort. Only start laying out on the computer when you are sure you've got it right.

Magazine pages

Magazine pages and newspaper feature pages are not so demanding on the reader. We are not screaming for the reader to start at a particular point, because we are providing a more leisurely read where the reader has already started to flick through the publication. They are already involved and so we can attract their attention more subtly with a clever headline or interesting picture. The entry point is likely to be much more obvious as there is likely to be only one story, and

Skating adventure nearly ends in disaster for eight-year-old

Brave Brian races to the rescue

An eight-year old boy was saved after falling through ice on a local lake. Now the boy's mother has hailed neighbour Brian Jones a hero after has dramatic rescue saved the boy's life.

Well written news copy is always tight, bright and right and fills the columns with interesting and easy-to-read stories. Who, what, where, when, why and how are always the key questions to answer and copy should ideally contain plenty of human interest.

Well written news copy is always tight, bright and right and fills the columns with interesting and easy-to-read stories with plenty of human interest.

Well written news copy is always tight, bright and right and fills the columns with interesting and easy-to-read stories. Who, what, where, when, why and how are key questions when it comes to good reporti and all that goes with ing andany a good question has caught out a liar.

Well written news copy is always tight, bright and right and fills the columns with interesting and easy-to-read stories. Who, what, where, when, why and how are always the key questions to answer and copy should ideally contain plenty of human interest.

Well written news copy is always tight, bright and right and fills the columns with interesting and easy-to-read stories with plenty of human interest.

Well written news copy is always tight, bright and right and fills the columns with interesting and easy-to-read stories. Who, what, where, when, why and how are always the key questions to answer and copy should ideally contain plenty of human interest.

Well written news copy fills the columns with interesting and easy-to-read stories. Who, what where, when, why and how are always the key questions to answer and copy should ideally contain plenty of human interest.

News copy is always tight, bright and right and fills the columns with interesting and easy-to-read stories. Who, what, where, when, why and how are always the key questions to answer and copy should ideally contain plenty of human interest.

Well written news copy is always tight, bright and right and fills the columns with interesting and easy-to-read stories. Who, what, where, when, why and how are the key questions and copy should contain plenty of human interest.

Well written news copy is always tight, bright and right and fills the columns with interesting and easy-to-read stories. A final paragraph should finish

ABOVE: Tim Dawson (aged eight) with his rescuer, neighbour Brian Jones. BELOW: The frozen lake in Carslake field near their homes that almost cost Tim his life.

Library axed in town council cutback

Local libraries are to feel the full effect of cuts as the County Council struggles to save more than £24m on its annual budget.

Well written news copy is always tight, bright and right and fills the columns with interesting and easy-to-read stories. Who, what, where, when, why and how are always the key questions to answer and copy should ideally contain plenty of human interest.

Well written news copy is always tight, bright and right and fills the columns with interesting and easy-to-read stories with plenty of human interest.

Well written news copy is always tight, bright and right and fills the columns with interesting and easy-to-read stories. Who, what, where, when, why and how are always the key questions to answer and copy should ideally contain plenty of human interest.

Well written news copy fills the columns with interesting and easy-to-read stories. Who, what where, when, why and how are always the key questions to answer and copy should ideally contain plenty of human interest.

News copy is always tight, bright and right and fills the columns with interesting and easy-to-read stories. Who, what, where, when, why and how are always the key questions to answer and copy should ideally contain plenty of human interest.

Well written news copy is always tight, bright and right and fills the columns with interesting and easy-to-read stories. Who, what, where, when, why and how are the key questions and copy should contain plenty of human interest.

Well written news copy is always tight, bright and right and fills the columns with interesting and easy-to-read stories. A good picture can also brighten the page. A good reporter always asks the key questions and copy should ideally contain plenty of human interest.

Well written news copy is always tight, bright and right and fills the columns with interesting and easy-to-read stories. Who, what, where, when, why and how are always the key questions to answer and copy should ideally contain plenty of human interest.

Factory theft

A thief stole copper piping after breaking into a disused factory.

The thief broke in through a window at the back of the premises on the Carslake industrial estate and took the pipe from the heating system. Police spotted the theft after being called to deal with the consequent flooding.

Drunken chip shop fight led to court

A man has been found guilty of common assault after a fight in a chip shop following a night of heavy drinking.

Jack Dimwit had been out drinking with friends since early afternoon, Newtown magistrates were told by prosecuting counsel and he had consumed numerous pints of beer and some whiskies.

Around 11.30 he was told to go home by the landlord of the Green Dragon in the town centre. He stopped off for fish and chips on the way down the High Street and got into an argument with another customer about who was first in the queue for food.

Although no-one was seriously injured, the police were called and Dimwit was arrested and held in the cells overnight.

Dimwit apologised to the court, "I had been drinking because my wife had left me and was not able to cope when I got into an argument," he said.

Magistrates found him guilty of assault and fined him £200 and bound him over to be of good behaviour for a year.

Thief stole pipe

A thief stole copper piping after breaking into a disused factory.

The thief broke in through a window at the back of the premises on the Carslake industrial estate and took the pipe from the heating system. Police spotted the theft after being called to deal with the consequent flooding

Parking pledge

Police and traffic wardens are to crack down on irresponsible motorists who are parking their cars illegally in Newton. Residents near the Carslake industrial estate complain about poorly parked cars blocking access and now police and wardens are to apply a zero-tolerance policy to parking restrictions.

Man hurt in late night milk float collision

A man was seriously hurt in a road accident after his car was involved in a collision with a milk float late on Sunday night.

John Denver, aged 42, of Wearing Street, Newton was driving home from visiting friends when he ran into the back of the milk float.

He had not been wearing a seatbelt and was thrown forward onto the steering wheel breaking several ribs and his leg. The car suffered minor damage.

Mr Denver is now recovering in hospital and hopes to be out within the next few days.

Milkman Mr John Pinter said that he always starts his round at 2.30am. He had just stopped to deliver at the first house in Topping Street when the car hit hard from behind. "The impact broke hundreds of bottles of milk," Mr Pinter said. "I had to go back to the depot for more. "Fortunately, the float wasn't seriously damaged."

A chip pan fire at a house on the Carslake housing estate was dealt with by the local fire service last Tuesday. There was no serious damage caused to the house in Bryants Lane.

Figure 6.6 The final stories are added and adjustments made.

even if there are several pieces of text, they are likely to be working together. Again the starting point should be the design of the entry point. For many magazine or feature pages, this will be the main picture; it is this that will draw the eye and bring the reader in to land. Whether the picture is of a favourite celebrity or some key activity, it needs to draw the reader in. This means the picture must dominate the page, and one of the easiest mistakes to make as a beginner is to use too small a picture.

The example I give in Figure 6.7 is a 'celebrity-style' feature with an interview and picture. The picture dominates the page and draws the reader in. The heading is also large, to clearly identify the entry point, and it overlaps the picture. The picture is cut away because the background tells us nothing about the picture; the picture is only of interest because of the facial animation and greeting smile that make us want to read the story. Cutting away some of the background accentuates this animation. It also allows us to take the hand out into the text, breaking up some of the vertical lines through the page. I cannot show the page in colour, but the picture, which was taken in Italy, is made up of warm sand colours, and this colour might well be continued into the heading, perhaps combined with a purple-blue, which is the natural complementary colour. This would emphasise the sandy colour and make it more vibrant and interesting.

The text would then run beneath the heading and around the pictures. The second picture and *standfirst* would be placed around the bottom of the main picture to break up the text. This page uses a standard four-column grid, and without the extra picture the page would look very flat. Using the picture allows us to start off with a wide *intro* and then break into a three-column setting across the bottom of the page.

Dropping the pictures so deep allows us to put a significant amount of text in without its appearing to be overwhelming. I think the text is just about short enough not to need help, but you could consider putting *drop caps* in halfway down the first column and halfway through the last column. Instead of drop caps, a crosshead might also help break the longer first column.

Often a feature is long enough to continue onto a second page or even more. You might then have to take a decision about whether to run the copy on or break it up. Readers will happily follow a feature through three or four pages, but it might be better to split the feature so that the main text can run through all the pages, forcing the reader to stick with it, but with sidebar and boxed pieces of text placed in the pages to allow the reader to break off and look at something slightly different.

Let's singa songa Julia

WOWING them in the West end after a triumphant run in one of TV's favourite soaps, Julia Frost is at the top of her game.

"Life's great for me at the moment," she says, "I can't think how it could get any better."

But this bright new star in the British theatrical firmament is no overnight success. "no," says Julia, "I'm afraid it's slog, slog, slog. You don't get anywhere in the theatrical world without putting in loads of hard work and convincing people you're able to do the job."

Julia started her theatre career after university, where she studied acting.

Julia Frost (pictured) has stormed the West End in her new musical "Whistle While You Work". Alison Webster talks to the new star and discovers that over-night success is any-thing but.

Theatre

She joined a small theatre group touring schools showing plays and educational material.

Carry on writing loads of material like this, well supported with quotes from the subject and other people who know her.

Carry on writing loads of material like this, well supported with quotes from the subject and other people who know her.

Carry on writing loads of material like this, well supported with quotes from the subject and other people who know her.

Carry on writing loads of material like this, well supported loads of material like this, well sup loads of material like this, well sup with quotes from the subject and other people who know her.

Carry on writing loads of material like this, well supported with quotes from the subject and other people loads of material like this, well sup who know her.

Carry on writing loads of material like this, well supported with quotes from the subject and other people who know her well supported with quotes from the subject and other.

Carry on writing loads of material like this, well supported with quotes from the subject and other people who know her well supported with quotes from the subject and other.

Carry on writing loads of material like this, well supported with quotes from the subject and other people who know her.

Carry on writing loads of material like this, well supported loads of material like this, well supported with quotes from the subject and other people who know her.

Carry on writing loads of material like this, well supported loads of material like this, well supported with quotes from the subject and other people who know her.

Carry on writing loads of material like this, well supported with quotes from the subject and other people who know her.

Carry on writing loads of loads of material like this, well supported material like this, well supported with quotes from the subject and other people who know her.

Carry on writing loads of material like this, well supported with quotes from the subject and other people who know her.

Carry on writing loads loads of material like this, well supported of material like this, well supported with quotes from the subject and other people who know her.

Figure 6.7 A feature page. Note the dominance of the picture and how this feeds into the headline to create an unmissable entry point.

Story counts

Story counts are an important consideration when designing pages. The correct story count for each page should be a careful balance between interest, size of page and material available. There should be a good balance between text and image and other design devices such as headings, captions and other display text. A feature page or magazine page may only have one story on the page or even two, four or eight pages, depending on its strength and the quality of the pictures. A news page for a newspaper or magazine will have a much higher story count. This will vary according to the liveliness required. A page with a major news story in a newspaper could have only one story on the page. A major UK train crash, the abduction of children, a major disaster could all be stories that require not just a page of their own, but a number of pages. However, the story would probably be broken up into a number of different pieces of text so that inside pages at least had several stories, headlines and pictures in order to maintain interest.

Not only does this allow the stories from different reporters to be kept separate, but it also allows for the views of different witnesses and different angles and positions on the story. By keeping the story count per page reasonable – even when it is all the same story – we maintain reader interest. The story count on a tabloid page will traditionally be between 5 and 7, and on a broadsheet it could be as high as 12. On a magazine news page, particularly one where none of the stories is especially strong, the story count could be even higher as the designer attempts to give the reader a lively and value-for-money experience.

Essentially, if the stories are not strong in their own right, then providing a high story count will often get round this problem. Readers enjoy a column of nibs (news in brief) as much as one strong story. If the stories for the page are not strong, then cut them drastically and keep the story count high.

Headings as display

Headings play a major part in any design. They signal entry points and lead the reader's eye around the page. Fashions for headings have changed over the years. The old-fashioned multi-decker heading has gone, to be replaced with more multi-purpose headings. A multi-deck heading is one with several headings, each different to the next, and should not be confused with the number of lines a heading has. A four-line heading is not the same as a four-deck heading, which is four separate headings relating to the same story. Hutt attributes this development to the likes of W.T. Stead and T.P. O'Connor, whom he labels the 'true pioneers of the New Journalism' (Hutt 1967: 36). The change to photosetting and *web-offset* opened the way for even more flexibility in display text. Headings were no longer limited to columns; different sizes and shapes could be set easily. The old-fashioned decks set 'full out and centred turn' (ibid.: 35) could now be set flush left or centred, and required wording to be carefully thought through to fit the space allocated. This meant that headings were no longer just a part of the story: while being involved with it, they were also separate from it – an active and dynamic part of the process of drawing the reader into the story.

Headings can now be used across different column widths. One heading could be used to link two stories, for instance, while another will pick up one element of a story, and a further sub-heading will break the columns beneath the *intro*.

When designing pages, you should try to avoid too much heading. Apart from taking up valuable space, too many headings on busy news pages mean inevitable clashes, making the page look ugly. Headings should be kept from other headings by text, rules or pictures. Avoid running headings for different stories together. Sometimes it is unavoidable, as in a single and double column down the page. Then you can try to ensure they do not clash by using different sizes, different fonts or, for instance, by parting two similar double-column headings from each other with a boxed single-column light heading. Headings should be signs to the entry point of a story, so any heading that is away from the intro should be avoided. Only if there is just one story on the page can a heading that is split from the story ever hope to succeed. Even here it is unlikely to work well.

Reversing headings to set them white on black or placing them on a colour tone patch, a textured patch or a part of a picture that provides atmosphere but no detail can often help lift a headline away from the rest of the page, and this is also a useful technique for emphasis. Patches of colour are identified by the Poynter Institute's research as good entry points (Garcia and Stark 1991: 25). But, as with all devices, they should not be used to excess. There should be a good reason for more than one tone or reverse heading on a page. More than one or two makes the page look like a patchwork and loses the novelty that you had hoped to obtain. Beware of using different typefaces for headings. All your heading type should be in the same family, with the possible exception of one or two headlines in something completely different as a *kicker*. Papers with serif headline faces often use a gothic (sans serif) face as a kicker, again to add emphasis and variety. Gothic-faced papers will use a semi-sans typeface such as Cooper Black. This is a heavy face in which the serifs are highly stylised. It works well with gothic faces, providing variety without looking out of place. The watchword should always be to use kickers sparingly; as with any other device, a little goes a long way.

The shape of headings, particularly on the lead story, does a lot to help the design of the page. The main picture and the lead heading are the two most likely entry points for a reader, and therefore if you can get them to work together, they are likely to draw the reader into the page just where you want them. There are a number of shapes that can be applied to a lead heading. Multi-line headings can be used: anything up to five lines on a three- or four-column heading. *Streamers* – headings that go across the full page – tied in with sub-headings over several lines but fewer columns can also make attractive page starts, especially if they are tied in with a good picture. Another device is the *strapline*: a heading above the lead heading in type of about one-third or a quarter the size of that of the main heading. Straplines are particularly useful where several pictures and several pieces of text all need to be tied together (see Figure 6.8).

Pictures on a page

The pictures on a page are as important as, if not more important than, the headings. Preferably, you should work on the two together, but if this is difficult, plan where you intend to put the pictures first and then work text and headings around them. Pictures, as I have said, are the most likely entry point for a reader. Provided a picture has been well chosen and appropriately edited, you will need to make it a reasonable size in order to ensure it has the necessary impact. Harold Evans's seminal book about pictures (Evans 1978: 3) has a picture of an aeroplane taking off. Only on close inspection can you see a stowaway falling from the jet's wheel housing. This is a picture that needs to be used in a large size in order to see the stowaway in the context of the jet.

Nearly all pictures worth using need to be of a reasonable size. The average holiday snap these days is printed at least 15cm by 10cm, and that is on high-quality photographic paper. If you are considering using a smaller picture (other than a mug shot), you should be asking yourself whether the picture is worth using at all. It also depends on what the picture is about; a passport-style picture of someone named in the story could be used as small as 3cm by 4cm, but any picture with several faces would need to be large enough for the reader to be able to easily identify the faces. A picture with small detail important to the story would need to be big enough for the reader to see that detail easily. This could mean that some photographs with lots of people or a wealth of detail would need to be six or seven columns wide. You would then have to justify to yourself that such a large picture is worth using. The wrong decision would be to use it in any case but to make it small; that just ensures you have a picture that no reader will be able to see, and the space will be completely wasted.

Drivers 'distracted' by roadside activity

Two killed in M-way pile up

By JOHN SMITH

TWO PEOPLE were killed and four others injured in a multiple pile up on the M62 yesterday.

The accident happened in fog near the Huddersfield turn off. Police believe that one of the drivers may have been distracted by activity at a building close to the motorway.

The two killed were Mr John Bates, of High St, Chorley and Mr Peter Sims of Bassenthwaite Lane, Oldham.

The injured were taken to hospital but were later released. They were said to be suffering from shock and minor cuts and bruises.

A police spokesman said: "Lorries were being loaded under bright lights at factories alongside the motorway and we believe that one of the drivers might have been momentarily distracted. With the fog so thick, a moment is all that it would have taken."

Four cars were involved in the accident and police were surprised that more were not drawn in. The spokesman said: "Luckily, the accident happened in the inside lane and so other drivers were able to avoid the crash fairly easily. It was also easy for us to remove the cars from the carriageway very quickly."

Police were on the scene in just a few minutes, according to witnesses and were able to prevent any further carnage.

The accident happened at 6.30am and so traffic was relatively light. The early morning fog lifted later on

The scene of the accident shortly after the crash.

The dice with death we 'take for granted'

Figure 6.8 A strapline above a multi-lane heading with a double-column intro.

Either use pictures at a size large enough to give them their full dramatic impact and to allow the reader to see what's in the picture, or don't use them at all.

It is possible to use more than one picture with a story, and often this is the only way to show the full detail. When working with several pictures on the same story, try to get some variation. Aim for different shapes and sizes so that you are able to make that part of the page appear livelier. The exception to this is if you want to use several pictures as a single block, in which case you could keep the sizes the same and place them alongside each other. You might also want to use several pictures for the purpose of comparison, and here again you might also use them in a series in the same size.

Text

Once the headings and the pictures are placed on the page, you need to start laying in the text. Most of this will be set in the standard body size for your publication, whatever that is. However, varying the type size and how it is presented will liven up the page and add emphasis to sections of the story. This is particularly important if the story is of any length – a feature page, for example. Whether it is for a newspaper or a magazine, the longer runs of text require careful handling to avoid presenting the reader with large areas of indigestible grey.

Intros as entry points

The first variation that can be made in the type size and presentation is in the entry point of the text. You should already have directed the reader to this point with headings and pictures, but it doesn't hurt to emphasise the start for the reader. This is often done by setting the *intro* in a larger type, possibly bold (see Figure 6.9). Sometimes, if the story is run over more than one column, or in the more flexible style of a magazine, the intro can be set over a wider measure than the rest of the text. This often allows a sub-heading or a *byline* to be set in the run of text (see Figures 6.10 and 6.11). Magazines can handle the intro right across the page, if the type is set large enough, but newspapers rarely go above 14pt for their intros and this tends to limit you to three or four columns (40 ems maximum) (see Figure 6.11). Anything wider rarely has the depth required to sustain it, and tends to look thin and unimportant. It also becomes difficult to read.

It's worth considering setting the *intro* in a different font to the body – sans serif, for instance – to emphasise the start (see Figure 6.10). It is usual to set the first or first two words of a story in capitals. This again helps emphasise the entry point for the story.

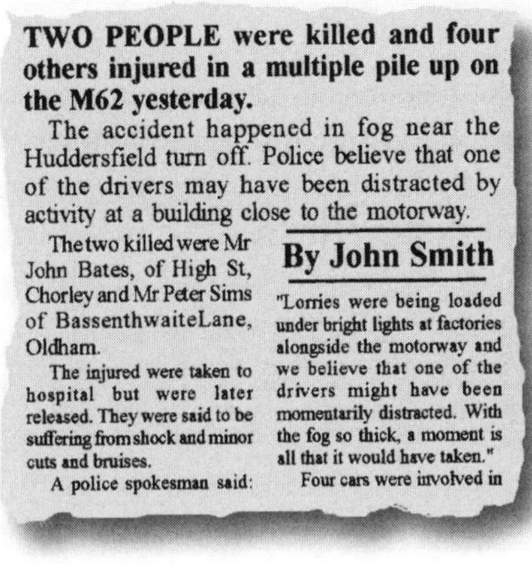

TWO PEOPLE were killed and four others injured in a multiple pile up on the M62 yesterday.

The accident happened in fog near the Huddersfield turn off. Police believe that one of the drivers may have been distracted by activity at a building close to the motorway.

By John Smith

The two killed were Mr John Bates, of High St, Chorley and Mr Peter Sims of BassenthwaiteLane, Oldham.

The injured were taken to hospital but were later released. They were said to be suffering from shock and minor cuts and bruises.

A police spokesman said: "Lorries were being loaded under bright lights at factories alongside the motorway and we believe that one of the drivers might have been momentarily distracted. With the fog so thick, a moment is all that it would have taken."

Four cars were involved in

Figure 6.9 A double-column intro. A standard double-column intro, with the byline placed in the shoulder to allow the second column to stand clear of the intro.

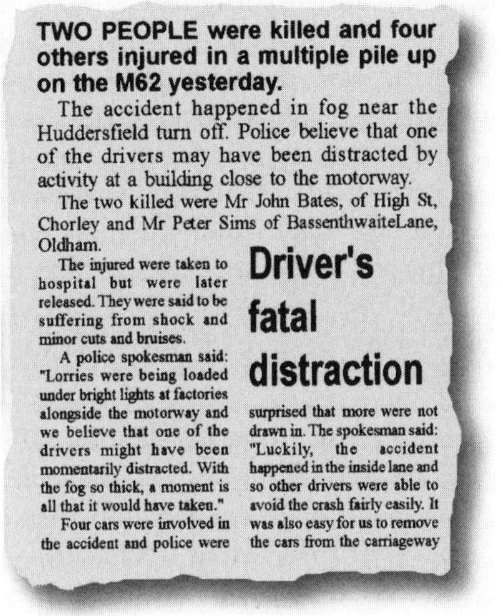

TWO PEOPLE were killed and four others injured in a multiple pile up on the M62 yesterday.

The accident happened in fog near the Huddersfield turn off. Police believe that one of the drivers may have been distracted by activity at a building close to the motorway.

The two killed were Mr John Bates, of High St, Chorley and Mr Peter Sims of BassenthwaiteLane, Oldham.

Driver's fatal distraction

The injured were taken to hospital but were later released. They were said to be suffering from shock and minor cuts and bruises.

A police spokesman said: "Lorries were being loaded under bright lights at factories alongside the motorway and we believe that one of the drivers might have been momentarily distracted. With the fog so thick, a moment is all that it would have taken."

Four cars were involved in the accident and police were surprised that more were not drawn in. The spokesman said: "Luckily, the accident happened in the inside lane and so other drivers were able to avoid the crash fairly easily. It was also easy for us to remove the cars from the carriageway

Figure 6.10 Double-column intro with secondary heading. A similar idea, but this time with a secondary heading. Note the use of a sans serif font for the first paragraph.

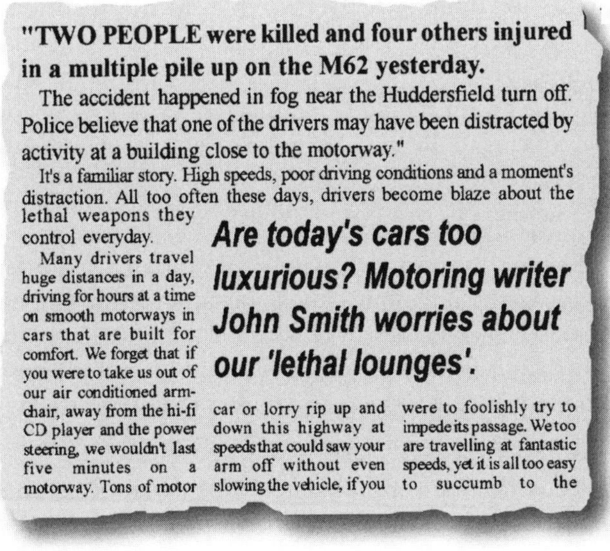

"TWO PEOPLE were killed and four others injured in a multiple pile up on the M62 yesterday.

The accident happened in fog near the Huddersfield turn off. Police believe that one of the drivers may have been distracted by activity at a building close to the motorway."

It's a familiar story. High speeds, poor driving conditions and a moment's distraction. All too often these days, drivers become blaze about the lethal weapons they control everyday.

Are today's cars too luxurious? Motoring writer John Smith worries about our 'lethal lounges'.

Many drivers travel huge distances in a day, driving for hours at a time on smooth motorways in cars that are built for comfort. We forget that if you were to take us out of our air conditioned armchair, away from the hi-fi CD player and the power steering, we wouldn't last five minutes on a motorway. Tons of motor car or lorry rip up and down this highway at speeds that could saw your arm off without even slowing the vehicle, if you were to foolishly try to impede its passage. We too are travelling at fantastic speeds, yet it is all too easy to succumb to the

Figure 6.11 A triple-column intro with a standfirst tucked into the shoulder. Running three columns of type immediately under the intro risks confusing the reader.

Running and shaping text

After the intro, the main run of text needs to be considered. Long runs of text usually need to be set over a wider measure than short runs (see Chapter 9). With modern computer setting it is also possible to wrap text around pictures and other items, often in quite complicated shapes. This is a technique (like most tricks) that should be used sparingly, but can add emphasis to a picture or graphic and brighten up a page. Text can be run over pictures and graphics to add emphasis, but this should also be used sparingly. Unless the text is set in a fairly large size, any underlying image is likely to make the text more difficult to read.

Nearly all longer stories need to be set in multi-columns. It is difficult to make hard and fast rules in design, but once you start moving into multi-columns rather than a single column drop, then it is best to avoid dropping the story too deep. Better to have four columns 10cm deep than two columns of 20cm. This doesn't mean that two columns of 20cm or longer should never be used, just that you should always look to see whether you can spread the story wider.

Text presentation

Once the text is laid onto the page, the work does not end there. The options available for dealing with the text are almost endless.

One of the standard choices for running text other than in the traditional column is to tabulate copy or put it into tables. This is ideal for sports results, league tables, TV listings, and so on. Any setting that is not narrative but a list of information in a standardised form should be considered for setting in this way. Tabulation allows you to set up columns within the column of your text to line up items of the same sort: team names or goals for or against, for instance. Tables allow for something similar, but in a boxed format.

Even if the text is a straight run of narrative, you might want to add emphasis to certain sections, either for editorial reasons – the paragraph you are emphasising is of particular importance – or for design reasons – it's there to keep the reader's interest and to give them a marker through the copy. Markers are useful because if the reader becomes distracted, there is a marker to remind them of where they were.

This emphasis can be added with drop caps, indented paragraphs, underlined text, emboldened text, italicised text, or by increasing the size of a paragraph (see Figure 8.12 for examples).

Other **types** of display

As well as being part of the story, other text elements can be used as design devices to break up long runs of text, to separate stories and to split pictures from each other and from inappropriate text. For instance, captions can split a picture from another picture or from text. Captions need to be used carefully. The convention is to place a caption below the picture, and you need to think carefully before doing anything else. Readers find it extremely irritating to have to locate a caption that is not beneath the picture. They want to find out who or what is in a picture, but the sub has decided to tuck it away on the other side of the page or put it in the text. It is possible to run the caption alongside the picture rather than beneath it; sometimes it is even turned through 90° to run up the side of the photo (see Figure 9.5). It is also possible to *pierce* the picture to insert a caption so that it covers a part of the picture that is otherwise a waste of space.

Bylines are another device that can break up an area of text or pictures. Bylines can be used in the shoulder of an intro to give the break into the second column. They can be used at the end of an introductory paragraph, or they can be large areas of display. They can be included in *standfirsts*, with or without a picture to make a large area of display. This would certainly be how a celebrity byline might be used. An article by Wayne Rooney on technique in a football magazine, for instance, or a newspaper's sports pages, would use a very large picture byline/ standfirst that might also incorporate the heading: 'Top of your game – David Beckham on how to add that little extra' (see Figure 9.3 for an example).

Some dos and don'ts of design

Setting out golden rules is a proven way to trip over your own good intentions, but there are some things one should always consider doing when designing pages, and so I offer my own golden rules:

- Choose your entry point with care and make it the focal point of the page.
- Break up long stories into easily manageable articles linked together by design.
- Use pictures and graphics wherever possible.
- Break up type to add interest.
- Consider using subheads and crossheads to add emphasis to sections of the text.
- Consider using bulleted pars, drop letters and bold pars to add emphasis.
- Keep things simple and easy to follow.
- Consider carefully how long each article should be, depending on your readership profile.

- Try to avoid clashing with adverts. Ads with large areas of halftone should be cordoned off using text. Text-based adverts could be put next to pictures.
- Consider how best to get over the information. For instance, an annotated aerial picture may do more to describe the scene of an accident than pages of text could hope to do. It will be the designer's job to arrange for the text and pictures to be turned into a diagram.
- Consider using just parts of a picture, or cutting out the image or overlaying it with type.
- Ensure that there is a suitable amount of white space around the headlines and any other elements.
- Ensure that there is always a caption beneath any picture. Readers get very irritated if they can't find the caption to a picture.
- Emphasise your entry point with larger intro type, bold faces, drop letters, etc.
- Ensure that the strength of your stories is reflected in the design.
- The reader should be in no doubt about where the story continues after it has ended in one column.
- Be imaginative in how you deal with the elements of a page.

Similarly, there are things that it is wise to avoid. Although it is all right to do these things occasionally if you've thought things through properly, generally you should try to avoid:

- Running headlines over adverts. Always break the space with text or pictures. If the space above a run of adverts is too small to be useful, don't be afraid to give it up and float the ads to the top or ask the advertising department to fill the space. Anything less than 6cm is going to give you problems.
- Running a headline next to another headline unless the stories are connected or unless you have some way of ensuring they are not connected, such as column rules or by using very different styles and sizes of font.
- Covering the page with lots of different typefaces. Too much variation will end up just looking a mess. It is best to limit yourself to one font and use varieties of it.
- Using cut-outs on a picture just for the sake of it. Whether the picture is cut away from its background or a section is cut out, it will lose context and start to look isolated. A cut-out used without a good reason usually looks ridiculous, because it is clear you are trying to edit the picture and the reader will wonder why.
- Turning copy to another page. It's a great way of ensuring the reader loses interest in the story.

7
Master pages, templates and style sheets

Master pages, templates and style sheets are devices within the main desktop publishing (DTP) software packages aimed at making life easier for designers and publishers. There are several desktop publishing software packages available, but the two most often used for professional publishing are QuarkXPress and Adobe's InDesign. These are now very similar packages doing the same job in much the same way. InDesign is claimed by some to be more flexible and intuitive to use, but those who prefer Quark claim that InDesign is more complicated. Most designers are obliged to use whatever software package their employer has bought. It's doubtful whether one system is better than any other all of the time; the key is always how good you are at designing publications and at getting the best out of the system you are obliged to use.

The importance and purpose of master pages and templates

Master pages are pages that are not actually printed out but ones that keep general information common to all pages in a publication linked to the master page. They are different from *templates* or copy pages in that they can be altered at any time during publishing and the changes will be reflected in the final publication and on every page of the publication linked to the master page.

There are usually two master pages per publication, one for the left-hand pages and one for the right, although it is possible to have more to allow for two or more sets of master pages with matching left- and right-hand pages. Any standard material that runs through the whole publication can be placed on a master page and it will appear on every page in the publication that is linked to that master page. So, if you were to put the page number on the top right-hand corner of the right-hand master page, that page number would then appear on every page. Since it is possible to instruct the DTP software to automatically match the page number as printed to the actual number of that page, this is an easy way to insert page numbers, or other header material.

Master pages are good for placing header material, footer material and any other logos, guidelines or material that go on every page throughout the publication. For every page you work on, you can then select whether it picks up a master page and which master page it selects.

Templates

As well as master pages, which can be used to set up headers and footers and regularly used material, it is also possible to set up templates. These are pages that are standardised and allow the editor or designer to select a style of page that is already part-designed. This saves a lot of work and potential for mistakes. If a standard page for your publication is 38.6cm by 29.2cm with 12mm margins, then it is easier to call up the standard page than to remember this detail every time you start a new page.

A template will first define the page size and margins. A newspaper might produce in both broadsheet (for the main publication) and tabloid (for the supplements). Templates would be required for both sizes of pages. The margins would also need to be fixed on the templates.

Next the template will contain the standard number of columns required. Thus, a news page in a consumer magazine might have four or five columns. The feature pages might have only three columns. Each column would have a space between it and the next column, and again the template would fix this according to the standard decided by the publication designer. Templates should carry all the information about a page that a designer will require. The designer can then call up the appropriate page and start work.

The templates can also be extended to pick up information that always appears on standard pages such as TV listings, advice columns, entertainments pages, and so on. This means that a TV listings template, for instance, will already have appropriate headings such as BBC1, BBC2, etc. in place. The standard space for reviews and pictures will already have frames placed on the page so whoever is working on the page can quickly insert the text and pictures and send the page. Some newspapers have even extended this to news pages so that there are half a dozen standard news pages that can be used to load news stories into, saving the trouble of getting each of them designed from scratch.

The only risk with using templates in this way is that many publications are starting to look very similar. If the editor decides to have a template for each news and feature page that already carry frames for headlines, stories and pictures so that the same design is always used, then there is a risk that each edition will start to look the same and news stories will be presented at the same strength regardless of their merit. Although computers and modern printing methods should give the designer more freedom, the use of templates has in fact often brought about a sameness to pages that is unfortunate. While using the same template for the TV listings day after day makes sense, always using the same design for page 3 will soon bore readers.

This is not to oppose the tidy look of a page that is adhering to the publication's house style, nor to not welcome the savings brought by standardised pages where the margins, columns and artwork are automatically put onto the page, but it is to deprecate the unwillingness, usually caused by lack of time, to use that framework imaginatively by tweaking the style where it will advance the design or by altering the standard templates for reasons other than necessity.

As well as fixing such items as margins and columns, a good template also includes a style sheet.

Style sheets

Style sheets are used in major DTP packages and in word processing packages. Anyone skilled in using one of the major word processing packages may already be familiar with style sheets, and their use in DTP packages is identical. Style sheets allow the user to pre-format paragraph and character styles. For instance, the standard body type that will be used in the publication can be called 'body text' and its *font*, size, *leading* and paragraph characteristics can then be pre-determined. Assume, for instance, that the publication is using Nimrod as its body type. The designer may have decided that body style would be 8pt Nimrod on an 8.5pt body, justified with standard *kerning* tables and a UK English dictionary. There might be 3pt of space before each paragraph and the first line of each paragraph would be indented by an em space. Hyphenation rules would be pre-decided. All of this can then be pre-formatted by defining a new style or editing an existing one. There will then be a style called 'body text' which can be easily applied to sections of text. Open the style palette in your software and click the style called body text, and that style will be instantly applied to the paragraph in which your cursor is sitting. If you want to apply the style to several paragraphs, just select them and click on the style. In order to load copy into the frame already to style, the style sheet can be selected when the copy frame is drawn onto the page. The copy will then be set in that style as it is imported.

There is no real practical limit to the number of style sheets that can be pre-defined and it would be normal for a publication to have predefined style sheets for all standard type elements: body text, *intros*, *bylines*, *standfirsts*, captions, headlines, crossheads, side-heads and so on (see Figure 7.1).

Figure 7.1 Style sheets on a page make-up system (InDesign). The menu at the centre allows adjustment of the character style, while the menu at the bottom left allows the paragraph style to be changed. These menus would not normally be open together; I've included both to show the range. The menu on the left of the dialogue box allows choices to be made.

Most publications set up the style sheets right at the beginning of the publication design process to ensure that subs use the predetermined styles available.

Each templated page should have a style sheet attached that keeps the standard house style, but also introduces any special styles for that page. The TV listings page, for instance, might have fonts and styles not used on other pages, and these should be available in the style sheet. If templates are useful (and they are), then style sheets are indispensable. To be able to quickly click on a series of paragraphs and then select a style and click on that, converting a block of type neatly and quickly to the appropriate style, is a real time-saver. Time spent developing style sheets is never wasted and always repays itself during the lifetime of a publication.

If ever you get to set up a new publication, do make sure your style sheets cover all the main options your house style is going to allow the designers.

8
Typography

Type is one of the most important design elements of any publication magazine but one that is often overlooked, particularly by the novice. Type plays a major part in the look of any publication. Subtle and imperceptible though it might be to the untrained eye, the face used in a publication plays a direct part in the way we perceive the published words. For any modern publication the design team will need to choose a *font* that will aid the reader as much as possible. It is our job as designers to ensure that the fonts we choose to use are as helpful as possible to the readers so that they can absorb as much of what has been written as is possible in the time available to them. If they become aware of the font, we are probably not doing our job properly.

To take an extreme example, if we were to publish in Old English characters, readers would perceive what was written in an entirely different way as compared to how they would perceive a publication set in some frivolous art nouveau face. (See Figure 8.1 for a comparison of different fonts.)

In the days of *letterpress*, there were other factors involved in the choice of font. The actual process of printing meant that great care had to be taken over the choice of type to ensure image clarity. Letterpress is a contact process with the type hammering into the paper at high speed. Only a font that could stand up to those pressures and still print legibly without the 'e's and 'o's filling with ink or the delicate serifs dropping off was of any use. Whole groups of type, called the legibility group, were designed expressly to provide a text type that would print true and be highly readable despite the rigours of the printing process. Fonts such as Ionic, Corona and Paragon took over from the earlier Times Roman faces. Each of them had different attributes but all of them tried to balance various factors: reproduction; colour; body size; readability.

Modern computer setting and *web-offset lithography* allow us much more freedom to choose whatever font we want. The type is no longer subject to the damaging punishment of the press, and delicate, insubstantial fonts can be used

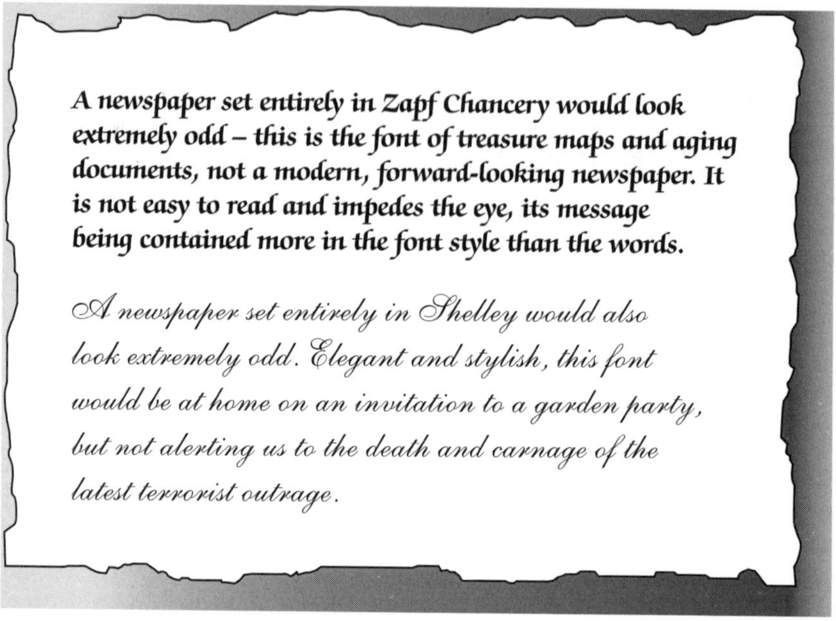

A newspaper set entirely in Zapf Chancery would look extremely odd – this is the font of treasure maps and aging documents, not a modern, forward-looking newspaper. It is not easy to read and impedes the eye, its message being contained more in the font style than the words.

A newspaper set entirely in Shelley would also look extremely odd. Elegant and stylish, this font would be at home on an invitation to a garden party, but not alerting us to the death and carnage of the latest terrorist outrage.

Figure 8.1 Fonts for different purposes.

if we want. However, the process of producing printed type in a computer system, particularly the proprietary systems available early on and the licensing systems involved, led to early complications that meant a publication designed in one font could often not be published because the printer was not able to match that font in the equipment being used. When computers were first used, it was expected that the printer would be a fixed character output, like a typewriter. The computer would send a code (typically ASCII) to represent a particular character that would then be printed out. This was improved slightly with the introduction of dot matrix printers, but neither of these was acceptable for publishing.

The early computer systems used for publishing relied on photocomposition, a method of setting type by photographing characters onto photosensitive paper or film from a negative master that contained pictures of all the characters required. The systems involved for this were expensive and meant that one publication's computer system could only set on that publication's output device.

The development of page description languages driven by the consumer market was an important step forward. Apple used PostScript to launch its range of laser printers, giving it a vital lead in the DTP market as maker of the first computer systems capable of true desktop publishing, producing pages that could be output to laser printers and other output devices. PostScript allowed the output to be described in a way that any PostScript-enabled output device could understand. But PostScript was complex and expensive, and required output devices with interpreters that were themselves complex. Publishers and printers both had to buy expensive PostScript software fonts and licences to ensure they were able to match fonts. Apple eventually decided to develop its own version and produced TrueType. Although this worked well, it was not allowed to use PostScript fonts because of the licensing arrangements, and so many of its DTP customers, who had already invested heavily in PostScript fonts, were not impressed. Instead, Apple licensed the system to Microsoft, which developed them, and when it launched Windows 3.1, which started the ability of IBM PCs to be able to mimic the graphic capabilities of Apple, TrueType launched the now ubiquitous Arial and Times New Roman. Many fonts are now available as either TrueType or PostScript, and these are now widely used in publishing. The introduction of DPT and the page description software and software fonts that lie at its core has allowed even the smallest publisher to produce its own publication with only a modest investment in equipment. A publication can now be produced in a small office, sent by email to a printer and have thousands of copies run off within a few hours.

What is type?

Type is a method of converting language into symbols that are readily understood by those trained to read. English uses a Roman alphabet and characters, and while this is far from the only alphabet or set of symbols used in the world, it is one that many people can decipher.

Whatever alphabet is used, however, there are two requirements:

1 that there is a symbol produced (or implied) using some form of ink or paint;
2 that there is a space for the character to live in that is not inked.

Both of these requirements are equally important, and we forget that at our peril. It is the contrast between the symbol and the space in which it is placed that makes reading either easy or difficult. For instance, a light green character on a light blue background is not easy to read and may well be impossible for someone who is colour-blind. The art director of a men's magazine who chooses to print green type on a pink background will be upset when scores of readers ring to complain about what they see as a blank page because they are colour-blind (a significant minority of men are colour-blind). Even those who are not colour-blind will not enjoy the experience because it will be difficult to make out the characters. While this might just be acceptable for one or two words –

a heading or caption, say – over several thousand words most readers would soon give up.

Even limiting the colours to black and white requires care. Research by Starch in the 1920s (cited in Tinker 1963: 129) showed that black type on a white background is read 42 per cent faster than white type on a dark grey background. In another study by Paterson and Tinker (cited in Tinker 1963: 130), white on black was read 10.5 per cent slower than black on white. The black on white was preferred by 77.7 per cent of the readers. Figure 8.2 shows some variants on the colour of the paper and how these affect the ease of reading the text.

When one of my newspaper offices first moved over to computers, there was much concern about the health and safety repercussions of working on-screen all day. It was possible for the user to decide how their screen displayed, using either black characters on a white background or white characters on a black background. It is no coincidence that while a lot of reporters happily wrote white on black (because we had been told this would lead to less glare and therefore be safer), most sub-editors changed to black on white despite the additional glare. Subs do much more reading than reporters and so legibility is much more important.

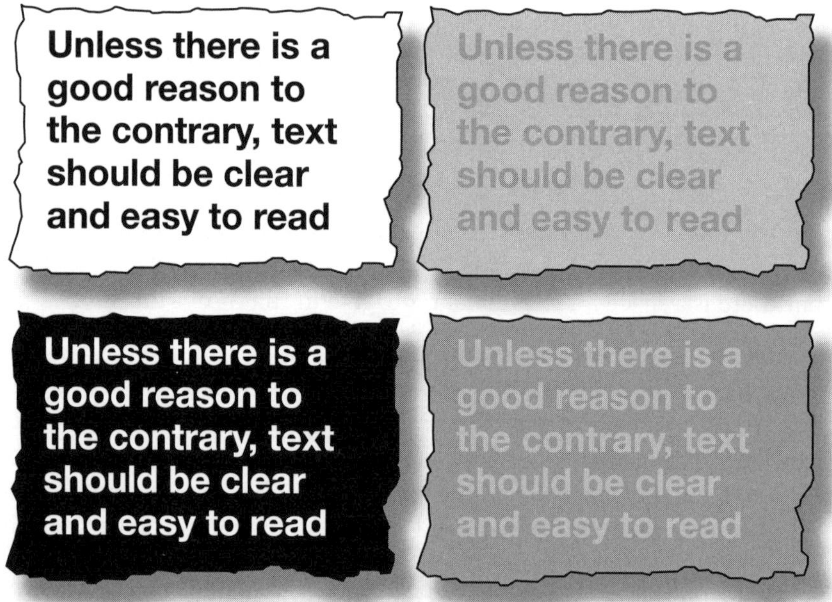

Figure 8.2 Paper colour is as important as ink.

The shape of the type itself is also important. When we are reading, we need to be able to quickly identify both the characters that we are reading and the words that those characters make up. We read by identifying word shapes, and good readers will identify up to three or four words in one scan. Being able to quickly identify the characters that make up those words is vital. Try deciphering someone's handwriting in order to see how important the shape of letters can be. Only if the type chosen is well designed and reproduced clearly in the publication will the reader be able to get the best experience.

For this reason, type is much more stylised than is perhaps realised. Moves to simplify type often only succeed in making it more difficult to read. Type was historically cast in metal (see Figure 8.3), and much of its terminology comes from this history. There are names for all the different parts of the type, but we only need to be aware that the size of type is determined by the metal block on which it is cast and that type has descenders, ascenders, serifs and an x-height. See Figure 8.4 for details.

Figure 8.3 Metal type. Note that it is a mirror image and that the body of the type is larger than the actual typeface.

Figure 8.4 Type and its parts.

What is a font?

A font is a single design of type, usually available in a range of different styles. This family of type often means that a type from the same font can be in roman, bold, italic, bold italic, condensed, extended, lower-case, small capitals, capitals, and so on. This means that even if you have decided to use only one font in your designs, there is still plenty of opportunity to adjust the way the type presents. A bold heading will look very different from a light (or roman) heading even in the same font. Choosing to present it in italic or extended can also make a huge difference.

Measuring type

Type in the United Kingdom and United States is measured in point sizes (the European continent uses the Didot system, in which the points are known as Ciceros). The point system is a measuring system in its own right, so comparisons with other measuring systems are just that, but there are approximately 72 points to the inch (28.34 to the centimetre). It needs to be remembered that the type measurement system was developed for use with metal type that you could actually see and measure. Since this type was cast in metal, the actual printing face was mounted on top of a metal block, and it was this block (or body) that gave type its size, not the actual size of the letters. This means that it is very difficult to measure the size of type once it is printed on the page as it is the space in which the type lives that we actually measure, not the symbol printed on the page. Added to this, publications shrink slightly after printing because of the damping process used to ensure the separation of oil and water, so what was set as 60pt might only be 57.6pt after printing. Figure 8.5 shows the variety of type size.

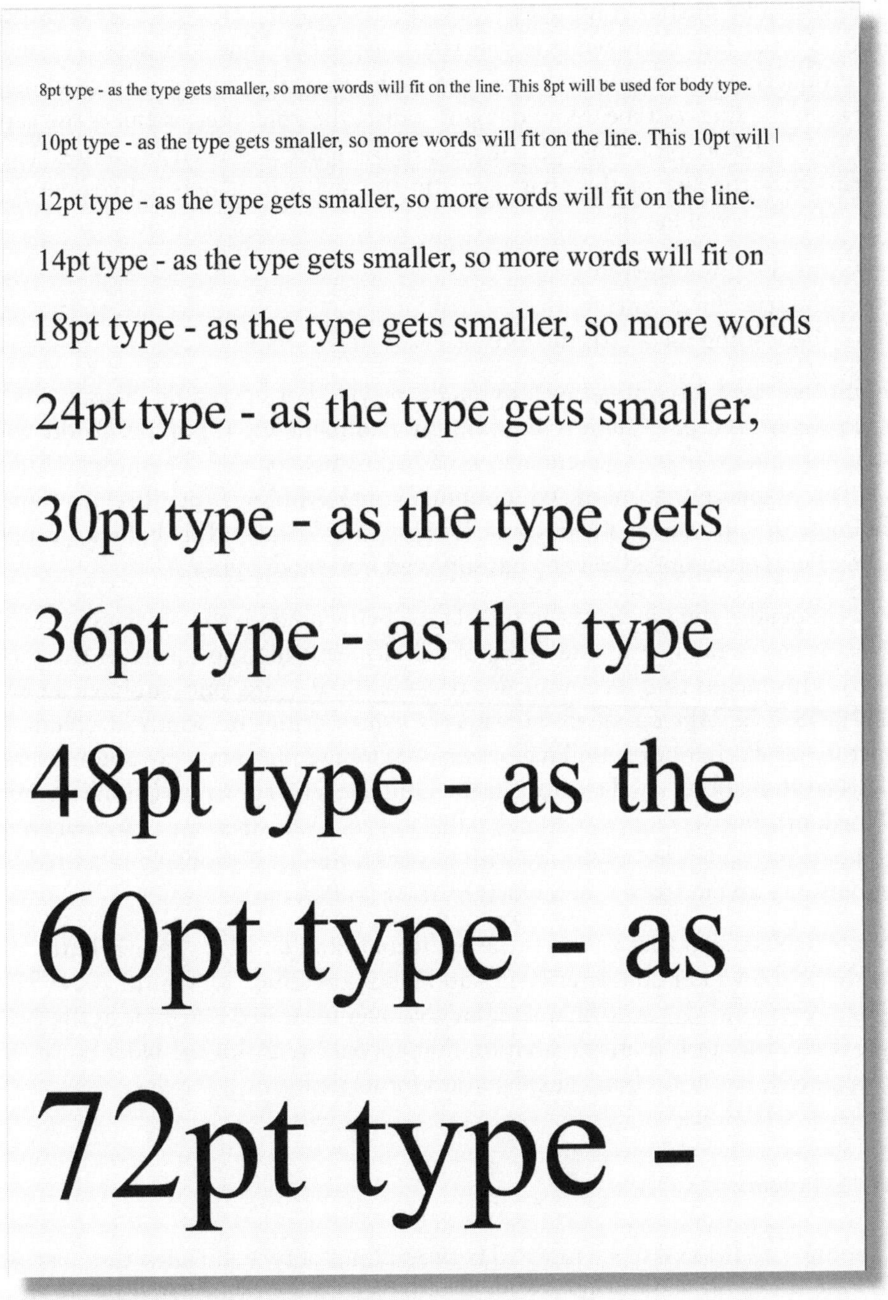

8pt type - as the type gets smaller, so more words will fit on the line. This 8pt will be used for body type.

10pt type - as the type gets smaller, so more words will fit on the line. This 10pt will l

12pt type - as the type gets smaller, so more words will fit on the line.

14pt type - as the type gets smaller, so more words will fit on

18pt type - as the type gets smaller, so more words

24pt type - as the type gets smaller,

30pt type - as the type gets

36pt type - as the type

48pt type - as the

60pt type - as

72pt type -

Figure 8.5 The variety of type size.

Things can be further confused when additional space is inserted between the lines of type. This is known as *leading* (pronounced 'ledding') because it used to be produced by inserting strips of lead or brass of the appropriate thickness between the lines of type. Nowadays, of course, the computer produces the gap, but most software programs will still refer to the space produced as leading. This means that the size of the character and the space in which it lives are the product of several factors:

- the design of the font;
- the size of the font;
- the leading used with the font.

Points are used for vertical measurement in type. For horizontal measurement the pica-em is used. A *pica* is an old-fashioned name for 12pt type. Before the point system came into general use, type had names for sizes: Pearl (5pt); Ruby (5½pt); Nonpareil, pronounced 'nonprul', (6pt); Minion (7pt); Brevier (8pt). Bourgeousi, pronounced 'burjoyce' (9pt); Long Primer (10pt); Pica (12pt). Only Pica (pronounced 'piker') has survived into modern usage.

An em-quad is the square of the size of type being used. In the old days of metal type, it was actually a square block of metal measuring the square of the type used. This means that an em-quad is not a particular size; one can have an 8pt em-quad or a 24pt em-quad. However, for measuring the width of columns, pictures and other horizontal measurements, we use pica-ems – a 12pt measure. This is often abbreviated to pica (in the United States) or to em (in the United Kingdom). We use ems (sometimes called muttons) as a measure to indent type. If a paragraph is indented (starts with a space), then it is probably indented by a mutton – an em space – or a nut (an en, or half an em).

Some books claim that an em is the width of a standard 12pt roman letter 'm' as this is the widest character (Giles and Hodgson 1996: 30; Quinn 2001: 81). This seems unlikely, as no character 'm' I've ever measured is as wide as the type size it's set in, nor is it an explanation that appears in any of the older books on typography, but it is a handy explanation for its name.

What is leading?

Leading is additional space inserted between lines of type. Imagine that you are writing notes on a standard A4 lined notepad. The space offered by the pad between the lines remains constant, but you could choose to write in very large or very small letters (see Figure 8.6). If you wrote small, there would be more space between the lines of script. If you wrote large, there would be very little room. Adding space between the lines by leading has a similar effect, adding or

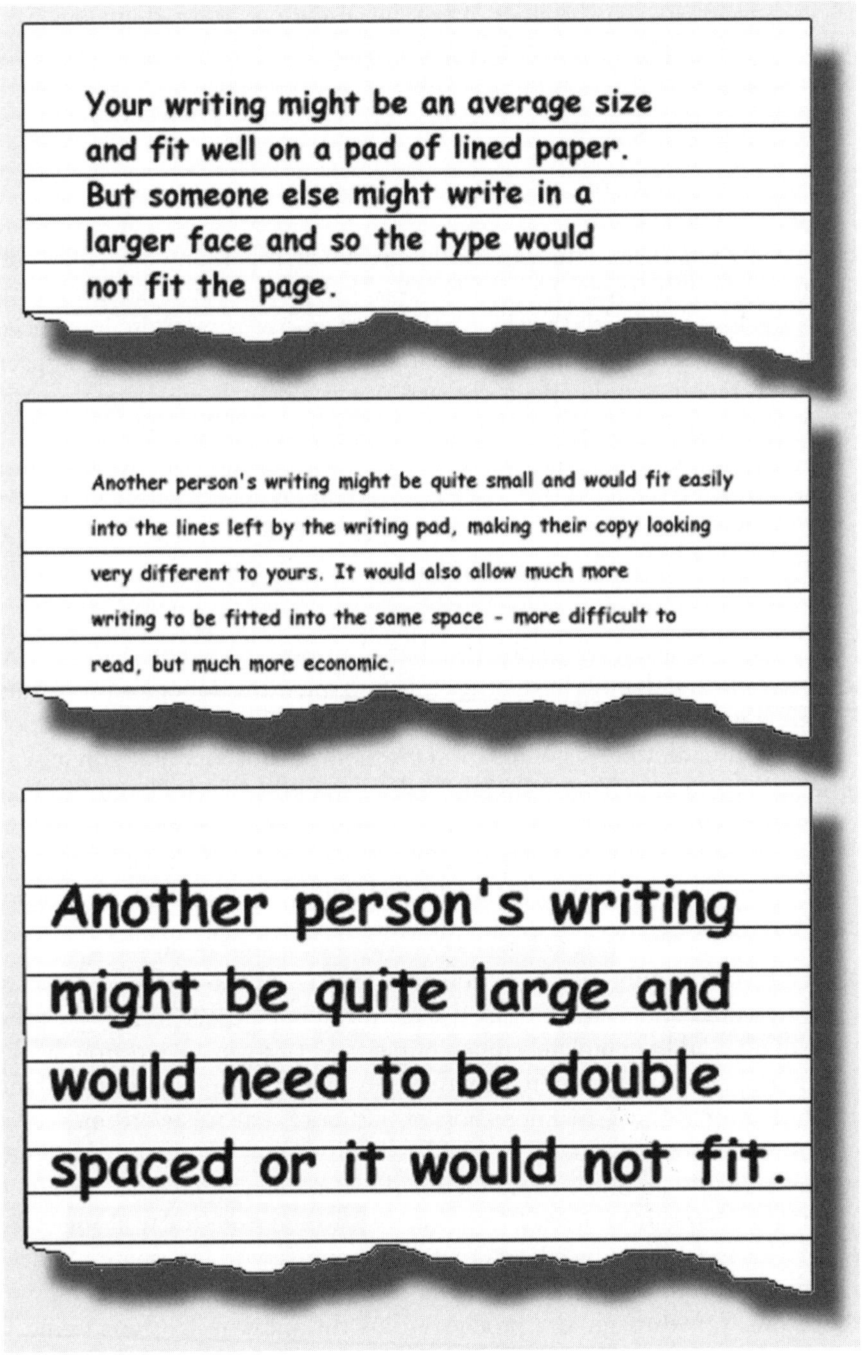

Your writing might be an average size
and fit well on a pad of lined paper.
But someone else might write in a
larger face and so the type would
not fit the page.

Another person's writing might be quite small and would fit easily
into the lines left by the writing pad, making their copy looking
very different to yours. It would also allow much more
writing to be fitted into the same space - more difficult to
read, but much more economic.

Another person's writing
might be quite large and
would need to be double
spaced or it would not fit.

Figure 8.6 Leading can be considered using a reporter's notebook as an analogy. The type size might vary, but the distance between the lines remains the same.

removing space between the lines of type. If, using my notepad analogy, you decided to double-space your writing, writing only on every other line, it would give the effect of inserting lead to the value of one of the lines.

White space and leading

White space is vitally important in the design of newspapers and magazines and is vital to the way the type looks and behaves. Just as one would judge a person partly by the house in which they live or the car they drive, one is also influenced not just by the type but also by the space in which it lives. The amount of space allowed to a type not only affects the way we interpret the message the type contains but also influences how easy the type is to read. Tinker (1963) quotes a number of studies, one by Paterson and Tinker (1940) in particular which shows that a little leading is a good thing as far as legibility is concerned. Adding 2pts of lead to an 8pt type improves legibility by 5 per cent. Interestingly, any increase of leading beyond this does not appear to improve legibility, according to Tinker (1963: 93).

However, just because leading thicker than 2 pt does not improve legibility, that doesn't mean it doesn't have other effects. Type with a lot of leading would inevitably have a lot of white space around it. This block of type would look unhurried and uncluttered, giving an impression of authority and gravitas. A traditional font such as Times Roman is often combined with plenty of white space by the broadsheets in order to give an impression of thoughtfulness and authority. A tabloid or gossip magazine, on the other hand, usually wants to give the impression of brashness, immediacy and liveliness. Tabloids tend to use fonts with large x-heights and minimum white space (see Figure 8.7).

Look in a couple of publications to compare adverts. Adverts have to say a lot in very few words, and so the font used is of crucial importance to reinforce the message or even add a completely different message. Copy in adverts from banks and insurance companies is often set with plenty of leading and space around the text. They want to give an impression of authority and trustworthiness. An electrical retailer of the 'stack 'em high, sell 'em cheap' variety, on the other hand, wants to give an impression of haste, the idea that special offers are being snapped up by bargain-hunters. If you don't get to the store today, it might be too late. This is achieved by adverts that are crammed with information, prices and pictures. The adverts don't say it – indeed, they often mention helpful staff ready to talk you through the product – but the message in the spacing is intended to give the reader the feeling of a busy marketplace brimming with bargains that need to be snapped up immediately or they will be lost to some other customer.

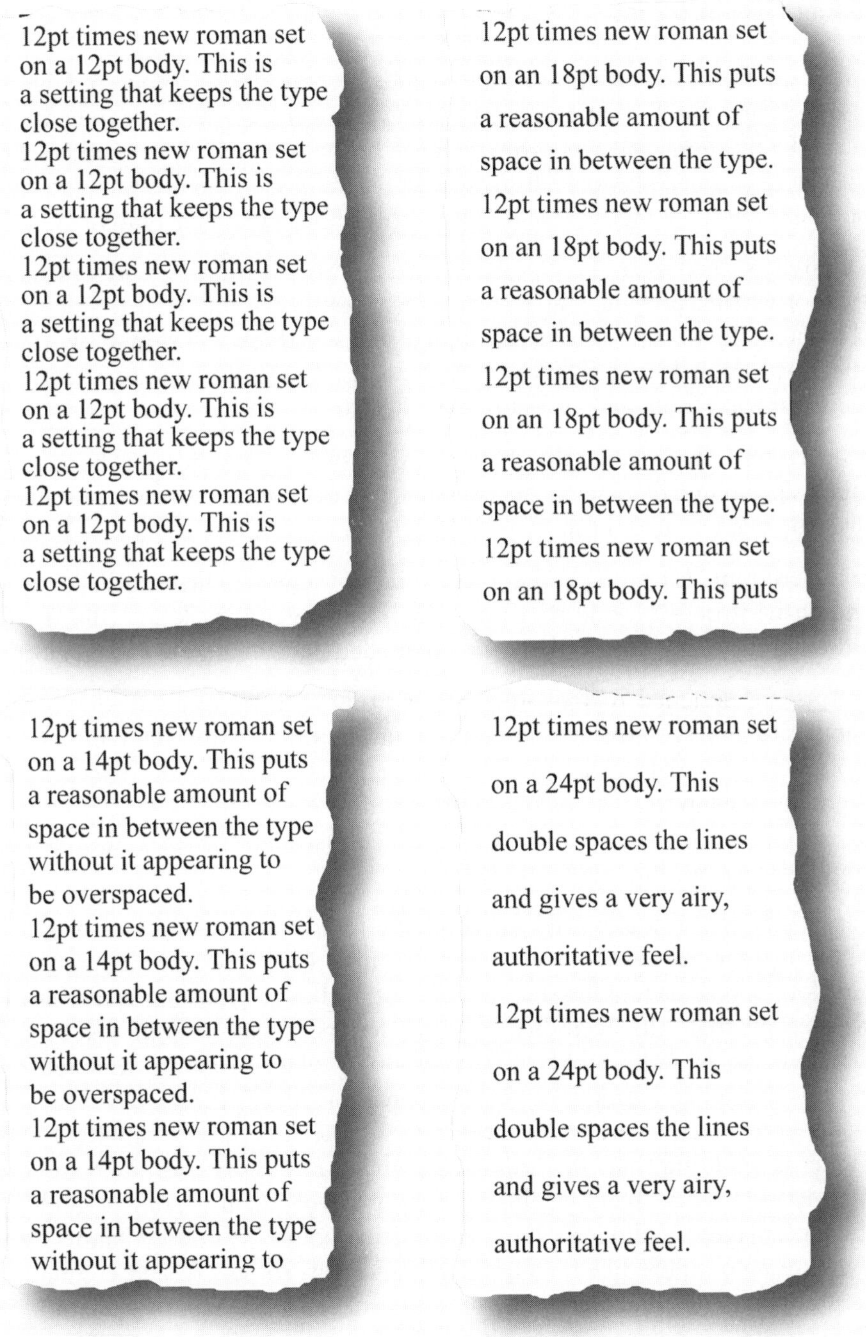

12pt times new roman set
on a 12pt body. This is
a setting that keeps the type
close together.
12pt times new roman set
on a 12pt body. This is
a setting that keeps the type
close together.
12pt times new roman set
on a 12pt body. This is
a setting that keeps the type
close together.
12pt times new roman set
on a 12pt body. This is
a setting that keeps the type
close together.
12pt times new roman set
on a 12pt body. This is
a setting that keeps the type
close together.

12pt times new roman set
on an 18pt body. This puts
a reasonable amount of
space in between the type.
12pt times new roman set
on an 18pt body. This puts
a reasonable amount of
space in between the type.
12pt times new roman set
on an 18pt body. This puts
a reasonable amount of
space in between the type.
12pt times new roman set
on an 18pt body. This puts

12pt times new roman set
on a 14pt body. This puts
a reasonable amount of
space in between the type
without it appearing to
be overspaced.
12pt times new roman set
on a 14pt body. This puts
a reasonable amount of
space in between the type
without it appearing to
be overspaced.
12pt times new roman set
on a 14pt body. This puts
a reasonable amount of
space in between the type
without it appearing to

12pt times new roman set
on a 24pt body. This
double spaces the lines
and gives a very airy,
authoritative feel.
12pt times new roman set
on a 24pt body. This
double spaces the lines
and gives a very airy,
authoritative feel.

Figure 8.7 Leading (the space between lines of type) can have a dramatic effect on the message.

Using type in design

There are five main families of type – old style, transitional, modern, Egyptian and contemporary – that represent the development of type over the past 350 years (Craig 1980: 31). Modern types have been with us since the middle of the twentieth century. However, from a design point of view a better categorisation of type is old style, modern, slab serif, sans serif, script and decorative.

Old style is the design of type used at the start of printing and representing the style of writing prevalent at the time. Scribes used quills, and therefore the characters they wrote were made up of a series of thick and thin strokes. This effect was mimicked in the type. Old style also has serifs – the little curlicues identifiable on fonts such as Times New Roman.

Modern types maintained the thick and thin strokes and the serifs but became much squarer and blockier as the need to carve or cast the type took precedence over the need to match the style of contemporary scribes.

Sans serif fonts (meaning without serifs) do not have the little curlicues at the end of the strokes. Nor do they normally have a mix of thick and thin strokes, although they can. They look even more modern and are simple and unadorned.

Scripts are designed to look like handwriting and are often used to mimic handwriting on such things as invitations and printed matter that is designed to look more personal or elegant. Decorative fonts cover a wide range and are there to have fun with. You wouldn't normally use a decorative font to set more than a few words; they are usually very difficult to read. However, they can add emphasis to a headline or caption.

Serif fonts are normally used for the body text of a newspaper or magazine. There is some debate about why this is. Tinker (1963: 64) claims that a sans serif font is read as rapidly as a seriffed font, although readers prefer serifs. He also accepts that '[t]he legibility of certain letters . . . can be improved by more judicious use of serifs' (ibid.: 42). Shipcott (1994: 46) claims that serifs do improve legibility, but does not cite a source for this. Either way, it seems that readers prefer serifs and find a seriffed font easier to read. Personally, I think Tinker is right and that the serifs seem to help us identify certain characters a little better; the eye seems to float along the top of the line, perhaps guided by the serif, making reading much easier. Another point about seriffed fonts is that they are much more likely to use thick and thin strokes to add emphasis to certain parts of a character. According to Tinker (1963: 42), this mix of thick and thin strokes helps us to identify characters more easily.

So why use sans serif? Although sans serif fonts are probably not so legible when grouped together in words, they are more perceptible as characters. They catch

A serif font (Times New Roman)

A sans serif font (Arial)

A CAPS ONLY DECORATIVE FONT (JUDAS)

A traditional font (Black chancery)

A handwriting font (comic sans)

A shadow font (Shadow)

A script-style font (Ariston)

A fun font – Bucaneer

A delicate, elegant font (Bodoni)

Figure 8.8 There are thousands of fonts.

the eye better from a distance and can be more easily distinguished from further away. Sans serif fonts are always a popular choice for advertising hoardings or road signs. However, although they are more perceptible and are easier to distinguish at a distance or in difficult circumstances, they are not so easy to read in a block. It is as though we can identify each letter more easily, but have to read them individually, while a serif font allows us to read a whole word, or even several words, at once. Because of this effect, reading a block of type in a serif font is much easier. We can read more, and read more quickly, in a serif font. For these reasons, newspapers and magazines often use serif fonts for body text and sans serif fonts for headlines. The easy-to-see headlines grab your attention, even from a distance, but the serif text is then easy and efficient to read.

The difference is like switching between shouting and talking. Shouting may well catch the attention and allow you to absorb short sentences quickly, but it very soon becomes wearing if someone is shouting at you all the time. The subtleties of the normal conversational voice are much more expressive for long periods of conversation.

It is no surprise that the optician's test card aims for perceptibility and is set in sans serif, while most books go for legibility and serifs.

Font styles and the iconic appeal of type

According to Tinker, most seriffed fonts read as easily as each other (ibid.). Yet there are hundreds of different typefaces available to the designer. Why is this, and why use one rather than another?

Most newspapers and magazines will try to keep to a handful of fonts for everyday use. This makes the newspaper easy to identify because readers become used to the look of certain fonts. Pages look much neater and are easier to read if there are only a limited number of different fonts on a page. However, every newspaper or magazine will occasionally use a decorative or unusual font to say something out the ordinary. Figure 8.9 shows how different fonts can be used to add an extra dimension to the message contained in the actual words used.

Display fonts of this sort should be used sparingly, but in the right circumstances they can really add to the message being conveyed.

Displaying and using type

Within any font there are a number of ways the face can be displayed to make it look different while maintaining the continuity of using the same font. These differences include using condensed, bold, italic, extended, bold italic or bold condensed type, and so on.

Using the same font but in these different formats gives the designer a wide range of materials. Bold and italic can be used to add emphasis to a word or

Sign up for a brand new life

The handwriting-style font helps make this headline personal.

all the luck of the irish

The typically Irish font emphasises the Irish element of the story.

STAY SNUG WITH YOUR GAS BOILER

The headline says: stay snug. The font emphasises the cold.

Figure 8.9 Using different fonts.

paragraph. Bold type is much more legible than roman type, while italic type (according to Tinker 1963) is far less easy to read.

Bold faces look like this.

Italic faces look like this.

An extended or condensed face changes the set of the type. The set is the width of individual characters. In the days of cast type, a foundry would produce condensed or extended faces, but these would normally only be bought by a publisher in one size, so an editor would talk about it as though it were a different font – Helios bold condensed, for instance. Things did not change with photocomposition, but with computers it is now easy to set a font not only to any size but also to any set width, and so to produce a Helios bold in 127 point and a set width of so many points (or say 90 per cent) is easy.

Adding extra definition to the font, such as bold, italic, shadow, outline, is also easy, often as easy as a keystroke on the computer. But you should avoid putting in a different emphasis just because you can. There needs to be a good reason for it.

Another major consideration is whether to set in upper case or lower case. Capital letters are sometimes called upper case because in the old days of hand setting of cast type, the boxes carrying the capital letters were in a case physically above those carrying the lower-case letters. Tinker (1963: 57) cites Starch as reporting that lower-case letters are read 10 per cent faster than capital letters. Readers also preferred lower case by 90:10. Tinker himself found even more startling figures, reporting that students read lower case 14 per cent faster (ibid.). He identified the shape of the words as one reason for this effect. In lower case, most words have a much more clearly identifiable shape than in upper case (see Figure 8.10).

Structuring text

The space around paragraphs and the space around words is as important as the space around individual characters. Paragraphs of type can be displayed in four main ways (see Figure 8.11):

- the right-aligned paragraph, sometimes called ragged left;
- the left-aligned paragraph, sometimes called ragged right;
- the centre-aligned paragraph, sometimes called ragged both;
- and finally, the justified paragraph.

Figure 8.10 Not only do capital letters take up more space, but they are also less easy to read. The lower-case word forms an easy-to-recognise shape, while the capital letters are just a block.

TWO PEOPLE were killed and four others injured in a multiple pile up on the M62 yesterday.

The accident happened in fog near the Huddersfield turn off. Police believe that one of the drivers may have been distracted by activity at a building close to the motorway.

The two killed were Mr John Bates, of High St, Chorley and Mr Peter Sims of Bassenthwaite Lane, Oldham.

The injured were taken to hospital but were later released. They were said to be suffering from shock and minor cuts and bruises.

A police spokesman said: "Lorries were being loaded under bright lights at factories alongside the motorway and we believe that one of the drivers might have been momentarily

TWO PEOPLE were killed and four others injured in a multiple pile up on the M62 yesterday.

The accident happened in fog near the Huddersfield turn off. Police believe that one of the drivers may have been distracted by activity at a building close to the motorway.

The two killed were Mr John Bates, of High St, Chorley and Mr Peter Sims of Bassenthwaite Lane, Oldham.

The injured were taken to hospital but were later released. They were said to be suffering from shock and minor cuts and bruises.

A police spokesman said: "Lorries were being loaded under bright lights at factories alongside the motorway and we believe that one of the drivers might have been momentarily

TWO PEOPLE were killed and four others injured in a multiple pile up on the M62 yesterday.

The accident happened in fog near the Huddersfield turn off. Police believe that one of the drivers may have been distracted by activity at a building close to the motorway.

The two killed were Mr John Bates, of High St, Chorley and Mr Peter Sims of Bassenthwaite Lane, Oldham.

The injured were taken to hospital but were later released. They were said to be suffering from shock and minor cuts and bruises.

A police spokesman said: "Lorries were being loaded under bright lights at factories alongside the motorway and we believe that one of the drivers might have been momentarily distracted. With the fog so thick, a moment is all that it would have

TWO PEOPLE were killed and four others injured in a multiple pile up on the M62 yesterday.

The accident happened in fog near the Huddersfield turn off. Police believe that one of the drivers may have been distracted by activity at a building close to the motorway.

The two killed were Mr John Bates, of High St, Chorley and Mr Peter Sims of Bassenthwaite Lane, Oldham.

The injured were taken to hospital but were later released. They were said to be suffering from shock and minor cuts and bruises.

A police spokesman said: "Lorries were being loaded under bright lights at factories alongside the motorway and we believe that one of the drivers might have been momentarily distracted. With the fog so thick, a moment is all that it would have taken."

Figure 8.11 Top left: text is ranged left. Top right: text is ranged right. Bottom left: text is centred. Bottom right: text is justified.

A justified paragraph requires the copy to have been hyphenated so that long words are not unduly squeezed trying to fit within a line. This can be a particular problem on the narrow column widths favoured by tabloid newspapers.

Newspapers use columns because they aid readability. A column width of 10 ems (almost 4 centimetres) is fairly normal, although quality papers sometimes have slightly wider columns while tabloid columns can be as narrow as 8 ems.

The optimum is said to be 15 ems. A column wider than this becomes difficult to read, as the eye has to scan the line in several jumps. Giles and Hodgson (1996: 137) say that a column width should be chosen with an eye to the paper's readership. This makes sense. Educated readers who can read quickly and efficiently will want a longer line so that they can read more in one go. A less well-educated readership for whom reading is more of a chore may find a narrower column width more acceptable.

The proportions of a character in any typeface are vital. The ideal character needs to be oblong rather than square. If the x-height is too large, the all-important ascenders and descenders become indistinguishable, making reading difficult. On the other hand, a large x-height makes the type appear larger and therefore easier to read, and it also means fewer words to each line of type.

A serif is the curly part of type that hangs off the ends. It adds definition to ascenders and descenders, making reading much easier. Since the ascenders and descenders are vital to our ability to read quickly, this is important and could be the reason why serif faces are more readable.

Type has a lot of work to do. It must allow the reader to pick up the words as quickly and as easily as possible without using up too much space. To do this, a face must be relatively small, but still be perfectly readable. The amount of space for each character also affects the speed and ease with which type is read. Too much white space around a character makes it as difficult to read as too little. Space between paragraphs breaks the text into bite-sized chunks. The same kind of space between lines makes the whole thing too difficult to read. Too little space and the words become cramped, crushing in on each other.

You need to give considerable thought to the type and spacing you use for any publication. The space between characters can be adjusted in two ways to ease reading. First is *kerning*. Kerning is when a character hangs over into the space normally reserved for another character. Characters such as 'f' or an upper-case 'T' need to hang over the vowels that often follow them, otherwise the space between the two characters looks odd. The software can be instructed to kern certain characters in appropriate situations to reduce the space between these letters. Sometimes, instead of kerning, ligatures are used. Ligatures are specialist characters that combine two ordinary characters in order to reduce the space required and to make the characters more readable. Sometimes a ligature is used for the characters 'fi' In order to avoid the dot on the 'i' clashing with the rounded end of the 'f', the dot is removed and the 'i' is brought closer to the 'f', giving 'fi'. Other popular ligatures include '&' (short for 'et', meaning 'and'), 'œ' for 'oe', and 'æ' for 'ae'. Scroll through symbols in your word processing package to find a whole range of interesting-looking ligatures.

Devices to add interest

There are a wide range of devices that can be used to improve the look and readability of a page or to add emphasis or urgency.

Drop letters. These are probably one of the earliest ways of providing an entry point. Monastic scripts used to be big on highly decorated and illuminated drop letters. They left the reader in no doubt about where to start reading. Modern drop letters, used judiciously throughout a piece of text, can keep it interesting, prevent it looking too grey and allow the reader to absorb the piece in reasonably easy-to-read segments.

Indented text. Another way to add emphasis or change the pace of a piece of text is to indent it. Indenting the first line by an em space gives a clear indication of where each paragraph starts. It allows the reader to quickly find their way back into the column of text and is a useful guide. Paragraph indents are not essential, but they are helpful to the reader.

A hanging indent is the opposite of standard paragraph indenting. Here the first line is run full out and the rest of the paragraph is indented, usually by an em space. This allows the text to stand away from the text in the left-hand column, giving plenty of white space and definition. It is a technique that is useful for extended captions or *sidebar* stories.

It is also possible to indent individual paragraphs. 'Full out' text runs right across the column, leaving only a little space before the next column. By indenting, you can increase the space and so, by increasing the white space, highlight that paragraph, pulling it away from the rest of the text. You can indent both sides or only one. Generally speaking, indenting both sides is more pleasing unless you intend using vertical scoring (see below) or the text runs alongside a picture or graphic.

Boxed text. If you want to box a piece of copy, you will have to indent both sides in order to give space for the box. Boxes give very definite emphasis and are useful for small stories that are worth more than their size would suggest. They are also good for sidebar stories – additions to a main story that are not too long but are deserving of more emphasis. Boxes can be complete, open (top, bottom or one side), shadowed or on tone (see the next paragraph) and come in a variety of rule sizes. An open box is useful if you wish to tie in the boxed story with something else: you can put the open side alongside the tied-in story. Rules thicker than 6pt would be extremely unusual and tend to look too heavy.

Boxes can be produced by reversing the copy or laying it on tone (either black on tone or white on tone), or by underlying with colour. All of these devices make the text more difficult to read, and so you should also consider using an increase in type size. It is also wise to use these techniques only for short runs of text.

Bold text. Emboldening text adds emphasis. A short story tied in with others or one you wish to lift from the page can be emboldened. This often works well with a light headline. Emboldening paragraphs within a story helps break up a long story and adds emphasis. You can even embolden a single word for emphasis.

Italic text. Italic text manages to add an ingredient of urgency to text. Italic can be used for emphasis but is better used where you want to introduce an element of breathlessness. Long pieces of italic (anything over 30 words) are very difficult to read, but short phrases or paragraphs can add real importance to the words. Italic is very useful in blurbs.

Underlined text. This also adds emphasis but is slightly self-important and not very fashionable. It is reminiscent of the slightly potty letter-writer who writes on lined paper in green ink with a mix of caps and lower case, underlining every third word. Still, underlined text is useful in small doses, and invariably with bold text.

Caps. Putting the occasional paragraph in caps (especially small caps) can add further emphasis. I would always use this with bold text to double the impact. Like underlining, it is somewhat unfashionable (although as it's been unfashionable for some years, maybe now is the time to revive its use).

Font breakers. Using a different font can be very dramatic, adding a lot of emphasis. Although sans serif faces are less readable because of their high perceptibility, a small paragraph of emboldened sans serif in a long run of text can really draw the eye, encouraging the reader to keep at it.

Staggered font size. Entry points can be emphasised with an increase in typeface. Increasing typeface size for *intros* can emphasise the entry point, and some papers use sizeable emboldened sans serif faces for their lead story intros because they are highly legible and mean the reader should have found the entry point and read the intro before they are really aware of it.

Vertical scoring. This ties in well with indents, especially when the indent is on one side only. The score fills in the indent so that the column sides are even but the rule (from 6pt to 18pt) adds heavy emphasis to the paragraph (see Figure 8.12).

Bulleted text. Bullets are also known as blobs, to give 'blob pars'. These bullets are devices at the beginning of each par. Usually they are round, but they can be any shape: square, asterisks, arrows, triangles, snowflakes, phones – the list is

TWO PEOPLE were killed and four others injured in a multiple pile up on the M62 yesterday.

The accident happened in fog near the Huddersfield turn off. Police believe that one of the drivers may have been distracted by activity at a building close to the motorway.

The two killed were Mr John Bates, of High St, Chorley and Mr Peter Sims of Bassenthwaite Lane, Oldham.

The injured were taken to hospital but were later released. They were said to be suffering from shock and minor cuts and bruises.

A police spokesman said: "Lorries were being loaded under bright lights at factories alongside the motorway and we believe that one of the drivers might have been momentarily distracted. With the fog so thick, a moment is all that it would have taken."

Four cars were involved in the accident and police were surprised that more were not drawn in. The spokesman said: "Luckily, the accident happened in the inside lane and so other drivers were able to

Witnesses

avoid the crash fairly easily. It was also easy for us to remove the cars from the carriageway very quickly."

By JOHN SMITH

TWO PEOPLE were killed and four others injured in a multiple pile up on the M62 yesterday.

The accident happened in fog near the Huddersfield turn off. Police believe that one of the drivers may have been distracted by activity at a building close to the motorway.

The two killed were Mr John Bates, of High St, Chorley and Mr Peter Sims of Bassenthwaite Lane, Oldham.

The injured were taken to hospital but were later released. They were said to be suffering from shock and minor cuts and bruises.

A police spokesman said: "Lorries were being loaded under bright lights at factories alongside the motorway and we believe that one of the drivers might have been momentarily distracted. With the fog so thick, a moment is all that it would have taken."

Four cars were involved in the accident and police were surprised that more were not drawn in. The spokesman said: "Luckily, the accident happened in the inside lane and so other drivers were able to avoid the crash fairly easily. It was also easy for us to remove the cars from the carriageway very quickly."

Police were on the scene in just a few minutes, according to witnesses and were able to prevent any further carnage.

TWO PEOPLE were killed and four others injured in a multiple pile up on the M62 yesterday.

The accident happened in fog near the Huddersfield turn off. Police believe that one of the drivers may have been distracted by activity at a building close to the motorway.

The two killed were Mr John Bates, of High St, Chorley and Mr Peter Sims of Bassenthwaite Lane, Oldham.

The injured were taken to hospital but were later released. They were said to be suffering from shock and minor cuts and bruises.

A police spokesman said: "Lorries were being loaded under bright lights at factories alongside the motorway and we believe that one of the drivers might have been momentarily distracted. With the fog so thick, a moment is all that it would have taken."

Four cars were involved in the accident and police were surprised that more were not drawn in. The spokesman said: "Luckily, the accident happened in the inside lane

Witnesses

and so other drivers were able to avoid the crash fairly easily. It was also easy for us to remove the cars from the carriageway very quickly."

Police were on the scene in just a few minutes, according to witnesses

Figure 8.12 Different ways of breaking a long run of type. Left: an indented, emboldened paragraph and a side-head. Centre: A drop cap in one of the paragraphs. Right: An indented paragraph with a vertical score and a crosshead. These tend to look better in a run of text than a side-head; they tend to give the impression of a new story.

as long as your imagination. They are usually used with indented text to give the impression of a hanging indent. Sometimes they are used like a drop letter and inserted into the first line or lines of the par. Where the bullets are dropped into several lines, they become a very useful device, allowing you to use bits of artwork or logos at the beginning of each par. For instance, a column of international nibs could avoid headlines by running the pars close together but with a globe of the world dropped into the first two lines of each par.

Bullet devices are good for:

- lists of items;
- short paragraphs one after the other;
- a short paragraph added at the end of a story that is separate from it but connected.

Bylines. Bylines – the name of the reporter credited with writing a story – give wide scope for breaking up text. Once only set in bold at the top of the text, they now come in all sizes, with rules or boxes, are added to *standfirsts*, included with pictures of the reporter – the only limiting factor is your imagination. They can be very useful for breaking up columns of text or placing at the top of a second column of text, underneath a double column intro (see Figure 6.11).

Standfirsts. Standfirsts are a round-up of events or issues in he main text event that explains why the article is there, written in under 30 or even 15 words in a way that makes a story sound irresistible. They are also a useful way of going over old ground that it would be wise not to take for granted.

Captions. Provided the caption for a picture is easy to find, you have a wide range of opportunities to break up a page with a caption. Different types, rules, reverses, etc. are all tricks that can make a page seem more interesting. A drop letter or word and sequential caption can be used here. A feature that sends a reporter or reader out with the army as it practises for a major campaign, for instance, might have a number of pictures that could be captioned as: DAY 1: the army sets up camp. DAY 2: and we're ready for manoeuvres – and so on.

Rules and borders. Rules and borders can be used to break up stories or to connect and add emphasis. Rules and borders can run into headlines, and through, into, under or over pictures and graphics. They come in a variety of sizes, shapes and designs: from the famous dotted rule (as in 'tear along the dotted line') to fancy borders with a variety of uses from holly borders for Christmas pages to fancy scroll borders. Rules come in sizes from 0.5pt to 24pt. Don't forget that there are tone rules, white rules and all the colours of the rainbow in between.

White space. Careful use of white space adds more emphasis than you would imagine. Compare the white space in the *Guardian* with the look of other papers and see the effect it has.

Crossheads. Crossheads and side-heads are great for breaking up long slabs of text. They can be used in a wide variety of ways but should be kept to the same style throughout a page. You can have fun with the crossheads, linking them together throughout the text by providing a running theme. However, you do need to be careful you don't spell out a message you didn't mean to. One sub's final message to the boss after his acrimonious departure was spelled out in the initial letters of crossheads throughout the lead item.

Devices should be used sparingly and with coherence. Too many differing devices will make a page just as unreadable as a page that is just one big slab of text.

9
Words in type

Although the choice of type used to set words is critical, so is the choice of the words themselves. The whole point of design is to sell the journalism contained on the printed pages, and it has been assumed throughout this book that the copy to be used is well written and well edited. I have relied on other books to discuss how to get these vital tasks right. But there are other writing and editing tasks required as part of the design process and it is important to know how to do these in order to produce a lively and attractive page.

Writing headlines

A headline is there to sell the story below it.

As we have discussed before, readers leaf through a publication looking for something to grab their attention – an entry point to draw them into a page. A good headline attracts attention and should make the reader want to read the story. A good headline should make the story sound like just the kind of thing they would want to read. This means that the headline should be aimed at the target audience: if you are writing a headline for the *Sun* or *Loaded*, there is not much point in writing a serious-minded headline or one that contains clever literary allusions; the reader either will be uninterested or will miss the point. The headline should contain cultural references that your readers will understand and want to relate to, it should excite them about a story that they will want to read.

The headline should tell the reader a little bit about the story – but not enough to let them think they know all about it and no longer need to read it! A heading or headline aimed at a young audience hooked on *The X-Factor* might say:

X-factor's
June dishes
dirt on 'Sico'

There are key words that are going to draw in the readers: 'X-factor' is an obvious phrase as millions of 15- to 30-year-olds watch this popular show. They are keen to find out what's going on behind the scenes. 'Dishes dirt' tells little but implies that there's some juicy gossip to come. The use of a name that will be known to the readers as one of the contestants that they either support or want to vote out, and certainly want to read about, will also attract attention. However, the headline does not go into detail. If the reader wants to know what the 'dirt' is and to learn about the gossip, they are going to have to read the article – and there is barely an *X-factor* fan alive who could resist that one!

Headlines need to be active. They should be in the present or future tense in order to keep them immediate and urgent. It also makes them shorter and simpler to read. By saying that June 'dishes dirt' (present tense), the headline is active and suggests that this 'dishing dirt' is a continuing process and one that is new and up to date. Although the interview must have taken place at least the day before, probably much longer ago if this was in a magazine, the present tense keeps it live and current.

Headlines must be sentences and should always contain a verb to provide action: June 'dishes' dirt. This verb is carefully chosen to give the correct balance of action combined with colloquial usage. It implies more than a verb such as 'telling' could: it suggests the narrator will get to the nitty-gritty, the material you really want to hear about, without equivocating or dressing it up in prissy language. Of course, whether the story actually goes into the depth of detail the reader is hoping for is another matter, but if the headline implies it, then the reader will soon get stuck in. Your choice of verbs in the story text is also vital, of course, but it is especially so in headlines, because you rarely have room for adverbs or adjectives, and so the correct choice of verb and noun is vital. 'Britney storms out' is much more expressive than 'Well-known singer walks out in a bit of a huff', even if we don't know where she walked out or what she walked out of.

You should avoid putting your opinions into headlines; they should explain the story, not your view of it. This means that there are words you need to be careful of. For instance, the phrase 'hard-left' (or 'hard-right'), applied to a politician, is widely used in a disparaging way. But there is no easy definition of what is hard-left or hard-right; they are relative descriptions that are used to disparage someone's political viewpoint in an attempt to dismiss it without proper thought. If the term is used by a politician about someone, then you could use it, but it is not a term you should use for your own description. A headline needs to be accurate and should avoid straying from the facts presented in the copy. The Press Complaints Commission (PCC) is as likely to uphold a complaint against a publication for an inaccurate headline as for inaccurate text. Jonathan

Aitken, a former MP, complained against the *Observer* in 1993 about the headline 'Aitken named in arms bribe case', saying that it incorrectly implied that he was involved in wrongdoing. The PCC accepted that:

> [T]he text of the story did give details of the extent of the complainant's involvement which made it clear that he was not 'named' in any sense of being involved with wrongdoing in the arms bribe case or evasion of US export controls.
>
> (PCC 1993: 8)

Journalistic jargon or clichés are another trap for the eager sub-editor. It is tempting to use journalese such as 'bid', 'blaze', 'slash', 'rap' or 'quiz' because all the papers seem to. This is sloppy writing and should be avoided. Fresh headings are bound to seem more attractive than jargoned headings such as 'Bravery bid in fire dash'. To show you how weak cliché headings can be, try the headline generator (Figure 9.1). Choose one word from each column and see what you get. There is no need to follow the horizontal lines, but you can only choose one word out of each column in that order. Some make more sense than others, but all work, more or less, and rely heavily on cliché.

There is also jargon that comes from other sources and specialist words that are not in common usage. These might come from politicians, showbiz stars, scientists or technicians. We should avoid using them if it is unlikely that readers will understand them. Of course, if you are working for *New Scientist*, then a reasonable smattering of widely used scientific terms would be acceptable in headlines and it would probably be difficult to write without them. Similarly, writing for financial publications introduces a specialist vocabulary that would need to be used. But try to avoid phrases or words with which the target audience of your publication will be unfamiliar. Acronyms or abbreviations are also potential trouble. 'PCC' might mean Press Complaints Commission to readers of the *Press Gazette*, but to the purchasers of the *Church Times* it would be Parochial Church Council. If you are sure that your readers will understand the abbreviation, that there is only one interpretation and that the abbreviation is widely used, then by all means put it in the headline. For instance, 'Aids' is probably more widely understood now than the name acquired immune deficiency syndrome from which it comes, and readers would certainly take longer to remember what the British Broadcasting Corporation is than good old 'BBC' or even 'the Beeb'.

A headline must make sense and it should also make sense line by line – or at least not imply something you did not mean. A famous wartime headline read:

French push bottles
up German rear

1	2	3	4	5
Disgraced	Hero	raps	babyfaced	love-cheat
Brave	Mum	accuses	royal	baby
Sad	schoolkid	praises	disgraced	boyfriend
Have-a-go	Mr Chips	angers	sexy	girlfriend
Happy	copper	burns	kinky	lads
Missing	cult	serenades	illegal	girls
Crazy	star	bedded	legit	son
Soccer	sex-pest	slaps	sweet	daughter
Disgraced	worker	shoots	sour	wife
Defiant	woman	saves	cruel	hubby
Disabled	Mrs mop	slams	gorgeous	blackmailer
Drunken	Dad	wins	obsessed	fortune
Sexy	stepmum	fights	rip-off	cash
Mystery	pensioner	hurt in	raging	child
Wicked	thug	rescues	dead	star
Wild	rocker	fires	angry	celeb
Depraved	athlete	sacks	old	Scrooge
Hairy	student	stabs	new	animal
Tubby	granny	bags	broken	babe
Skinny	DJ	babies	bitter	hunk
Racist	yuppie	quits	slighted	maniac
Cruel	hubby	steals	shamed	killer
Barmy	wife	loses	shattered	thief

Figure 9.1 A cliché-headline generator.

(or so Sellers claims (1968a: 98)). Read as three lines, this makes better sense:

French push
bottles up
German rear

Read a headline out loud. Are there hidden meanings? Does slang turn it into something that will be sniggered at? Good editors have dirty minds and a wide appreciation of slang, both obscene and regional. They need it to avoid headlines such as

Jilted lover loosened boyfriend's nuts

which was written about a court case concerning a man who tried to scare off a rival by loosening the wheel nuts on his car. Another example concerns a TV advertising campaign against pickpockets based around the slogan 'snatch of the week'. This came to an abrupt end a few years ago, presumably after someone pointed out that Midlands slang made this advert 'snigger of the week' in some parts of the country where 'snatch' meant something very different.

A headline must fit the space available for it. These days you will usually be writing the heading direct onto the computer screen and you will be able to see whether the chosen type size 'busts' (is too long) the headline or leaves it 'shy' (too short). It is important to try to keep the size of type to match the design. It can be very tempting to reduce or expand the size of the heading type in order to ensure that a good heading fits the space available, but this is bad practice. It might be all right to run 60pt as 58pt in order to allow it to fit, but better still, get the right words that will fit. It is also tempting to condense the face or expand it in order to fit a heading. Again a small amount might not be noticeable, but changing the fit by more than ±5 per cent means that the coherence of style implicit in the type will be lost.

The shape of a headline is also important (see Figure 9.2). The balance between different lines of heading in a multi-line heading will affect how the page looks. If there are only two lines, then they should both fill the space fairly well and certainly should not be more than one column shy. Both lines should be of similar length. Three-lined headings should tend to have the middle line shorter than the other two as this looks more balanced; the same applies to multi-line headings.

With multi-heading display, always write the main heading first so that it can tell the story, with any straplines or subsidiary headings written later. Make sure you do not repeat the same word in any of the other headings, and avoid punctuation. If you must put things in quotes, then single quote marks should be

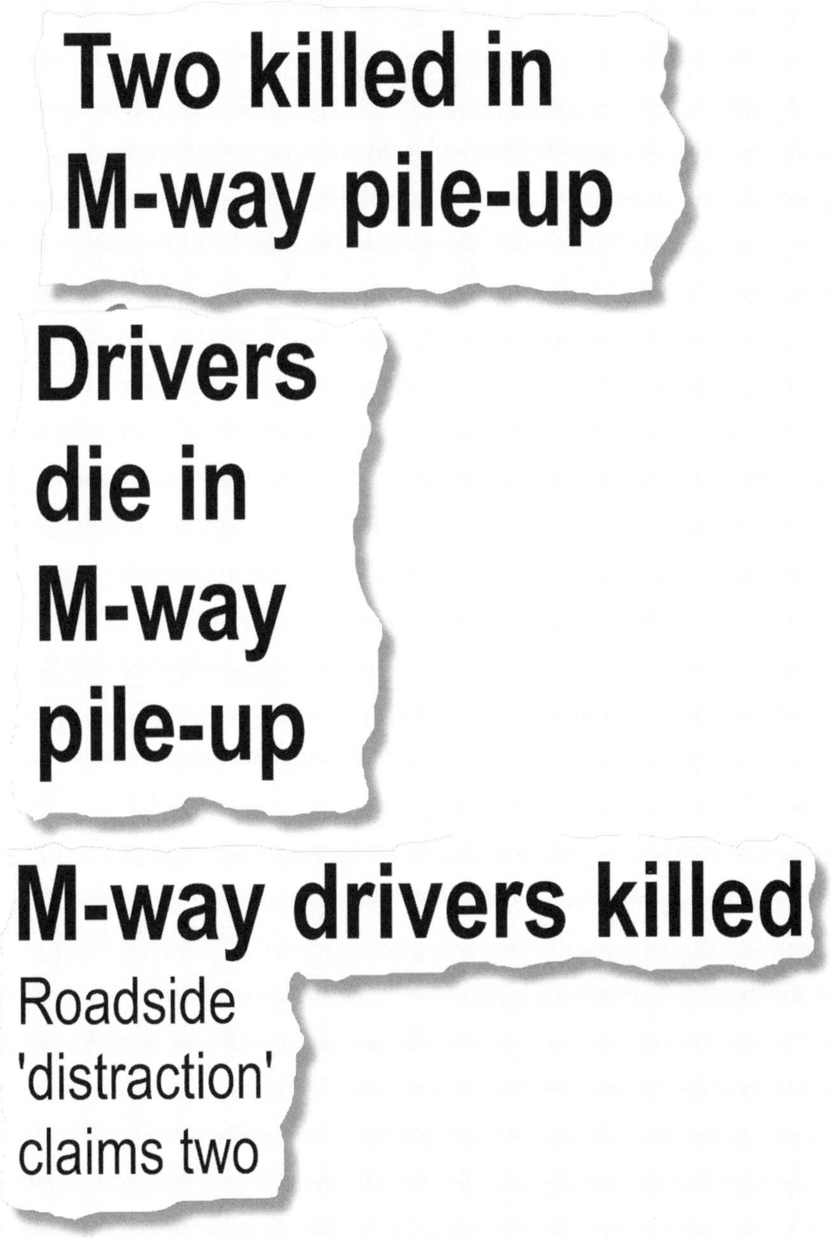

Two killed in
M-way pile-up

Drivers
die in
M-way
pile-up

M-way drivers killed
Roadside
'distraction'
claims two

Figure 9.2 Top: a two-line heading. Both lines need to be about the same length and certainly should not be more than one column shorter than the other. Centre: four lines. The top and bottom lines need to be the longest of the four and should be of similar length. Bottom: a two-deck headline. The second deck should be about half the type size of the first deck. Try to keep the lines of the second deck of equal length.

used. Normal punctuation rules apply, but you should avoid headlines that need punctuating. Do not put a full point after the heading.

Normal rules about capital letters apply, so do not use cap starts for words unless they are proper nouns or the first word of a sentence. Check finally that the heading fits, has no double meaning, is legally safe and makes sense.

The heading must come first on any page, and if this means rewriting the *intro* after the heading has been finished, then this will have to be done. Often the obvious heading is in the intro or sounds very similar, and so the intro needs to be rewritten to avoid repetition.

Different styles of heading

The several different types of heading have their own particular names and uses, but all are there to allow the designer to prevent the text running through from one heading to the next.

Kickers

Kickers use a completely different style of font in order to give a story a particular emphasis. This is the same kind of emphasis that TV tries to inject with the 'And finally . . .' type of news item. You should only use one kicker font per page, allowing a particular story to stand away from the rest, giving it a distinctiveness even though its heading style and content do not make it the top story on the page. Often the kicker font will be sans serif when the usual font is serif, or vice versa. The *Sun* used to use Cooper Black as its kicker, a bold font with heavy, stylised serifs that stood up well against the heavy sans serif fonts used throughout the rest of the page.

Multi-column headings

Single-column headings carry little weight and are generally used to introduce small down-page stories. However, they can be inserted within a block of text either to split it or to add emphasis, either as a heading or as a device to carry a strong quote or reinforce a part of the story. Nowadays, most headings cover several columns, from the down-page double column to the multi-column lead heading. The broader the heading, the stronger the display and the more material required as support beneath the heading.

Multi-line headings

There is no real limit to the number of lines a heading can take up, although it is rare to see one deeper than six lines, and most are between two and four. The more lines there are, the narrower the heading will normally be. A full-page *streamer* dropping down four lines would look extremely odd and over-heavy no matter how important the story. On the other hand, a single-line streamer will probably require an additional heading to give the appropriate emphasis. Generally we can say that the average lead headline fills 10–12 column widths. The average second lead heading would probably fill 6–10 column widths.

Writing standfirsts and bylines

There are a variety of text devices used on pages by designers to assist the reader to navigate the page and attract the reader into a story. *Standfirsts* are the first device usually used. A standfirst is a cross between a headline and the *intro* to the story; it often also combines a *byline* – the name of the story's author. The standfirst is more likely to be used on a longer story, probably a feature or news backgrounder. It is particularly important in magazines.

A standfirst is usually presented in a font size that is larger than the story text, but much smaller than the headline. Anything from 14pt to 30pt could be considered normal, although a larger font is possible. It is possible to use much more detail in a standfirst than in a headline and it will often contain one of the more interesting anecdotes used within the story (see Figure 9.3). So, a story about how a celebrity overcame their drug addiction might have a headline such as 'My heroin hell' followed by a standfirst that said:

> My family had left me, my life was a mess. I had lost my job and I lived in squalor. What had happened to my golden life as TV's soap queen? Spenders star Jane Zilfur talks to Chris Frost about celebrity, fame and drugs.

This relatively short but easy-to-spot entry point gives readers key elements that allow them to decide whether or not they want to read the story, although of course if the designer and editor have done their job properly, the reader will hardly be able to resist.

If a standfirst is used, then the traditional *intro* (probably the one that the reporter had written) needs to be changed, otherwise it is likely to conflict with the standfirst. The editor needs to ensure that the headline, the standfirst and the intro fit together as a whole.

Standfirsts often contain bylines, and sometimes picture bylines (see Figure 9.3). Bylines are seen as a reward for good work by most journalists, and getting a byline is still considered important. However, it is now unusual to find unbylined stories in magazines and even in newspapers; if the story is of any length, a byline is normal. If the byline is not included in a standfirst (or there is no standfirst), then a byline might be included at the front of the text, or even in the text. If it is at the start of the text, it might be just a straight 'By Chris

Driving oui
lethal loung

Today's roads are busier than ever whilst our cars are more comfortable. JOHN SMITH wonders if they are too relaxing for our own safety and whether we should go back to the hard times of yore.

Lethal comf

Today's roads are busier than ever whilst our cars are more comfortable. Motoring correspondent CHRIS FROST wonders if they are too relaxing for our own safety.

Figure 9.3 A byline standfirst and a picture byline standfirst.

Frost' in a bold version of the body text, or it could be a more detailed description: 'Special report by Chris Frost, Education correspondent', or 'An exclusive report by . . .' (see Figure 9.4). If the name is to be included in the text (and this really is a style issue – how does your publication do these things?), then it might have '. . . writes Chris Frost' at the end of the intro paragraph.

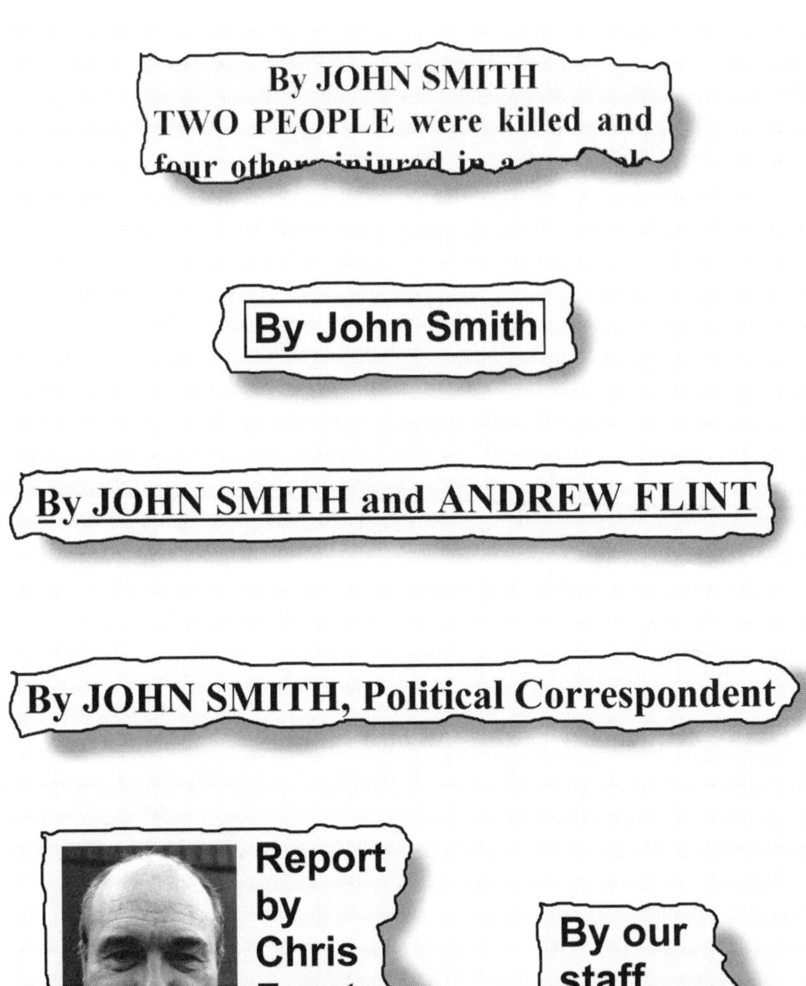

Figure 9.4 A variety of byline styles.

Captions

The caption is another text device that needs to stand out from the general run of text. This can be achieved either by making it slightly larger or by putting it in bold, italic or a different font. Italic can add emphasis but has been out of fashion for some time now. This must partly be because it is difficult to read, but also because it appears fussy and old-fashioned. No doubt it will become fashionable in some retro move, but probably not for a while. By setting the caption in a sans serif face against a seriffed body text, particularly if it is emboldened, the caption stands away from the body text and there can be no confusion about its being read in with the text.

Captions are usually provided with pictures or graphics to explain details within the picture (see Figure 9.5 for caption ideas). If you need a caption to explain a picture, then maybe it would be better not to use the picture, so do consider carefully what goes in the caption. If there are people, objects or places that need description, then describe them. The usual format for a photo of people is to put: 'pictured from left to right are: xxxxx'. It is worth remembering that while sub-editors sometimes get bored and like to put captions in odd places – up the sides of the picture, within the border, hidden in a section of the picture or in another column – readers never get bored with having captions in an obvious place where they can find them easily. If someone wants to know the name of the person in the picture, they don't like searching for captions and we should make them easily available.

A caption is there to help the reader make sense of the picture, and if it requires too much explanation, it's worth considering whether to use the picture at all. As discussed in the next chapter, a picture should be capable of telling the story, and the caption should only be there to fill in the details, usually explaining who is in the picture. A caption should be adding to the picture, not saying the same thing. It can offer detail, or describe what happened before or what is about to happen. We should be confident that the picture and caption tell the whole story.

LEFT: The town centre that will have to be demolished to make way for the new motorway. Protestors are set to blockade the centre from Saturday.
OPTOMETRIST

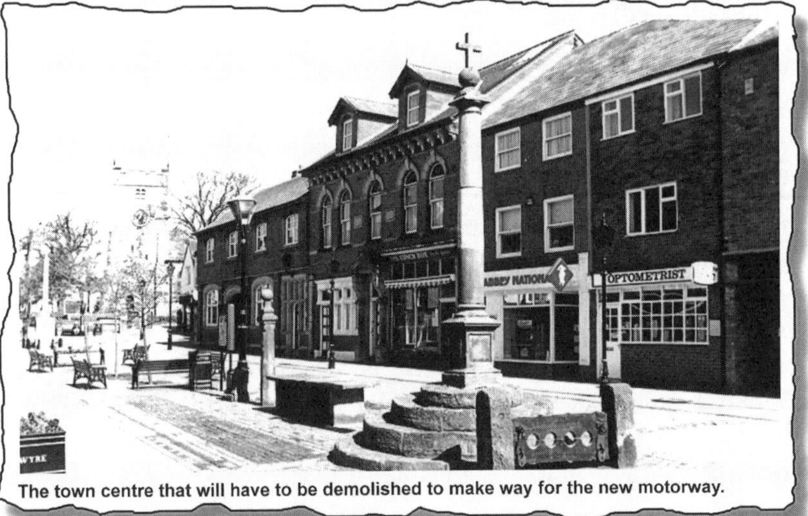

Figure 9.5 A variety of caption styles.

10
Using pictures

Pictures are one of the key elements of a page. It is pictures that draw a reader into a page and help to guide them through the page and the material on it. This means that considerable care needs to be taken in the choice of pictures and how they are used.

'A picture's worth a thousand words' is an oft-used phrase, but one that has the wrong emphasis. In publication terms it must be turned on its head: a picture must be worth its space in words before we should consider using it.

This often becomes difficult in a local paper, trade journal or in-house publication. A national newspaper or magazine has at its disposal dozens of top photographers desperate to illustrate all the really good stories – and has the budget to pay for them. But a small publication may have to rely solely on freelance photographers who are constantly asked to cover boring but difficult-to-get-out-of presentations, awards and retirements. Good photographers who make these bread-and-butter pictures exciting, original and worthy of publication are rare and well worth a good salary. Unfortunately, they rarely get it – at least on the publication that they start working for.

You may also be forced to take your own pictures. Digital cameras, with their direct links to computers, make this job easier technically but still difficult creatively. The National Union of Journalists has traditionally opposed this practice for the very good reason that good writers don't often make good photographers and vice versa, because no one has the time to do both jobs well. However, employers are often keen that reporters should take photographs, and it is certainly right that good reporters should be aware of the importance of good images to go with text for print or website. There is a big difference between knowing what makes a good picture and having the time and talent to take one. That said, good reporters should always carry a cheap camera, even if it's only a disposable instant camera, in case something dramatic happens. The poor quality of some of the video from the London Underground disasters of 7/7 did not prevent its being used, because it was all there was. Better to get a poor picture than no picture at all.

Editors of local newspapers or small specialist magazines also find that they are often pressured by an advertiser or good contact to produce or use boring pictures of award ceremonies or products. There is also the view, still widely held on local papers, that faces sell papers. A group shot of 30 local people in a picture will sell 30 papers, so the wisdom goes. I can't help thinking that people are a little more sophisticated these days. Those 30 might well buy the paper, but another 80 might cancel their subscription because they are fed up with boring photographs of groups of people.

It is also the case that this continual exposure to boring pictures makes it difficult for the editor choosing or editing pictures to make the best use of something different when it does come along. It is all too easy to think of pictures merely as three- or four-column space fillers. It is always important to examine each picture as it is presented and decide whether or not to use it on its merits. A good picture uses the space allotted to it in the best way possible. A good picture should:

- illustrate and illuminate quickly and effectively what the story is all about;
- underline the emotive side of the story;
- hint at action;
- allow the reader to identify with the people in the story.

It may well be that one picture can do all these things, but such pictures are rare. Usually, more than one picture is needed to describe the full spread of a story.

It is up to the editor to decide whether one picture is used to illustrate one aspect of a story, or whether more than one is used. The decision will depend on the story, the pictures and the space available.

Making a point

Pictures can be used to ram home a point made in the page display. If the picture is worth that magic thousand words, then use it. Nothing makes the point about the carnage and waste of life in the latest war or terrorist outrage more strongly than a picture of the dead and dying; nothing sums up the triumph of a World Cup victory better than a jubilant captain carried shoulder high waving the trophy at the team's supporters.

Picture selection is a difficult and subjective task. Explaining why a picture works with a particular story is complex. Any picture that is worth its place on a page must be paying its way with added information for the reader. It must help us to describe what is going on. An aerial picture of the site of an incident can help readers picture the place, particularly if it is a rural area where immediate identification is difficult, unlike towns, where an address will often suffice. But even here, a map and picture of the premises can often make things clearer. Pictures of objects can aid identification.

An archaeological find, for instance, can be pictured much more easily and to better effect than by description. People too can be better served by pictures. A description of the outlandish style of Lady Gaga will never call her to mind as well and as quickly as a picture.

Similarly, no amount of cunningly crafted prose is going to say as much about the courage of Falklands war veteran Simon Weston as a picture of his face complete with its unnaturally tight skin grafts criss-crossing the few remaining tufts of hair left on his head. One picture of this man sitting comfortably, at ease with his disfigurement, says more about his courage and ability to come to terms with his fate than any amount of writing could.

Pictures have a major part to play in setting the emotional agenda of a piece. Whether they are pictures of widows weeping at a pithead mining disaster or the triumphant smile of the sports victor or the mouth-twisting absorption of a picture-painting toddler, they all add something to the reader's perception of what has happened.

Choosing pictures to go with stories and features becomes a way of emphasising and underlining the areas of the story that are strongest. Harold Evans believes there are three tests for a publishable picture and that a picture without any of them 'should be rejected as junk'. The three tests (Evans 1978: 47) are:

1 animation
2 relevant context
3 depth of meaning.

Evans is not suggesting that you must have all three at once, although a picture that did could well be a winner. Animation gives activity and a lively picture that invites the reader to discover more, although Evans makes it clear that by animation he doesn't mean activity but life: 'a set scowl or a closed eye may give animation to a picture' (ibid.: 69). Relevant context helps to explain what is going on or adds extra information and so supports the story, while depth of meaning also supports the story, adding more information but also bringing in the emotional element, to help us feel more about the story.

You should never use a picture with a story just because you have got one. Only if the picture adds to the story should you consider using it. Does the picture add to our understanding of what is happening? Does it help to emphasise what has happened? Does it add to our feeling of identification?

Take the example of the murder of a child. We will certainly want a picture that will show the murder spot, be it a house or a trampled piece of field. This allows people to firmly fix in their mind where the incident took place – either as a place they know, or know of, or at least as the type of place. They probably know of somewhere similar in their own locality.

The Mainwaring murders in which a father and daughter were killed and their bodies dismembered and left in the garden were covered by all the popular tabloids with a huge aerial picture of the modest semi-detached home with its suburban garden on the front pages. Millions of readers had similar homes; the Mainwarings, the picture confirmed, were just ordinary people like you and me.

A picture of the victim and, if possible, the nearest relative will also be required. This is particularly important for local papers, where many readers might recognise the picture. But it is also important for national papers, where the picture allows us to relate to the victim. It could have been us, or our child, or our mother. Since these pictures are often snapshots from the family album, the pictures show the victim smiling or laughing incongruously. This can add to the poignancy of the story by confirming that the victim is a real person enjoying the same things as the readers. Pictures of murder weapons or the police scurrying back and forth can also add context and animation. Nor is it any different for features. Whether the story is about the latest fashion or diet craze or the advantages of the latest piece of technology, imaginative pictures can add to the overall strength of the article.

Whether a picture shows someone making a pot from clay for *Crafts Magazine*, or a tearful mother hugging her kidnapped child in a True Life Tale, or a photo of the Rubens picture that has just sold for a record £50 million, it is bound to say more about the event than even the best-written piece could manage. But a picture of 20 safety officers receiving their certificates from their employer probably adds nothing to the story and will require a large amount of space that could be better used for something else, unless of course the magazine is aimed solely at safety officers in that company. However, an animated demonstration of how they won their certificates might well provide a strong focal point for the page for a more general publication.

Occasionally you will get a picture so good that it requires a different slant than that suggested by the copy. If so, don't be afraid to follow this line. Really good pictures have a massive impact and sometimes the copy must play second fiddle to this. This is why TV quickly became the dominant medium for news.

Shape

One of the first decisions to be made about a picture is what should actually be in it and what shape it should be. The photographer decides what will be in the picture for a variety of reasons: news value, artistic merit, colour and shape, for instance. The editor needs to decide what should be in the picture on the basis of the story and the rest of the page. Not only will the editor need to consider the content of the picture, but he or she will also need to consider the shape. Some shapes work better than others in a publication. Changing the shape of a picture can often dramatically influence the way the picture looks and therefore how the story is presented and ultimately how the page is shaped (see Figure 10.1).

A tall picture can look dramatic because it presents us with a view that is different from the normal one. Our eyes allow us to see in landscape format; we have a very broad view, spanning almost 180° in a horizontal form. But our brow prevents us from seeing too high, presumably on the basis that there's not much up there to see apart from sky and the sun, which is more likely to blind us. A picture that is tall rather than wide is therefore unusual and likely to appear dramatic. That doesn't mean a wide picture is wasted, however. Often, cutting a horizontal picture into a vertically shaped frame would mean missing out a lot of the information we want to include – for exactly the reasons I've just explained.

Be careful not to cut out a picture's setting. A face could have been photographed anywhere. To cut out the part of the picture showing the gas chamber in which a convicted murderer was about to be executed is to waste the picture. Even white space around a picture can add emphasis, particularly if the subject is looking out of the side of the picture.

The shape of a picture can add a lot to the way both the picture and the page look. An unusual shape can add drama and interest to a page. This could be as easy as making it very wide or very tall, but it could involve shaping the edge of a picture in an unusual way against the type so that the type wraps around the picture, emphasising certain attributes.

Square is the most boring shape. A square picture can be a good picture but it struggles to make the best of itself within an all too symmetrical frame. Although a picture will attract attention on the page (as any picture does, according to Garcia and Stark 1991), it will not give the feeling of drama or interest that an unusually shaped picture or block of pictures will do. This is something of which those in the entertainment industry are well aware. They know they can add dynamism to their movie products just by producing them on a wide screen. TV is aware of this dimension as well. The new wave of television sets are all wide-screen. Even your holiday snaps come on oblong-sized paper in order to add impact.

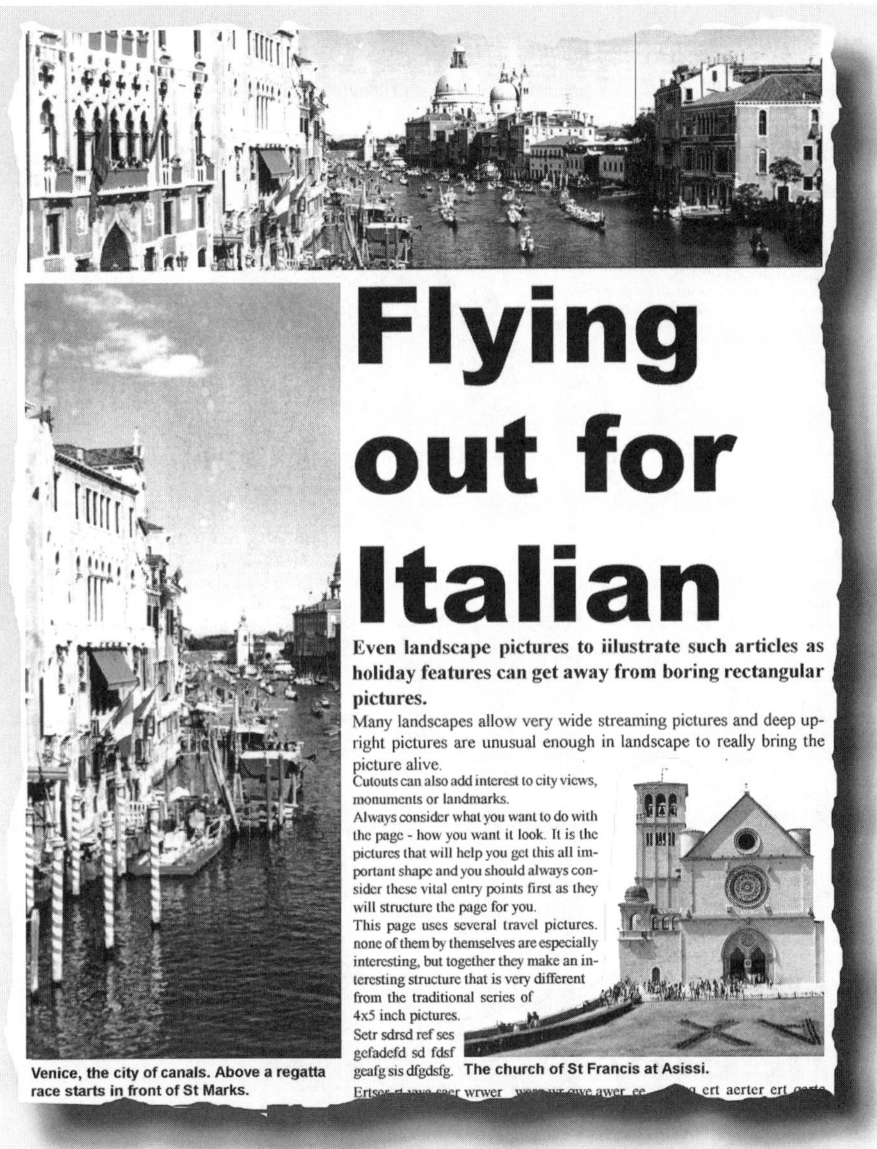

Flying out for Italian

Even landscape pictures to iilustrate such articles as holiday features can get away from boring rectangular pictures.

Many landscapes allow very wide streaming pictures and deep upright pictures are unusual enough in landscape to really bring the picture alive.

Cutouts can also add interest to city views, monuments or landmarks.

Always consider what you want to do with the page - how you want it look. It is the pictures that will help you get this all important shape and you should always consider these vital entry points first as they will structure the page for you.

This page uses several travel pictures. none of them by themselves are especially interesting, but together they make an interesting structure that is very different from the traditional series of 4x5 inch pictures.

Setr sdrsd ref ses gefadefd sd fdsf geafg sis dfgdsfg.

Venice, the city of canals. Above a regatta race starts in front of St Marks.

The church of St Francis at Asissi.

Figure 10.1a The pictures you choose for a page need to be the best pictures and in the most interesting shapes.

Common wisdom has it that a 4:5 ratio is the ideal, but you will find that other ratios can also work well.

A good photographer will provide an editor with a variety of shapes: wide or tall. Study them carefully and decide which adds more impact. Often, a wide

Town centre in car park battle

A car park is set to be built across the centre of a landmark town centre.

This type of picture allows the shape of the buildings to be used to break up the normal rectangular shape of a picture. Rather than cut out part of the picture, the much lighter left hand side can sit behind the double column text of the intro. This type of setting requires care as the picture may make the text much less legible. You should keep text off dark areas and use in a slightly larger size, but it does allow for different shapes of picture.

In this example, the text is wrapped into the picture, but it would be possible to just lay it over the top, if the background were not too dark.

Biker kids raise cash for needy

Motorcycling enthusiasts as young as three are to hold a special biking day to raise cash for a local children's home...

This tall picture has been deliberately made as long as possible in order to lengthen perspective and make a dramatic picture from a static pose.

The photographer took the picture at an unusual angle and included a very young child, building up the cuteness factor.

By rotating the picture by up to 12 degrees it has been made as deep as possible to drop well down the page.

This gives a stong diagonal that adds a feeling of action. The motorbike neatly frames the subjects.

Story: Chris Frost
Picture: Lewis Elliott

Sian Birch, leader of the charity workers with young helper, Emma Frost.

Figure 10.1b Picture shapes play an important role in determining the visual shape of a page. Try to avoid square pictures.

picture will allow for more action, as most action we are interested in tends to be in the horizontal plane.

You can also *pierce* a picture so that text or another picture or graphic is inserted into the picture. This can also add emphasis. It is worth remembering that picture shape is the overall shape, not just the shape of an individual picture. If you have a block of pictures together, then it is how they work together that is important, not the individual shapes.

Cropping pictures

What a picture frames is of vital importance. Everyone has been at an event when a famous person, or perhaps even someone we know, has been centre stage; it could be a concert, perhaps, or the graduation of a favourite relative. Flashbulbs pop and hundreds of pictures are taken, but we know that when the films are developed there will be a picture of the stadium or graduation hall with the subject of the picture a dark and distant dot in the centre. If we could cut out the bits we don't want, such as the ear of the person in front or the large section of audience, the picture that is left would be perfect. This is the process photographers and editors go through all the time, because although photographers try to ensure that they have correctly framed what they think the picture should be, they are not always aware of the angle the editor has decided to take. It is also possible that an archive picture is to be used, and this would have been taken for a different purpose altogether. Sometimes, of course, we are obliged to use photographs from amateurs which are not well framed. An early cropping decision can completely change a picture (see Figure 10.2).

The editor then has to decide which section of the picture needs to be produced on the page. It might be that the photographer has taken a group photograph, but we only want to use the two people standing in the centre. We would then crop off the people on either side (see Figure 10.3 for an example).

Zooming in on the action is often a good way to make a picture look more exciting. We are better able to see what is going on, and getting in very close makes for an angle that is unusual and adds interest. You need to be careful that you are not cutting out important context. Get in too close and although you'll know what's in the picture, for the reader it might seem to be one of those 'guess the identity' pictures that appear in puzzle magazines where a magnified picture of an everyday object leaves us guessing.

Occasionally there might be unavoidable sections of a picture that are distracting or of no value at all. We then have a choice of either piercing the picture to fill that space with text or another picture, or trimming away the background,

On your marks!
Even gondoliers find time to
relax and enjoy a regatta.

Figure 10.2 Cropping and changing the shape of a picture can make a huge difference to the way it looks on the page. Instead of being just a typical landscape, this travel picture has been cropped upright, making the scene appear much more dramatic. The caption and headline have been laid over the sea and sky to maximise the space.

Figure 10.3 Just because you have a picture of three people, that doesn't mean your picture has to include them all. If the story concerns only one of them, edit the others out and, if necessary, enlarge the portrait you need.

leaving parts of the subject of the picture standing outside of the frame. This is a useful technique. It makes the subject look larger than life and pulls them away from the background. It adds an illusion of depth to the picture and allows you to make the subject of the picture slightly larger than the space actually allowed for the picture. The *Daily Mail* is very fond of this technique and uses it extensively, favouring full-figure portraits that require quite a lot of space if the subject is to be seen at a reasonable size. Cutting away the frame and allowing the figure to stand clear is a good way of coping with the problem of space (see Figure 10.4).

Figure 10.4 Cutting away some of the background has several effects. The image can appear larger and the subjects more active, as though they are climbing out of the picture. The unhelpful, dull background is markedly reduced and becomes much less obtrusive.

Diagonals

Diagonals are important to a picture. They add drama and excitement; they suggest movement and action. Imagine a runner on the starting blocks. The body is diagonal across the picture. As the runner sprints away, the diagonal continues, with the body thrust forward and the arms and legs adding additional diagonals. The picture conveys action and we want to know why this person is running. If they are wearing sports gear, then it will be clear that they are playing a sport, but the picture will still be dramatic and interesting because it involves action (see Figure 10.5).

Animation

Too many pictures on newspaper pages tend to be static. TV and film producers found out a long time ago that people prefer to watch action. If action cannot be produced by the plot, then it can be produced by the framing. If two people are talking, the producer might get them to walk so that action is introduced in that way. If they are sitting in armchairs talking, a film producer might use extreme close-ups or cut quickly between the two, or use still other devices to make the scene more visually interesting. TV producers find this more difficult

Figure 10.5 You don't have to have photographs from a Premier Division football match to fill your publication with lively, action-packed pictures. Both these pictures have strong diagonals that start at the bottom left and finish on the top right. Both tell the story of youth football.

to do on some current affairs programmes without making them seem contrived, but even here, attempts are made to liven up things by cutting from close-ups to long shots, from one camera to another. Imagine watching *Question Time* or *The Graham Norton Show* with only one camera placed at a distance so that you could see everything without changing cameras. The picture would soon get boring. Instead, the producers use several cameras, and although in both *Question Time* and *Graham Norton* there are just a series of talking heads, the cameras cut in for close-ups so that we can pick up telling facial expressions, zoom out to show us the audience or change view and direction to give a feeling of pace and action.

We can't provide movement in publication pictures (although websites can use video to provide moving pictures to support the published edition), so we have to make sure that even static portraits of people contain animation by being an unusual shape, taken from an unusual angle, containing gestures or actions, or being framed unusually to contain additional information. That's why the traditional Budget Day picture of the Chancellor of the Exchequer holding up the famous red dispatch box used to be so popular; it's a bit clichéd now, but it still provides more interest and information than a mug shot of the Chancellor that could have been taken at any time. Watch the news when famous people are surrounded by the press; see how the flashbulbs flicker and hear the shutters clash as the star moves his or her head or makes a gesture.

Scaling pictures

One of the first tasks for a page designer is deciding on the size of the main picture that will become the entry point for the reader. The Poynter Institute's eye-tracking research shows that readers are drawn into a page by the picture or pictures (Garcia and Stark 1991). The picture is therefore important to a page design and usually becomes the page's entry point, drawing the reader in and then directing them to the start of the main article. The size of the picture is important in this exercise. If the picture fills the whole page, there will be nothing else on that page, although this could well draw the reader onto the opposite page. This is a lot of space, however, and when the copy taster is deciding what should go on a page, it is a juggling act to balance the relative importance of a picture against the copy that is competing for the space.

On the other hand, if a picture is too small, then readers will not be drawn to it on the page and will not be able to make out much of the information in the picture. A picture of a single person can normally be used in a smaller size than a picture of a group of people, for instance, because in order to be identifiable the people in the picture need to be of a certain size.

However, we would not put a picture of a person on a page and then use a small size just because it is one person. You need, as always, to consider why the picture is being used and what you hope to say with it. If it is there merely to show what the person looks like, then it only needs to be as big as is required for that purpose. If it is there to add drama, context and animation, and to draw the reader into the page, then it may need to be much bigger (see Figure 10.9 for an example).

Once the size of the picture has been chosen, the picture needs to be scaled. Just because the photographer has provided the picture at a certain size, we don't have to use it at that size. We can make it smaller or larger. We can also edit the picture (select the section we want to use) as discussed above and then make it smaller or larger. On an electronic system it is easy to scale the picture once it has been edited. The picture box is drawn to the correct size and the picture is then imported into that frame. Always remember to ensure that the frame has the same proportions as the picture. If the frame proportions are different, you should never stretch the picture to fit as this is nearly always detectable if it involves shrinking or stretching by more than a small percentage. This means that people can end up looking unusually thin, or – more damagingly – unusually fat. Making a person look fatter than they are is a certain way to be flooded with complaints, quite apart from being a distortion. Always try to ensure that you crop the picture so that the proportions of the picture and the frame are the same. That doesn't mean the picture and the frame need to be the same size – you might be reducing or enlarging the picture – but the proportions need to be the same. If the picture is 20cm × 24cm and you are intending to use it at half that size (or a quarter, if you are talking area), the frame will need to be 10cm × 12cm.

Cropping and scaling in Photoshop

Pictures in hard copy

You might occasionally be presented with a proper photograph to use on a page. In order to ensure that the picture is only scanned in at the maximum resolution required, consider what part of the picture you want to use and its possible final size before scanning.

Ethics and pictures

Now that picture desks have become fully electronic, there is little that you can't do to edit a picture. Take off a person's hat? Easy. Bring two people closer together? The stroke of a cursor key. This raises considerable ethical questions.

Occasionally a picture will require retouching by artists to remove blemishes or to cover up identification marks on vehicles. It can sometimes be tempting to use such retouching to change a picture. Doing so should be avoided.

It's very important to take care with library pictures. If you are using a picture of a person or landmark, check that the picture is still up to date. Using a picture of someone as they looked 10 or even 20 years before will not be too helpful. If that is the only picture, then you might decide to still use it but you should always make it clear that the picture is out of date. When the police are searching for a missing person, newspapers have often used a picture that looks very little like the person being sought. Extra information could make all the difference: adding 'The missing person pictured happily at home a few years ago when her hair was still brown and not blonde' makes it clear that the picture is out of date and that the missing woman's hair colour has changed.

The same is true of landmarks. If it is essential to use a picture of a landmark that is out of date (a nearby building that has been demolished, for instance) and a new picture can't be taken or the existing picture cropped to fit the new circumstances, then the only sensible approach is to make it clear that the picture is a library photo and so is out of date.

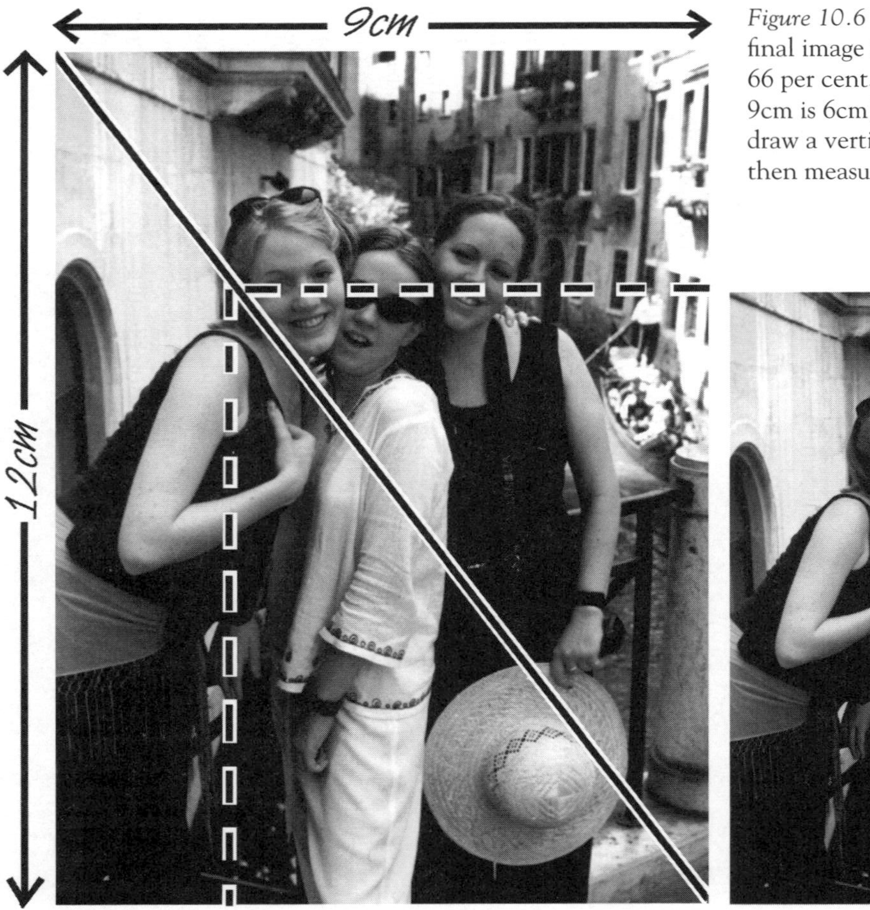

Figure 10.6 The original picture needs to be scaled so that the final image is smaller at only 8cm high. This means reducing to 66 per cent. We can either calculate the width (66 per cent of 9cm is 6cm) or we can draw a diagonal through the picture, draw a vertical line of 8cm (the height of our final image) and then measure the horizontal line, to find the width.

Special effects

Occasionally a picture needs to be changed to get the full effect required. This change could involve flipping the picture so that what was the right-hand edge becomes the left. This allows a picture to face into the page that would otherwise be facing out. It is a technique that needs to be handled with care. Hair partings, moles and scars now appear on the wrong side, and those are the subtle signs that give away a flipped picture. You can also change a picture to lay a texture over it, bleach the picture or change the tonal values in some other way so that you can disguise some part of the picture, perhaps. You can also paste two or more pictures together, to give the appearance of a much wider picture area. It is possible to darken a picture, leaving only the area we want the reader to concentrate on at the normal brightness and contrast (see Figure 10.3). All of these effects could be used to illustrate a story.

There is a discussion of the ethics of interfering with pictures in Chapter 9, but with modern software such as Photoshop you can do almost anything to a picture. To illustrate a feature about soccer hooligans, for instance, you might want a large picture of an after-match riot. You may have one in the library, but that would be of a specific news event and it might put you at risk of a libel suit if the participants' identities were obvious. Texturing the picture or bleaching it (see Figure 10.7) to remove the tones, leaving only black and white, might leave the impression of a riot (the picture might even be improved: stark black-and-white might be better than photographic realism) without identifying people and leaving the paper at risk of a libel suit.

A feature on divorce, for example, might be illustrated with a wedding picture torn down the middle. Getting a wedding picture from the library would do, but the identities of the couple would need to be disguised in some way.

This kind of interference with pictures is acceptable, but it is also possible to make major changes to pictures using Photoshop and engage in a kind of manipulation that could mean you risk having a picture that is untruthful and therefore unethical.

Graphics

Graphics have become even more important these days. The use of computer systems has allowed quick and easy access to graphic packages that can easily be placed on a page to illustrate a story. Whether it's a pile of cash to make a breaker on a Budget Day story, or a drawing of a plane taking off to illustrate a holiday story, there's plenty of material about. What is more difficult is specially drawn

Figure 10.7 Filters can dramatically change the look of a photograph. Left: normal; right top: coloured pencil; left bottom: dry brush; right bottom: mezzotint.

artwork. This will normally be produced by the art department, but you will need to brief them about what you want and when you need it. The quality of work they can offer may well depend on the amount of time they have, so it is worth deciding on a graphic as soon as possible. Any story involving a clear grasp of special locations is worth considering for graphics. Anything with figures or a large amount of detail might also benefit from a graphical interpretation (see Figure 10.8 for an example).

Finally, any story without any other good pictures should be considered for a graphic. Figure 10.9 shows a graphic I have produced to illustrate my point. It takes two fairly limited pictures, one of the 'victim' and one of the 'scene', and ties them into a graphic to show where the 'body' was found, only a short distance from where the 'victim' went missing.

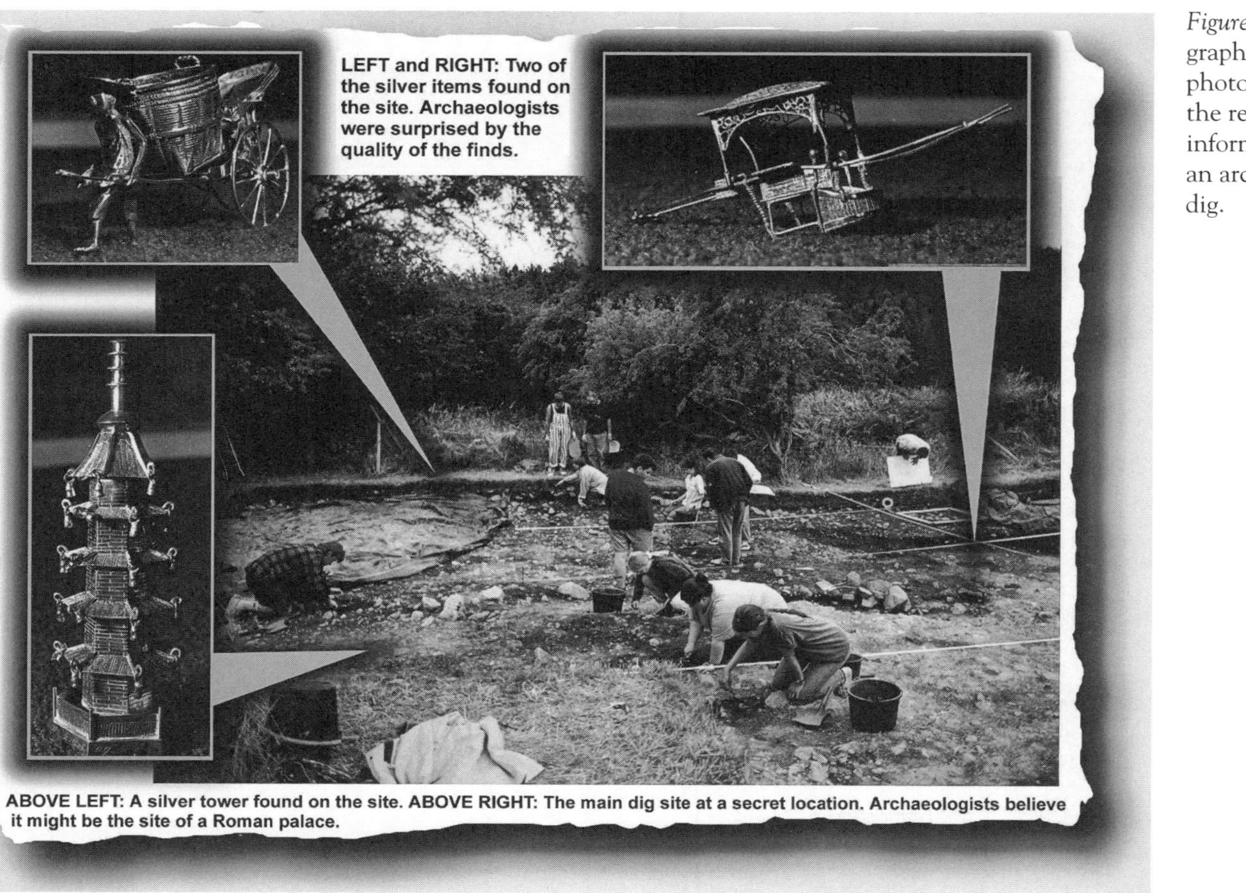

LEFT and RIGHT: Two of the silver items found on the site. Archaeologists were surprised by the quality of the finds.
ABOVE LEFT: A silver tower found on the site. ABOVE RIGHT: The main dig site at a secret location. Archaeologists believe it might be the site of a Roman palace.

Figure 10.8 A graphic using photographs to offer the reader more information about an archaeological dig.

Figure 10.9 A picture graphic.

11
Using colour

Colour plays a major part in our lives because we have well-developed colour vision, yet colour has come only relatively recently to newspapers, and even magazines have been published in full colour for only about 40 years. Much of this move towards colour was initially driven by advertisers. According to Favre and November (1979: 80), surveys among consumers showed a marked improvement in attention-getting when colour was used:

	Four-colour ads %	*Black-and-white ads %*
The ad was seen	57	43
The brand was identified	43	28
The text was read	22	16

With figures like these, it is no surprise that advertisers were clamouring for publications to switch to full colour as soon as possible, and so even newspapers that resisted moving to colour because they feared it would damage their brand image, making them appear more populist and frivolous, were eventually obliged to introduce it.

Our eyes are receptive to light through cells in the retinas called rods and cones. Rods perceive the relative brightness of a light wave and are not influenced at all by its colour, while cones detect the hue of the light wave, telling the brain how much red, green and blue light energy there is. Each cone detects all the colours, but some are much more receptive to one part of the colour spectrum than another and this allows us to detect the difference between various colours. Our cones are particularly receptive to red, green or blue, according the theories of Helmholtz (cited in De Grandis 1986: 14), and we detect other colours by measuring how much red, green or blue is contained in them. The wavelength of 570nm, for instance, stimulates the red, green and blue cones in a ratio of 2:7:7 to give the impression of pure yellow (ibid.).

Colour comes to exist when light bounces off an object. That object will contain a pigment that absorbs some of the light in a particular colour range. What is left is then reflected back to us, or, in the case of a transparent material, passes straight through. White paper absorbs little of the light and reflects nearly all of it back. Black objects absorb the majority of light. Colour doesn't exist in a dark room, because if there is no light, there is no colour. A wall might be painted with a pigment that reflects only green, but if there is no light to reflect, then it is black.

Because we see red, green and blue light, television sets and computer displays also use this RGB principle. The display screens use liquid crystal and matrices of transparent, thin-film transistors to produce pixels containing tiny elements that emit light, one red, one blue and one green, to give the impression of a particular hue and intensity. White light is made up of appropriate proportions of those three colours. Each multi-coloured pixel then combines with other pixels to give the total picture. A Full HD TV, for instance, has a pixel matrix of 1,920 × 1,080. A typical WXGA computer screen or HD-ready wide-screen TV has 1,280 × 720 pixels.

Hue, saturation and value

As well as the actual colour being displayed, the hue, we need to be aware that there are other ways of altering how we perceive colour. We may like a nice red, but we might prefer it lighter or brighter, or duller or darker. Hue is the type of colour being described. In good light, you can distinguish up to 500 different hues.

The saturation (or chroma or intensity) is the amount of that hue. In printing, 100 per cent would be complete colour, 0 per cent would be grey – no colour at all. A very dense colour has a high saturation value; a low saturation value would give a grey muddy colour. A stormy day prevents the transmission of light from an object and mixes it with light reflected from moisture in the atmosphere, and so things in the distance tend to look grey and washed out.

Value (or lightness or brightness or tone) is the relative brightness of a colour. As a colour's value approaches 100 per cent, it becomes whiter; at 100 per cent it is white. At 0 per cent it is black.

The value will determine how vibrant a colour is. Look out on a bright sunny day, and often the colours look washed out because the white light reflects and makes colours look lighter. Take a walk after a rainstorm during the day and the colours will look bright and vibrant as the light gives a value of 50 per cent. At night the low light levels do not give your eyes enough information. The value is low and things will tend to look black.

The psychology of colour

Colour is very important to us and its effect on our lives is significant. Colours are associated with emotions. Blue is calming but cold. Yellows and reds are associated with warmth and speed. Greens are more neutral and are considered nurturing. Rooms in which you spend time should be green or beige or brown. Value is important too. Rooms with bright light tend to have vibrant colours or are tending towards white. Rooms with soft lighting will reduce the colour value to make the hues less threatening.

Rank

Colour plays a part in everyday social interaction, with rank and place often being designated by colour. School uniforms are coloured, as are the outfits of sports teams. Rank can be defined by colour, as in the bishop's purple and the scarlet of a Roman Catholic cardinal. Political parties define themselves by colour, and many companies these days oblige their staff to wear uniforms designed in the company's brand colours.

Symbolism

Colours are also symbolic. We all recognise the red and yellow of fire, the blue of water and the green of nature. Map-makers use these colours to mark out tracts of water or forest. We would be more likely to use green on a gardening column than red.

Red is easy to spot and so is used on postboxes and, until recently, on telephone kiosks. Consequently, red came to symbolise the Post Office. Yellow is often used to represent Easter, and red and green are traditionally symbolic of Christmas.

Colour interactions

Objects of the same colour look different, depending on their setting. The light reflected back into a room will be affected by the colour it is reflected from. A blue surround will add a blue hue to a white object, while a red background would give it a red hue. Different colours together give each other different properties.

This effect can be extended. If you work for any length of time on a computer with a monochrome green screen, your eyes' red receptors are underused. If you see something red soon after, it will appear more intense than usual. If you have an unusual and vibrant colour scheme on your computer desktop, you've probably noticed this effect. In the early days of computer use, when screens were a monochrome green, it was not unusual for people to find it took up to 30 minutes to lose the faint red haze that normal lighting added to everything.

Some colours, called complementary colours, work well with others, making them stand out better. It is no surprise that Heinz baked beans are packed in a tin with a blue-green label. The blue-green is on the opposite side of the colour wheel (a theoretical circle of colours that artists use to guide them in the use of colour) to orange. The blue-green makes the orange of the beans look more vibrant and appetising. Green would also have helped emphasise the orange (although not as well as the blue-green), but as green is the colour of mould, it is usually avoided in food packaging.

Colour separation

Although television, computers and our eyes work on the red/green/blue principle, this additive method (where different colours of light are added together) does not work for printing. Paints are pigments, so that the red ink allows only red light to be reflected. If we mixed blue paint (which only allows blue light to reflect) with green paint (which only allows green paint to reflect) and red paint (which only allows red light to reflect), then no light would be reflected and the colour would appear to be black.

The printing process uses pigments – inks that essentially lay down a series of colour filters, which don't add, but instead subtract, colours. The printing of the colour red merely subtracts all other colours from reflecting from that area of paper. Adding green and red light together on a TV screen gives yellow. If you were to mix green and red paint (or ink), you would filter all light except that which could filter through the two coloured inks and you would get a dark muddy brown. Additive colour principles use the presence of light in all three primary colours to produce white and their absence to produce black.

When we are using pigments, we are not adding light together; we are subtracting light by preventing it from reflecting from the pigment surface. In traditional colour theory, as used by artists, there are three pigment colours that cannot be mixed from other colours and so are considered primaries: red, blue and yellow (Zelanski and Fisher 1989: 15). By mixing the primaries, you get secondary colours. Mixing red and blue gives purple; mixing blue and yellow gives green; and mixing yellow and red gives orange. However, we are not working with paint when we print; we are working with transparent pigments of ink (the same applies to the transparent pigments of colour photography). This allows us to use the secondary colours generated by the additive principles of RGB, although we use ink in a subtractive way, filtering out colours rather than adding them as we can do with light on a TV set, so the filters we use are cyan, magenta and yellow. Mixing red and blue light gives magenta; mixing red and green gives yellow; and mixing green and blue gives cyan. When all these secondary colours are present, they print black; when all are absent, they print white (provided you are using white paper).

Add yellow and cyan inks together and you will get the primary colour of green, because the inks will have reflected only yellow light (a mix of red and green) and cyan light (a mix of blue and green). Since the yellow pigment will have absorbed the blue light reflected by the cyan pigment, and the cyan pigment will have absorbed the red light reflected by the yellow pigment, only green light is left to be reflected. Remember, the inks are transparent, so you do not block the reflecting power of the other; you only filter it, so the green light can reflect through both pigments. If the pigment were paint, it would not reflect through both. We make paint to cover over all the colours beneath the top layer.

Although the secondary ink colours used for printing are magenta, cyan and yellow, black is normally used as well. This is because of deficiencies in inks. Although the theory says combining the secondary colours should give black, in fact the best possible is a muddy brown. The addition of black ink allows the printer to produce pure black and to alter the value of the colours from full black to white. The black can then be used to print the black type that still tends to be used for text, ensuring that the printer doesn't have to struggle to get the four colour plates in register to print the delicate type. Imagine trying to represent black type by laying four colours one on top of the other for 6pt type. It is much easier to use black, which will also give much better results. Black is represented by the letter K, so this four-colour process system is often known as the CMYK system.

The use of colour in print

Colour is now widely used in print. Years ago it was an expensive and therefore little-used luxury. Magazines switched to serious use of colour in the 1970s and they were followed by newspapers towards the end of the 1980s. There are now very few provincial or national papers not making extensive use of full or process colour.

There are two main areas for colour use: pictures and tonal variety. Both are important, but for different things. If we were producing a fashion spread, for instance, it would be vital that the pictures were in full colour so that the reader could get the full effect of the fashion. Pictures of carnivals or theatrical productions also tend to look good in colour.

On the other hand, a TV listings page might not need colour for the pictures or graphics but could be made much easier to read by using colour to separate out items from each other. Colour patches could be put behind each channel listing so that a light yellow might emphasise the ITV channel while a light pink could be used to support BBC1, for instance.

This means that if we have a colour page, we should be considering not only whether we are using colour or monochrome pictures, but how we are going to use colour to support both the pictures and the text.

Colour is particularly useful in tone patches, rules, boxes and highlights. It tends to be less useful in display faces and type, or at least for any length of type. A drop cap or a small crosshead can look good in colour, but at the end of the day we have to remember that we are trying to help, not hinder, the reader, and a long run of coloured text, particularly if the value (or lightness) is very high, is not going to be easy to read.

Black on white is still the easiest way to present type and to read it, and you change that at your peril. Using coloured paper, coloured type or a heavy type patch often reduces legibility. In tests carried out by Karl Borggräfe (cited in Favre and November 1979: 50) to see which colours worked best together, the following taxonomy of colour mixes was discovered, starting with the most legible and working through to the least legible.

Black on yellow
Yellow on black
Green on white
Red on white
Black on white
White on blue
Blue on yellow
Blue on white
White on black
Green on yellow
Black on orange
Red on yellow
Black on red
Blue on orange
Yellow on green
Blue on red
Yellow on red
White on red
Red on black
White on orange
Black on green
Orange on white
Orange on blue
Yellow on orange

Orange on black	Red on orange
Yellow on blue	Red on green
White on green	Green on orange

As you can see, black on white comes pretty near the top, although the list suggests that a yellow panel behind the black type would improve legibility (which is why important signs warning of danger are usually printed black on yellow). This choice of colour is clearly one that would work well, but remember that the yellow panel we could provide in a publication would have a dot screen and this might not improve legibility. Magazines normally have better-quality paper and so a finer raster dot, and this effect would be less noticeable than in a newspaper. In both types of publication, however, you need to be careful about reversing type out of a colour background, because if the type is too small, it will be swamped by the raster dots of the background.

Mixes of red and green or orange and green were seen as the worst in the list above, with blue and red close behind. This might be, in part at least, because red, blue and green have slightly different focal lengths. This means the eye cannot focus on all the colours at the same time. This leaves the edges of the letters a little fuzzy, and this can both be disconcerting and make the type hard to read.

Colour as definition

Colour can help you define an area, whether it is text or picture. The Poynter Institute's eye-tracking research shows that colour draws a reader into a page (Garcia and Stark 1991). Colour can be used in pictures, in text or as a background colour. Placing type on a patch of light yellow pulls that text away from the surrounding white paper and certainly sets it apart from another block of text set on a light red patch.

It is tempting when you first start using colours to use big, bright splashes of colour, but this can be a bad idea. Apart from making it difficult to print – large areas of heavy colour take longer to dry and are more likely to cause problems on the press – these big areas of colour compete with each other for the reader's attention. They can make a page look over-busy. Colour often looks better in light shades that draw the eye but don't dominate it. This is particularly true in newspapers, where there is little space to be wasted. The page needs to be filled with type or pictures, and so colours have to be directly involved with the picture or the type. Having heavy colour patches beneath type makes black type difficult to read, and I've already warned about reversing type out of colour patches. Laying colour against pictures also needs to be done with care. Putting a border around a picture can be helpful if the colour used matches a key colour of the subject, because it will help emphasise the subject, but using a colour that pulls away from the subject is not helpful, unless it is a complementary colour that again will emphasise the colour of the subject.

Drop caps can be printed in a strong colour, as can side-heads or crossheads. Captions, *bylines* or *standfirsts* can be made to stand away from the rest of the page by printing them in colour. It's best to use a hue with a relatively low saturation and a low value so that the colour has a strong density that makes it stand away from the text without being over-vibrant.

It is also possible to use gradient patches. Gradients are where the patch starts at one value and across the width or depth of the patch changes to another value, so the patch might start light and end up dark. A gradient patch can also start out as light in the centre and end up dark at the edges or vice versa. As well as changing the lightness, you can also change the hue or the saturation (or all three) through a gradient to give a number of effects that will add emphasis to certain parts of the page.

Colour as brand image

An important use of colour is as a brand image. Coca-Cola's brilliant red is perhaps one of the more famous examples of a brand colour, but there are plenty of other organisations and corporations, not to mention nations, that use colour as a brand or identity.

Your own publication might well have corporate colours that need to be included in the publication. This would be particularly true if you were producing a publication for a company, to be distributed among customers or employees. We regularly identify things by colour, and these colours should be included in a publication.

It also means that we might need to be careful about using certain colours on a particular story. If we were designing a page on personal finance, for instance, there might well be an advert for an insurance company near this that would be published in that company's corporate colours. We should therefore try to avoid using that combination of colours on the page to ensure that the editorial is not accidentally linked with the advert.

However, to run a travel item about the United States using red, white and blue, or an Italian food feature using red, green and white, would be a perfectly sensible thing to do, as the symbolism involved would be immediately recognised by most people and it would emphasise the national identity.

12 Publishing ethics

Ethics in journalism start from the moment a reporter asks their first question. From then on, everything a journalist does should be guided by their professional morality. This doesn't necessarily mean that there is only one standard that applies to all. Professional morality may vary depending on whom one is working for. The morality on the *Sun* may be different from the morality applied on the *Guardian*. Whether one is better than the other is for the individual to judge. That said, there are some basic standards laid down in the code of practice of the Press Complaints Commission (PCC) and the code of conduct of the National Union of Journalists (NUJ).

There is not enough space here for an in-depth discussion about professional morality and ethics. There are several books that discuss journalistic ethics (Frost 2011; Keeble 2001; Kieran 1998) if you want to know more. For the purposes of this chapter, it is assumed that you will want to consider the journalistic virtues of fairness, responsibility and truth in all your professional work.

Ethics of display and design

Designers and editors do not particularly need to consider the morality of gathering news. They are presented with stories already sourced and written. Sub-editors of course will want to reassure themselves that the codes of practice have been adhered to, and if there are any apparent breaches, a good sub will approach the news editor or the reporter concerned to discuss the matter. If this does not resolve things to the sub's satisfaction, he or she should raise the matter with the chief sub or, if necessary, the editor.

Provided the copy is ethically based, however, very few of the code of practice clauses apply to the ethics of design and publication.

The PCC's code covers:

1 accuracy
2 opportunity to reply
3 privacy
4 harassment
5 intrusion into grief or shock
6 children
7 children in sex cases
8 listening devices
9 hospitals
10 reporting of crime
11 misrepresentation
12 victims of sexual assault
13 discrimination
14 financial journalism
15 confidential sources
16 payment for articles.

Provided the copy offered for publication has adhered to these code elements in itself, you can see that there is little directly in the code for the designer to worry about. But this does not mean that there are no ethical dilemmas for the designer – far from it.

The main areas of concern are: has any additional text been dealt with fairly? Are captions accurate? Do headlines avoid sensationalising the copy? Have pictures been unfairly manipulated? Has undue pressure been brought to bear on whether to use the copy or spike it? Perhaps there has been pressure to cut the story or use it on a particular page. Perhaps an advertiser would like it to lie alongside a particular advert.

Are the pictures a true and accurate reflection of what took place? Have they been manipulated unfairly? Are they appropriate to use in this context? Does your publisher own the appropriate rights to whatever it is you are thinking of publishing? Are the copy and/or pictures being used suitable for the audience to whom they are being offered.

Copyright

Copyright, as with so many things, is both an ethical and a legal matter. Essentially, there are two main rights involved with copyright:

1 moral rights: that is, the right to determine whether copy or pictures are used and whether they can be altered;

2 intellectual property rights: the right to make money from the copy or pictures by selling them to people, or the right to publish them.

These two rights are separate and different. I can sell my intellectual property rights to anyone I want; I can even give them away. I cannot sell my moral rights. In the United Kingdom the Copyright, Designs and Patents Act 1988 protects the moral rights of authors, photographers and other creative workers. If you produce a piece of creative work, you have the right to be identified as the author; the right not to have work subjected to derogatory treatment; and the right for every person not to have work falsely attributed to them (Carey 1996: 106). Much of this does not apply to those who write for magazines or newspapers, however, as they are employed by their publication to do these things and the rights go to the publication, not the author. A reporter does not have a cause for action just because they did not get a *byline*. The writers of books, music or plays do have such rights because they work for themselves. The same applies to freelance reporters.

Since news reporters do not have any moral rights over their work, they often forget that other creative workers might. So if you want to use a photograph, or quote a poem or the lyrics to your favourite song, you need to be certain you are not breaching someone's copyright. Even TV programme titles are subject to copyright and it is not unknown for the BBC's lawyers to send a sharp letter to a newspaper using a programme title in a headline on a story that is not about that programme.

However, the property rights involved in an intellectual work can be sold, so it is possible to buy the right to use a picture, song lyrics or a story. A freelance reporter may not have the moral right to insist on a byline or prevent derogatory treatment, but they do own the copyright and can therefore sell it to anyone they wish. They can sell it for ever or they can sell a licence to use it. Normally a freelance would want to keep the copyright so that the right to use the story can be resold to another outlet.

For instance, a freelance reporter might have covered an interesting court case and, being the only freelance there, might then sell the story to a number of newspapers and magazines. None of these would own the copyright, which would stay with the reporter (although the newspapers and magazines would have copyright in the typographical arrangement of the page concerned), but they would be allowed to use the story in that edition of the paper. The reporter might then seek additional payment if the paper wanted to put the story on its website or syndicate it to other newspapers around the world.

Although much of this work is standardised, you need to be certain what it is you are buying should you negotiate with a freelance or agency for their copy or pictures. Do they own the rights and are you buying just what you need?

There's no point in buying rights to publish on the website if you don't have a website.

Things are not always in the seller's favour. Many newspapers and other news outlets now attempt to take all rights from freelances by sending a cheque for submitted work that has a stamp on the back saying that cashing the cheque accepts that the news outlet now owns all copyright rights on the piece of work. The National Union of Journalists has been very busy over the past ten years trying to negotiate acceptable settlements to prevent what it describes as a 'rights grab'. Although it has many deals with publishers, there are still quite a few multinational corporations that pay fees appropriate to single first use of copyright material and then attempt to take all future rights over the material as well.

It is always important to check who owns the copyright. For instance, when something newsworthy happens, such as the murder of a young child, reporters often try to get pictures from relatives. The picture offered might be one of those standard school pictures. They are usually the best quality and show the child looking clean and well scrubbed. The copyright on these is usually owned by the photographic studio, and if you use it without checking, you may well be breaching the studio's copyright – something for which it can sue your paper.

Often, photographs such as school photos, wedding photos, photos taken on cruise ships, photos taken at night clubs or photos of holidays are copyright of the photographer. The photographer is the only one entitled to make copies of the work, which is how such photographers make their money: selling prints to customers. You are not entitled to make copies without permission. Check with them first and negotiate a copyright payment. Remember that the market rate applies and a rare photograph might be very expensive. One-off photographs of celebrities doing things they shouldn't be doing or other one-off news events where there is only one picture can net the copyright holder hundreds of thousands of pounds and continue to be a good earner for years to come. The clip of film of John F. Kennedy being assassinated in Dallas was the subject of a court case a few years ago to establish ownership by the family of the man who took it; it was said to be worth millions of dollars. Another case involved the iconic picture of Che Guevara, which has become an emblem of revolution since the 1960s. The photographer had been happy for it to be used to support revolution, but was not happy when it was picked up for commercial gain by a drinks company, and he sued. Both cases netted the copyright holders millions of dollars. It is likely that the amateur videos of the 11 September attacks on New York's twin towers could also earn their copyright holders millions.

Pictures taken from Facebook are another popular way of getting pictures of people in the news, but Facebook insist that users assign it the copyright, and so it is possible it might start suing publications that lift pictures from its site.

The main defence we have against suits for infringement of copyright is fair dealing. Fair dealing is where the copyright material was used for the purposes of reporting current events or criticism or review, provided it is accompanied by a suitable acknowledgement. Thus, there is no problem about reporting a speech by the prime minister made in public since we would be clearly acknowledging who said what. If the speech was made in private and the media was refused permission to report it, we might have more of a problem. A speaker does have copyright over his or her speech. However, provided it was in the public interest, we could report the substance of the speech and perhaps even use sections of it. According to Carey, the 'courts have shown a willingness, in exceptional cases, to allow a defendant to avail himself' of the defence of public interest when reproducing a speech (1996: 106).

Fair dealing means acknowledging the source. If, for instance, you were reviewing a play, it would be acceptable to publish a small section, provided you made it clear that that is what it was and who wrote it. You might also use stills from a movie in order to support a review. Again these need to acknowledge the film and its director. In practice, of course, the movie-makers would normally provide you with a press pack that would include pictures for you to use free of copyright payments. Using a picture with the consent of the copyright holder is fine, provided that you are sure that the person providing the picture is the copyright holder and that there are no other considerations. A complaint to the PCC from a couple concerned that a topless photograph of their daughter, taken when she was only 14, was published without consent in *FHM* magazine led to a reprimand for the magazine when the PCC upheld the complaint. The magazine said that it received 1,200 photographs each week from or on behalf of women posing topless or in lingerie. It had put in place no procedures to ensure such a situation did not reoccur.

Plagiarism

Plagiarism is similar to stealing copyright in that it involves passing off the work of others as your own. In these cases it is often less clear that the work belongs to someone else. The work may have been rewritten, or the plagiarism may involve stealing someone else's ideas. There is no copyright on ideas or on news events. If there is a big fire in your town and an opposition paper publishes news about it first, it cannot then sue you for copyright if your paper also publishes a story about it – unless you use the rival's story or pictures. However, it is not unknown for journalists to rewrite someone else's story or to lift pieces of copy. Often this will be done because one paper or magazine was able to interview someone that the other publication did not get to. Lifting the quotes and using them in your own publication is plagiarism. Plagiarism is a difficult area. It's perfectly acceptable to use quotes from a speech by the Chancellor of the Exchequer in a story taken from a live TV or a radio broadcast. Taking photographs of a live TV broadcast is also acceptable, and many publications have used pictures of major live events taken from TV transmissions. It is fair dealing that allows us to use such pictures, or use the TV as the source. Taking photographs from the television of a live transmission of a news event, provided the pictures are acknowledged, is now well within existing case law (Carey 1996: 105). Publishing a list of classified information from another publication would not be covered by fair dealing. If your rival (or the local *Yellow Pages*) published a list of local restaurants and your publication simply copied this list and presented it as its own, this would be both plagiarism and breach of copyright. (For further advice, see Mason and Smith 1998: 102.)

Editing pictures

Editing pictures carries the same duties and responsibilities as editing text. Inevitably you are going to have to make editorial decisions. There is no such thing as an objective picture. A photographer has had to decide which pictures to take, where to point the camera, what to frame and when to open the shutter. He or she then has to decide which pictures to offer to the picture desk. Once the editor has them, he or she has to decide which pictures to use, how many, how they will be cropped and what size they will be. Figure 12.1 shows a perfectly reasonable picture of a wine-tasting but the editor is able to make a number of choices about picture use from the whole picture as presented by the photographer to a number of different pictures. Looking around the picture from top left to bottom right, we have several different scenarios: the husband asking for his uninterested wife's opinion; the enthusiasts considering the offering; the disappointed drinker; the carefully laid out tools of the trade; and finally the session leader, keen to teach and drum up trade. All are different points of view from the same picture.

As well as editing choices, it is very easy these days to alter a picture to show whatever you want. Modern photographic software makes it easy to make major changes to a picture. One famous example involves the *Sun*. It carried a story on the front page about a monk who had fallen in love with a woman and had been asked to resign. They obtained a picture of the monk and the woman walking down the street. But they were not close and the man was in ordinary clothes. In an attempt to make the story clearer, the *Sun* manipulated the picture to show the man wearing a monk's habit, and holding the woman's hand. The *Sun* later admitted: 'We have superimposed the monk's habit to make it clear to the readers that the story is about a monk' (Frost 2000: 137) (see Figure 12.2 for a picture that has been changed).

Figure 12.1 The original picture (top left) can present several different stories – so which one is true?

Figure 12.2 A picture can be altered to a very large extent. But is it ethical to change a picture as much as this? Removing the defenders alters the reality.

But even if a picture is not manipulated, it can still distort the truth. A simple example involves the party conferences. Each year the political parties gather at the seaside to discuss policy and to hear a rousing speech from their leader. Photographers take thousands of pictures of the leader and other key party figures. Even if they are just sitting on the platform, their expression can be very telling and can be used to illustrate a point. During the late 1990s, several photographers managed to get a picture of former Tory leaders Margaret Thatcher and Edward Heath sitting close to each other listening to William Hague, then leader of the Conservative Party, make his speech. Both were caught coincidentally looking at their watches with expressions of apparent boredom. It was a picture that made several of the newspapers, and was being used as a comment on the new leader's speech.

Politicians soon learn to take extreme care about their hand gestures and facial expressions when in public. Any major politician making a speech soon learns that there is little that can be done to prevent the press choosing an image to suit their message. When a major politician makes a speech, each photographer will take scores of pictures. This ensures that the news desk will get the kind of expression they want. This will be either a picture to match the tone of the speech, or a picture to match the tone of the report. Choosing the right picture can change the truth of the story and is an important editorial and ethical decision.

Pictures themselves can be unethical and so should not be used. The *Hartlepool Mail* was criticised by the PCC in 1997 for using a picture of a child taken at a funeral, as it breached the PCC's code on children (PCC 1997). Any picture taken with a long lens should be considered carefully before use; the PCC may well require the editor to explain why using the picture was in the public interest. Moreover, any picture taken of the subject in a private place should be considered very, very carefully before use. The PCC will almost always take the view that such pictures should not be used. In one important case a photograph was taken inside a café for an advertising feature. A customer complained that his privacy had been invaded, and the complaint was upheld. In another important case a photographer joined police for a raid on a private home looking for stolen sat-navs. The photographs identified the home and the complainant's son, even though his face had been pixellated. The PCC decided that there was no public interest justification in publishing the pictures as no arrest had been made or stolen goods found.

Although publishing pictures in news reports does not necessarily need the permission of the subject, permission is certainly needed if the pictures have not been taken in a public place. Always check that a picture was taken in a public place or that permission was given for it to be taken. It can be wise to pixellate out a person's face if identity is not important to the picture, to ensure that their privacy is not breached. You should pixellate out the number plates of cars, and house numbers or names, as a matter of course (see Figure 12.3).

You should also be careful of using archive pictures for purposes other than those for which they were taken. Although the permission of a subject is not required, using a picture out of context could lead to complaints or even a lawsuit. One former colleague used an archived wedding photograph to illustrate a divorce by electronically tearing the picture in two. The couple, who still lived happily together, were mortified and a full apology had to be made, together with a compensatory payment.

Editing text

Editing text can also alter the truth. A certain amount of editing becomes inevitable: stories are too long for the space available, priorities change and a

Figure 12.3 Pixellating number plates or house names can spare people embarrassment.

good story may have been overtaken by an even better story. This means the story as written by the reporter may need to be cut. It may also need to be merged with a story from a different reporter, or it might need to be split into three or four stories to be presented in the way the editor has decided. Even if the copy is largely untouched, it needs to be checked and facts confirmed if there are doubts. All of this means that the text used will be different from the text offered. Since the offered text will already be full of subjective decisions made by the reporter, it is possible that the sub-editor is taking the copy even further from the truth by amending it again. It is by no means unusual for a reporter to build up a news story as much as he or she dares – stretching the truth close to breaking point – only for a sub-editor to take the story and, assuming that the story is straightforward, stretch it even further, taking the elements the reporter has hinted at and making them appear to be unarguable fact.

Not only can a sub put mistakes and unethical elements into a story, but he or she can also be responsible for removing them. While it will not always be possible to spot errors of fact or be able to tell whether the reporter was unethical in gathering a story, text that is clearly comment or is discriminatory should be removed. For instance, the PCC upheld a complaint in 1997 against *Time Out*, which had run an article about 'sitting next to the "nutter on the bus"'. The PCC (1997) said this was not in the spirit of its guidance on mental illness.

Headlines

Headlines are one of the main trouble spots for fair reporting. The headline is there to sell the story, but often it goes much further than the story would allow. When writing a headline, a sub-editor needs to be very careful that it does not become sensationalist or inaccurate. A number of complaints made to the PCC concern headlines rather than stories.

Headlines, captions, *standfirsts* and any rewritten material can also breach the PCC's code of conduct in terms of accuracy, discrimination and intrusion. It is new copy, and although the facts have been gathered by another person, it is very easy for an over-eager sub to introduce errors in the new text. Since it is often the headline or even a caption that the reader sees first, errors here can have more impact than errors in the story.

Taste and decency

Taste and decency is a difficult area and not one that is covered by the PCC except for issues around suicide. The PCC has taken the view that matters of taste and decency are outside its area of responsibility, and it is probably right to do so. When it comes to factual publications, questions of taste and decency involve nudity, bad language, depictions of sexual activity, war, terror and other forms of violence. It has to be accepted that controlling these is easier for publications than it is for television, which has the whole range of factual and fictional programmes to contend with.

The main problem area for publications is pictures: pictures of naked people, pictures of sexual activity, pictures of violence and pictures of a bizarre and possibly distasteful nature. Although pictures of this sort have always been seen as a problem of morality, it is not morality that we normally measure when trying to decide whether to use such pictures or articles. In the end, it comes down to the audience, and this makes life much easier. Instead of a long debate about whether it is right to censor such material or wrong to try to titillate the audience, provided the publication is attempting to present the truth without glorifying it or commercialising it, then the right line will usually be taken. Showing pictures of the aftermath of a terrorist bomb with pictures of the dead and mutilated may make difficult reading, but they do spell out the truth of what happens in such horrific circumstances. On the other hand, inventing a story about people's supposed 'sexploits' on holiday destination aircraft illustrated by pictures of topless 'air hostesses' is the sort of *Sport* commercialisation of sex that appeals, thankfully, to only a small market. (In fact, the *Daily Sport* ceased publication in April 2011.)

Ignoring the fringe publications such as *Bizarre*, which makes a point of using such material in a titillating way, most publications know that it is the sensibilities of their audience that determine how far they can go in the presentation of nudity, violence, bad language and sex.

Cases of complaint in the past have included stories about inquests that contain too many details; pictures of decapitated heads or executions in various African civil wars; a burned-out Iraqi tank with the dead commander still at his post in the turret; and naked children fleeing a napalm attack in Vietnam. All of these were used in various publications and were either supported or criticised. But all of them said something about the truth of the story and, although they may have pushed the limits of their readers' sense of good taste, most of the readers understood the reason for using them.

Bad language, when used in quotations and sourced, may also be acceptable, depending on the readership. What one could use in *Loaded* or *Cosmopolitan* is not what may be acceptable in the local weekly; it's all down to the readership.

Conflicts of interest

Conflicts of interest can occur for a number of reasons. *Copy approval* has long been a feature of A-list celebrity interviews, but the idea is creeping further down the chain. A letter to the *Press Gazette* in July 2002 from a sub-editor of a trade magazine asked other sub-editors whether they had been instructed by their editors to give copy approval. The letter explained that this particular trade magazine gave copy approval on articles about key figures in that industry.

While it is not unusual, and is probably good practice, to check quotes with an interviewee, it is not acceptable to give copy approval. This automatically implies that the person has the right to change the copy, and few can resist doing so. This means the copy ceases to be the publication's view of the truth and becomes the source's view of the truth. While we journalists have to accept that the view we give is one-dimensional (ours), we are attempting to be fair and present all sides of the truth and give a rounded report. This is not something the source is concerned about. Their only viewpoint, ethically, practically and commercially, is to present themselves in the best possible light. The problem with copy approval is that it is a vicious circle. If access to certain key players, whether A-list celebrities or captains of industry, is limited by copy approval, then stories that do not have approval will be published only rarely. Access to these people for interview will be limited to those prepared to toe the line. As more and more publications give in to copy approval, so more and more sources will ask for copy approval and more and more publications will be obliged to give copy approval. In the end, copy about anything that people actually want to read about will be nothing more than sanitised public relations.

Pressure from advertisers

Pressure from advertisers can range from something as relatively innocuous as asking for a positive story on the company to sit alongside an advertisement to asking for changes in the copy or copy approval. This can be the case particularly in *advertising features*, where the advertiser is paying for space alongside editorial material. The Newspaper Society advises publications to put 'advertising feature' in reasonably sized type over any page that has editorial tied to advertising, but this does not stop the advertiser from thinking they have bought the editorial as well as the advertising space. Once, when I was designing and subbing an advertising feature, the advertiser rang and demanded to be read the copy. I politely refused, but they were insistent and said they would pull the ad if they had not read the copy, even though they claimed they did not intend to change the copy. I pointed out that if they did not intend to change it, then why did they need it read to them? In the end I refused and they said they would pull the ad. I immediately told the editor (a vital thing to do in the circumstances; the final decision is always the editor's). To his credit, he supported my decision even though the advert was pulled. I'm sure he had to take some flack for it later, and it was a brave decision.

There is also a more general concern with advertising. Most publications depend heavily on advertising for their commercial success. This can make them nervous of carrying stories about advertisers or potential advertisers. This leads to an implicit pressure not to carry stories that attack advertisers.

Pressure from proprietors

There is often pressure from proprietors or editors to protect advertisers from adverse publicity. They may also want to protect another part of the organisation from bad publicity or to promote another aspect of the organisation. Again, the pressure here might be direct or implied. The *Sun* and *The Times*, for instance, are owned by Rupert Murdoch, who also part-owns BSkyB. The number of plugs for BSkyB carried in the *Sun* and *The Times* as news led to *Private Eye* carrying a regular column called 'I BspyB', which published plugs for BSkyB carried in the copy of those two papers.

Many publications are now owned by larger corporations which have other holdings that they would like plugged from time to time. There is also the question of personal contacts. Many proprietors or editors are members of the establishment. This can be a double-edged sword. They know the right people, they mix with them and this is good for business and it's good for newsgathering, but it also means that they get to know people and may be asked for favours: to publish or, sometimes, to not publish.

When one is working for local papers, it is very difficult not to be involved in the local community – nor is it a particularly good idea for a journalist, particularly an editor, to be detached from the local community. Editors send their children to local schools. They belong to local charitable committees and possibly local political parties or campaigning groups. This will also influence what appears in a particular publication.

Bribes and corruption

While accepting a wad of fivers in a brown paper envelope as a bribe is clearly wrong, accepting cheap deals or discounts is not as obviously wrong as accepting a bribe. Receiving or accepting freebies (free holidays, cars, meals, books or CDs, and so on) may be unavoidable. How else could most local newspapers afford to review new cars or holidays without freebies? But you have to consider how this influences the final copy.

Defamation

Defamation is a large part of media law but one I can only touch on here. You should ensure you are fully familiar with the law of defamation by reading an appropriate law book or attending a course.

The law of defamation is there to protect a person's reputation. It is designed to provide reparation to that person should anyone publish material that might damage their reputation unfairly. The aim of the law of defamation is not to prevent publication of material that might be damaging, but to try to repair the damage caused. Since the truth can damage a person's reputation, establishing that what was published is the truth is not enough as a defence. You must also prove that it was reasonable to publish that truth. This defence is called justification.

Another defence against defamation is called *privilege*. This is where the defamatory remarks are made in a public forum such as Parliament, court or a council meeting and that the publication reports those remarks in a fair and contemporaneous (timely) manner. This is designed to ensure open reporting of public debate. Parliament could probably not function if its members were at risk of a suit for defamation every time they opened their mouths. Parliament has its own strict rules about what members can say about each other.

Defamation in permanent form is known as libel; in non-permanent form it is known as slander. Journalists are usually sued for libel.

Another defence against a suit for defamation is *fair comment*. This is where comments are made in the form of an opinion based on true facts and are made in fairness and without malice on a matter of public interest. The comments could be anything from a review of a local amateur dramatic production to an analysis of the Chancellor's latest budget.

If a publication is threatened with the courts over an alleged defamation, an offer of amends can be made. This can be used as a defence in court if the plaintiff refuses to accept. The offer of amends must include a published apology and a payment of compensation. Since the cost of a libel suit is high, this is often the route taken by a publication. Defending a libel suit involves the High Court, and costs of solicitors and barristers can easily get into six figures. If you lose, you also have to pay the plaintiff's legal costs, and a large payment may be ordered by the court. Losing a high-profile libel case can cost several million pounds.

It is important that any slur on the reputation of a person is not included in a headline or caption or any other text written by the designer or sub-editor without approval from the editor. It is not unknown for copy to be legally safe but for the headline to lead to a lawsuit. Don't use library clippings to add information to a story without checking them thoroughly first. Prior publication is not a defence against a libel suit. Consent to publication is a complete defence against a libel suit, so if you can get the person concerned to sign an approval form, that can be useful.

Children

Pictures of children need to be dealt with particularly carefully; there are some strange people out there. Using a picture of a sporting champion or gala queen is fine, but you should be very careful about giving details, particularly addresses. If it is possible for some ill-wisher to find the child's address or phone number, the child may well be subjected to offensive phone calls – something most journalists would prefer to avoid happening. Identifying children involved in stories that concern their welfare also needs to be considered carefully. Often the story is really about the issue involved, and identifying the child is unnecessary.

Addresses

You should always be careful about publishing addresses, particularly of people who are vulnerable by virtue of belonging to a particular group. Celebrities are unlikely to be put at risk by having their addresses published, but police officers, serving members of the armed forces, judges and others may be at risk if their addresses are published. Others who are at risk include those at pre-published events such as weddings, honeymoons, funerals or prize-giving ceremonies. Telling people that a particular house is likely to be empty at a certain time is to invite the local burglars around.

13
Design masterclass

The idea of the design masterclass is to look at a range of pages from contemporary publications and examine why they are good examples of their type. I am suggesting not that the examples here are the best pages ever, but that they are good examples of the designer's art produced to a deadline to solve specific problems in a pleasing way.

I have tried to pick a range of examples covering newspapers and magazines, but I have limited myself to eight. These cover news pages in magazines and newspapers as well as some feature pages in both types of publications.

Where possible I have tried to identify detail, but the aim of this section is not to produce a page designer's version of a train spotters' fanzine, but to identify good practice and show how professionals have gone about the job of designing pages that are attractive to readers.

Figure 13.1: a tabloid front page: *Daily Mail*, 11 October 2002

Front, full colour, tabloid

This *Daily Mail* page is typical of the publication both in its design and its copy-tasting choices. Aimed at a female audience, the story concerns the first birth in the United Kingdom from a frozen human egg. The story is the only one run on the page and fills the bottom two-thirds of the page. The top third is taken up with the *titlepiece* and a large *blurb* advertising an inside news feature about how lottery money is spent. This takes a highly polemical standpoint with which the editorial team believes readers will sympathise; however, its weight on the front page is something against which the lead story needs to battle for attention, hence the dominance of the picture and headlines.

Daily Mail

FRIDAY, OCTOBER 11, 2002

North West Edition 40p

ARCHER'S DIARIES
PAGES 60-61

How your Lottery money goes to Rwandan potters, Yorkshire male prostitutes and Irish travellers – but is denied to British war heroes

SEE PAGES 18-19

NORTH WEST ONLY / WIN A CHRISTMAS LUNCH ON THE NORTHERN BELLE TOKEN PAGE 78

ICE BABY

Emily, first child born from a frozen egg, could revolutionise how women have children

By **James Chapman**
Science Correspondent

SHE weighed in at 7lb 13oz after a straightforward natural delivery.

But it is what happened even before Emily Perry's mother became pregnant that makes the baby unique in Britain – and could revolutionise the way women approach having children.

For the egg that was to become Emily was taken from Helen Perry's ovary and kept frozen for an astonishing six months before being gently thawed for a test-tube fertilisation. It made Helen and her husband Lee the first

Turn to Page 2, Col. 3

Family delight: Emily contentedly in the arms of her parents Lee and Helen Perry

MAGENTA CYAN BLACK

Figure 13.1 A tabloid front page: *Daily Mail*, 11 October 2002.

The page is in colour and the blurb is an orangey yellow against a teal-blue background. The 'Archer's diaries' and 'Northern Belle' blurbs are white on red. The picture is in full colour, but the rest of the page is black on white.

The lead heading uses a traditional serif face in about 220pt for the *streamer* and 42pt for the second *deck*, which is a seven-line double-column heading. The streamer is very limited for space, despite going across the entire page. Only 11 characters are available for this heading, leaving the sub-editor with little choice but to go for a label heading; 11 characters are not enough for a subject and a verb, unless you are very lucky. The designer is relying on the second deck to act as both a headline and a *standfirst* with an extensive 14 words (about 80 characters). This heading is followed by a discrete *byline* for the science correspondent. This tends to imply that the copy has a greater authority than would be the case if it were written by a general news reporter. Underneath the heading is a short double-column take of copy. The entry point is clear, because there is no other copy-sized text on the page. It has a larger-sized bold intro with caps start and no indent.

The main picture takes a quarter of the page, filling the bottom right. It is a semi-*cutout* so that the couple stand slightly outside the frame, making it appear as though they are climbing out of the frame, adding animation and increasing the image size. If the whole picture to be used was the same size as the family, much more room would be required. As it is, the family edge into the 12pt border that surrounds the story and into the caption and heading.

So little copy is used on this page that a *turn-to* line is required, inviting the reader to continue the story on page two. Since there is no other story on page one, this invitation to turn over carries little risk that the reader will turn before finishing other stories on the page. It may even be of some advantage in that they are now more likely to start reading page two and are less likely to drift off to another page and miss the early news pages. This page ideally suits the *Mail*'s audience: middle-England women, who hold traditional, establishment views and who are aspiring to a better lifestyle. The chance to produce children on demand at a time that suits them best will worry their conservative instincts yet appeal to their aspirational desire to be in control of their lives.

The story is presented in a narrative form that is often seen in the *Daily Mail*. It sits beneath a heading that is presented in a traditional *font* that is easy to read. The whole page is attractive, well balanced, clear and unequivocal. Like most *Mail* pages, it is a fine example of the designer's art and is a model front page.

Figure 13.2: a tabloid news page: the *Sun*, 26 April 2011, page 7

Right-hand page, full colour, tabloid

The *Sun* has the highest readership figures of any British national newspaper, even beating its now-closed Sunday stablemate, the *News of the World*, in 2010. More than 7.7 million people read the *Sun* on average throughout 2010. Of these, 57 per cent were men, and 56 per cent were under the age of 45. Two-thirds of readers are C2DE on the social scale, reinforcing the stereotype of the *Sun* as the readership choice of 'white van man'.

This page is a typical inside, right-hand page. As with all *Sun* pages, display values are high, and pictures and heading take almost 70 per cent of the page. The page is divided, with a single column to left being removed for a run of two stories. This column of grey text with two pictures cut slightly shy of the full column width separates the splash story from the leader page on the opposite left-hand page, which contains a colourful cartoon. The single column is headed by a picture, which helps prevent the headline clashing with the headline on the main story. Otherwise, the single column story is straightforward body text headed by four lines of heading held up by a byline.

The story at the bottom of the column has two lines of heading. The *Sun*'s standard body style is applied with no difference in the first paragraph apart from a cap start without indent. This makes the entry point clear, but without over-emphasis. Neither of these stories is particularly exciting, and indeed both may well have come from publicity material issued by the manufacturers. The choice of a story about high heels initially seems slightly odd in a newspaper with a male dominated readership, but of course it may be men who are keener on women wearing high heels than women. The popularity of the TV show *CSI: Crime Scene Investigation* explains the placing of the second story.

This column is essentially designed to ensure that maximum impact is given to the lead story splashed down the notional six columns remaining.

The page starts with a seriffed heading in red (the colour of blood) caps. The second line of the heading emphasises the horror of the incident. The caps heading is in 96pt or so and allows a count of 14 characters. This is a pretty tight count in which to tell the tale of daredevil stunts gone wrong. The nature of the event at a bank holiday family show in Kent is emphasised with the first two words; the second two tell of the nature of the event; and the fifth and final word tells of the event's fatal outcome. It's a straightforward headline, but it tells you all you need to know about the story. The heading is placed over the skyline of the main picture, which is toned to fill the rest of the page. Other pictures and the text are placed over it with a neat 2pt white rule around the

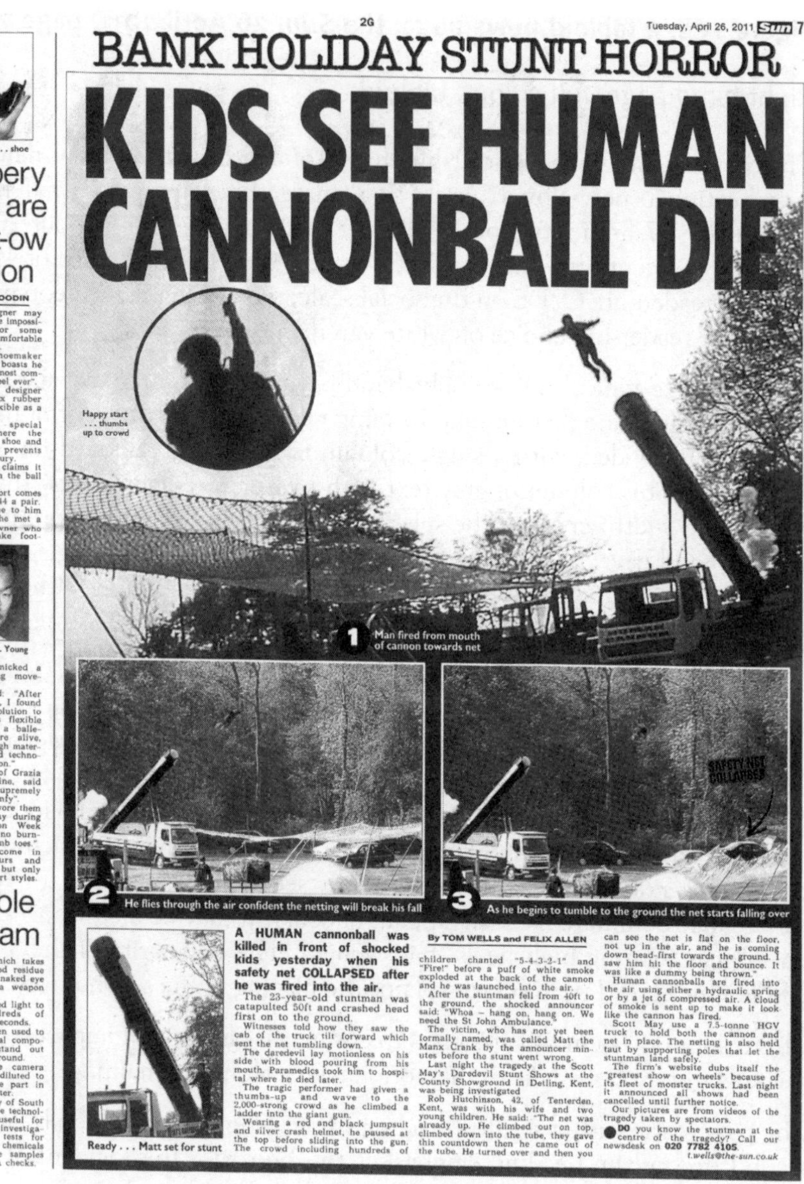

2G Tuesday, April 26, 2011 Sun 7

BANK HOLIDAY STUNT HORROR

KIDS SEE HUMAN CANNONBALL DIE

Happy start . . . thumbs up to crowd

1 Man fired from mouth of cannon towards net

2 He flies through the air confident the netting will break his fall

3 As he begins to tumble to the ground the net starts falling over

Ready . . . Matt set for stunt

A HUMAN cannonball was killed in front of shocked kids yesterday when his safety net COLLAPSED after he was fired into the air.

By TOM WELLS and FELIX ALLEN

The 23-year-old stuntman was catapulted 50ft and crashed head first on to the ground.

Witnesses told how they saw the cab of the truck tilt forward which sent the net tumbling down.

The daredevil lay motionless on his side with blood pouring from his mouth. Paramedics took him to hospital where he died later.

The tragic performer had given a thumbs-up and wave to the 2,000-strong crowd as he climbed a ladder into the giant gun.

Wearing a red and black jumpsuit and silver crash helmet, he paused at the top before sliding into the gun. The crowd including hundreds of children chanted "5-4-3-2-1" and "Fire!" before a puff of white smoke exploded at the back of the cannon and he was launched into the air.

After the stuntman fell from 40ft to the ground, the shocked announcer said: "Whoa – hang on, hang on. We need the St John Ambulance."

The victim, who has not yet been formally named, was called Matt the Manx Crank by the announcer minutes before the stunt went wrong.

Last night the tragedy at the Scott May's Daredevil Stunt Shows at the County Showground in Detling, Kent, was being investigated

Rob Hutchinson, 42, of Tenterden, Kent, was with his wife and two young children. He said: "The net was already up. He climbed out on top, climbed down into the tube, they gave this countdown then he came out of the tube. He turned over and then you can see the net is flat on the floor, not up in the air, and he is coming down head-first towards the ground. I saw him hit the floor and bounce. It was like a dummy being thrown."

Human cannonballs are fired into the air using either a hydraulic spring or by a jet of compressed air. A cloud of smoke is sent up to make it look like the cannon has fired.

Scott May use a 7.5-tonne HGV truck to hold both the cannon and net in place. The netting is also held taut by supporting poles that let the stuntman land safely.

The firm's website dubs itself the "greatest show on wheels" because of its fleet of monster trucks. Last night it announced all shows had been cancelled until further notice.

Our pictures are from videos of the tragedy taken by spectators.

● **DO** you know the stuntman at the centre of the tragedy? Call our newsdesk on **020 7782 4105**.

t.wells@the-sun.co.uk

Flex appeal . . . shoe

Rubbery soles are stilett-ow solution

By VINCE SOODIN

A SHOE designer may have created the impossible dream for some women – a comfortable pair of stilettos.

French shoemaker Raphael Young boasts he has made "the most comfortable high heel ever".

The ex-YSL designer says his R-Flex rubber soles are as flexible as a "ballerina" flat.

They use special technology where the softness of the shoe and leather sole prevents twisting and injury.

Raphael also claims it cuts pressure on the ball of the foot.

But the comfort comes at a price – £344 a pair.

The idea came to him in 2009 when he met a shoe factory owner who wanted to make footwear that mimicked a natural walking movement.

'Nourished' . . . Young

Raphael said: "After trials and tests, I found the technical solution to make shoes as flexible and comfy as a ballerina. Shoes are alive, nourished through material research and technological innovation."

Kay Barron, of Grazia fashion magazine, said they were "supremely flexible and comfy".

She said: "I wore them for a whole day during London Fashion Week and there was no burning pain, or numb toes."

The shoes come in different colours and two heights – but only peep-toe or court styles.

Invisible CSI cam

A CAMERA which takes pictures of blood residue invisible to the naked eye could become a weapon against crime.

It uses infrared light to capture hundreds of images within seconds.

Filters are then used to identify chemical components which stand out from the background.

In tests, the camera detected blood diluted to as little as one part in 100 parts of water.

The University of South Carolina said the technology could be useful for crime scene investigations. Current tests for blood use toxic chemicals that can dilute samples too far for DNA checks.

Figure 13.2 A tabloid news page: the *Sun*, 26 April 2011, page 7.

Courtesy of the *Sun*, News Group Newspapers, and reprinted with their kind permission.

two pictures. In order to give a sequence of events, the picture captions are numbered. The text is broken into three columns, making it easy to read, with a clear entry point signalled by a bold sans serif font. The captions are also sans serif, but the text is white to sit on the dark tones of the picture below. It's a straightforward, bold page that gives you what you need quickly and easily. The pictures are from readers who have sent in mobile phone video, and the *Sun* takes the opportunity to seek extra information by asking whether readers knew the stuntman, giving a phone number and email address.

Figure 13.3: a small-scale magazine fashion page: *Glamour*, October 2002

Left-hand page, full colour, 17cm × 22.5cm

Glamour is one of the magazines that publishes in small scale with a page of 17cm × 22.5cm. Such magazines are only slightly larger than A5 and are designed to fit easily into a handbag or pocket. Pagination tends to be high; the October 2002 issue that is used here runs to 370 pages. This size is about two-thirds the normal magazine size, and it would be interesting to discover whether the average reader feels cheated in any way. By use of smaller pictures and display headings, each page manages to be a replica of those of larger competitors, giving the impression that the same amount of material goes on each page but that there are almost double the number of pages. The size seems to be popular, and the October 2002 issue contains an editor's letter boasting about *Glamour*'s success: 'With 520,000 readers every month, we are far and away the most popular, best-selling women's mag in Britain.'

The page chosen is headed 'The Glamour Challenge'. A twin-deck heading quickly sets the scene that this is accessible fashion that the reader can buy in her lunch hour.

The page does not waste space. The models are cut off at the neck by the caption describing the event the outfit is chosen for. So economical are the writing and design that it takes me more words to describe the text than there are words on the actual page. The pictures of the outfits are large; most of the depth of the page is used by these pictures, but, cleverly, those all-important accessories with their small details are enlarged and placed over the models' feet. Small captions are inset on shadowed labels giving price and stockist, and a total cost is placed at the bottom of each of the four columns.

This is a page that knows what it is doing and gets right down to it, cutting out all the frills and ruthlessly removing everything that is not needed. The reader

Fast GLAMOUR

THE GLAMOUR CHALLENGE

UNDER £100 IN UNDER 1 HOUR

Four amazing-value, head-to-toe outfits you can snap up in one lunch-hour splurge

WEDDING RECEPTION

Dress £60 Unique at Topshop

GLAMOUR SUPER-CHIC

Beaded purse £15 Accessorize

Shoes £25 Freemans

GRAND TOTAL £100

POOL PARTY

Peacock beaded top £45 Topshop

Cord miniskirt £14.99 H&M

Mirror bag £20 Oasis

Two-strap mules £20 Choice catalogue

GRAND TOTAL £99.99

ROCK CONCERT

Beaded cami top £35 Oasis

Elasticated hem jeans £34.99 H&M

Earrings from £6.99 madaboutjewellery.com

Court shoes £23 George

GRAND TOTAL £99.98

COCKTAILS

Dress £41 Mango

Sequin bag £12 Dorothy Perkins

Ankle-strap shoes £35 Marks & Spencer

GRAND TOTAL £88

Styled by Victoria Taylor. Still lifes: Simon Vinall. For where to buy see Stockists, page 354

224 GLAMOUR

Figure 13.3 A fashion page in a women's magazine: *Glamour*, October 2002, page 224.

wants to know what the page is about, and she is told within 3cm of the top of the page. Readers want to see what the outfits look like so most of the page is used to show them, with enlargements of what would otherwise be difficult-to-see detail on shoes, handbags and earrings. The captions are relatively unobtrusive, placed in spaces that do not carry much information. There is a small caption down the inside of the page naming the stylist and photographer and explaining where to find details of the stockists. The captions themselves carry a minimum of information – price and stockist – but it is all most readers need. The page is in full colour (as are all the pages in *Glamour*), so the reader can see the colours for herself. It is assumed that if the reader is interested, she will be happy to visit the shop and see the outfit for herself, so telling her details about materials, sizes, alternative colours, and so on is clearly seen as a waste of space – and there is no space to waste on a page this small. The colours used on the page blend well with the outfits. The left-hand dress is bright red and the skirt and top outfit alongside are a deepish orange. The other outfits are black, apart from the jeans, which are a typical blue. The column headers and footers are mixed in dark orange or light orange, and these colours are also used in the heading. These colours brighten the black outfits and accentuate the colours.

All in all, it is a well-put-together, cleverly-thought-through page. It wastes no space and presents the reader with exactly what she needs. According to *Glamour* (October 2002: 13), the magazine won the Total Publishing Awards 2001 for Best Designed Consumer Magazine, and, if this edition of the magazine is a good example, it deserved the award.

Figure 13.4: a tabloid local newspaper page: the *Gazette* (Blackpool), 2 April 2011, page 3

Right-hand page, full colour, tabloid

Despite being reduced in size by the 4-centimetre-deep puff for Monday's paper, discreetly cut off by distinctive colouring, and a small advert, this page still manages to pack in six stories without any sense of crowding. The main picture takes a large proportion of the available space, leading the eye firmly into the centre of the page where the reader will automatically hunt for the entry point on the left, clearly signposted by a byline, neatly underscored, a cap start and a larger-than-body-size font. The heading is dropped in white at bottom of the picture, somewhere where it is not going to interfere unduly with what we need to see.

A second picture is laid askew into the side of the main picture breaking into the text run. Although this narrows the text, making it more difficult to read, it

www.blackpoolgazette.co.uk

The Gazette, Saturday, April 2, 2011 3

FRIER FLINTOFF!

From cricket to calamari for the England star – don't miss Monday's Gazette

FOUR-YEAR-OLD WHO NEARLY DROWNED REUNITED WITH HIS RESCUER

By JULIA BENNETT

PULLED TO SHORE: Craig Arnold with four-year-old Thomas Pacey-Blezard and (inset below) with his mum Sharani Picture: MARTIN BOSTOCK

Thank you, my lake hero

A LITTLE boy who was rescued from drowning in Stanley Park lake has been re-united with his hero.

Thomas Pacey-Blezard was riding his new bike down a hill when he lost control and somersaulted into the deep water.

When passer-by Craig Arnold saw the four-year-old plunge into the lake, he thought nothing of diving in after him.

The 37-year-old grabbed Thomas, who was under water and cannot swim, and pulled him ashore to re-unite him with his frantic parents and younger brother.

Mr Arnold, of Hereford Avenue, Marton, said: "We were feeding the ducks with my little girl and the next minute we saw this little boy whizzing past really fast. He hit the fence and did a somersault off his bike into the water.

"The boy was splashing about and going under the water, he had a big coat on which seemed to be weighing him down.

"I just jumped into the water and pulled him out. I didn't really think about it, it was a natural reaction, it was over in seconds.

"He was very shocked and upset, he didn't really know what was going on."

Following an appeal in The Gazette to find the mystery hero, Thomas and his mother, Sharani Pacey-Blezard, managed to meet Mr Arnold to say a special thank you for saving his life.

Mrs Pacey-Blezard, who lives in Alston near Longridge, said: "We're so grateful for what he did. His quick reactions saved Thomas and we want to thank him.

"I'm a landlady at a pub so we're going to give him and his family some vouchers to have a meal there."

Craig's partner Louise Elgee, 42, who was with him at the time of the rescue on Monday, March 21, said she was very proud of her "hero".

She said: "It was such a dangerous situation, it could have been fatal if no-one was around to pull him out.

"Craig did a wonderful thing though, I keep playing 'Hero' by Enrique Iglesias to him."

julia.bennett@blackpoolgazette.co.uk

in brief

Theft suspect arrested at flat

POLICE hunting a man in relation to a theft, swarmed a flat on Whitegate Drive in Blackpool.

Riot officers forced their way into the property at 9am yesterday after a 33-year-old man refused to open the door.

The man was arrested on suspicion of theft of a laptop and affray. A 44-year-old woman was arrested on suspicion of affray following yesterday's incident.

A dog warden was also drafted in after a Staffordshire Bull Terrier was discovered at the premises. The dog was taken to kennels.

Pub burglary

A BURGLAR stole copper piping after breaking into a disused pub.

The thieves climbed up the outside fire escape at the Blue Anchor Inn on Fleetwood Road in Greenhalgh and managed to get into the building through the roof.

They removed radiators from the wall and took copper piping before leaving the building via the fire escape.

The burglary was discovered around 3pm on Thursday.

Competition

NOMINATE your mum in a Mother's Day contest.

Bon Marche in Cleveleys wants to find the Fylde's 'Mum in a Million'. Visit the shop to pick up a nomination form.

All entries need to be in store by tomorrow.

Storage fire

A FIRE broke out at a storage depot in Lytham causing damage to the building. Crews were called to the property on Preston Road shortly after 7pm last night. Nobody was injured.

Raid finds £11,000 of cannabis in loft

A POLICE raid in Fleetwood found cannabis plants worth up to £11,000 being grown in a loft.

Preston Crown Court was told light emanating from a trap door attracted police to the "garden" which had 69 plants at various stages of growth.

Christopher Cummings, 26, of Broadway, Fleetwood, had been committed to the crown court by magistrates in Fleetwood after admitting a charge of producing and supplying cannabis.

David Traynor, prosecuting, told the court that on October 22 last year police entered the house at Broadway and discovered a "fairly sophisticated set up for the growing of cannabis".

Lights were rigged up and there was ventilation and ducting and items used for the growing of cannabis.

Plants were at different stages of production.

There were 25 seedlings, 38 small sized plants, four medium sized and two large plants.

The potential yield of the 44 established plants was 1,344 grams with a street value of between £7,500 and £11,500.

Mr Traynor said Cummings came home during the search and made full admissions.

Richard Haworth, defending, said Cummings' crop was predominately for his own use. He would have supplied two family members and a friend and was going to freeze part of it.

He said: "It was a one-off cultivation."

Judge Norman Wright adjourned sentence for further hearing regarding the supply aspect of the case.

Cummings was bailed until that hearing on May 27.

Figure 13.4 A tabloid local newspaper page: the *Gazette* (Blackpool), 2 April 2011, page 3.

does add interest and activity to the page as well as picturing his mother who is quoted in the story.

The heading is in 72pt and the white seriffed text is outlined in blue allowing it to stand distinctively from the picture. A blue border pulls the story away from the page, and this is helped by the blue patch strapline run in white caps.

The rest of the page is pretty pedestrian but none the worse for that. A run of news in briefs sits under an 'In brief' piece of artwork while the *anchorpiece* (the story holding down the bottom of the page) is a straightforward run of three columns spread over the normal space of four columns on this standard six-column layout. A single line of heading holds the story in place.

The 'news in brief' items all have a cap start and a sans serif face, setting the heading style away from the serif font used on the rest of the page.

Figure 13.5: feature in a women's magazine: *Woman & Home*, April 2011, page 47

Right-hand page, full colour, A4

The women's magazine is hugely competitive and knowing your target audience is crucial. *Woman & Home* is very clear about its target: it's aimed at 35-plus women 'who don't want to be pigeonholed'. Its emphasis, it claims, is very much on real women rather than the cult of celebrity. The magazine's website says it is 'especially geared to those with teenage children and older, who perhaps need help to rediscover their own priorities, hopes and dreams'.

The edition I've used for this masterclass is that of April 2011 and features actress Caroline Quentin on the front page. At 50, Caroline is the ideal celebrity for this magazine. No longer facilitating men behaving badly, she has portrayed plenty of working women with families on the screen and is one herself in real life.

In common with many women's magazines aimed at the more mature woman, articles about successful women are a regular favourite with readers. This article is headed 'Keep your hat on' in alternate pink and black. This theme is used on the rest of the page with black text and fuschia pink to complement the cobalt blue dress of the author. The entry point is clear and marked by a pink cap letter dropping down four lines and a bold intro, but after that the text is a straight-forward run of sans serif text set ragged right and shaped around the picture. The font is a reasonable size but has plenty of *leading*, giving a clean and easy-to-read look. This is not a magazine that wants to draw attention to its readers' deteriorating eyesight.

my secret passion

Keep your hat on!

Novelist Jessica Ruston on why she's determined to make millinery mainstream

The burly Polish removal man, looking unused to transporting such light loads, trooped down my front path to the van with four hatboxes stacked up in his arms. His mate followed with another two. It wasn't until I moved house and had to put most of my possessions temporarily in storage that I was forced to confront what I now admit is an obsession.

There's my all-time favourite, a little black top hat that perches on one side of my head. It has a sweep of veiling covered with little, multicoloured fuzzy blobs that bob gently in front of your eyes as you walk, hiding you from the world and making you feel girlishly flirtatious. I also love the chutzpah of the fuchsia one, which has a flourish of feathers. My mum found a shop that sells these inexpensive but unusual hats, and buys them for me when she sees them.

And I mustn't forget the clean, sleek lines of that perfect Philip Treacy trilby, a much treasured gift, the hat that makes me feel as though I'm a lady detective in a Hollywood noir movie, wearing a tightly belted trench coat and smoking cigarettes from a tortoiseshell holder. I haven't smoked for over six years, and I'm more Brighton beach than Sunset Boulevard, but that's the thing about hats – they have the power to transform.

My passion for hats started when I helped out in the costume workshops of the Royal Shakespeare Company during summer holidays. I steamed and hung and folded costumes inside their huge warehouse, and the sense of dressing-up that hats can give you has never left me.

My first serious hat was purchased with my allowance, saved up as a teenager. It was made of deep-red taffeta, with a black grosgrain trim, and a floppy, wide brim. I bought it from the covered market in Oxford, and nothing had ever made me feel more grown-up. From then on, I was hooked on hats.

I'm on a mission to drag hat-wearing from the back of the closet and into everyday life

So when I was dreaming up the heroine for my latest my novel it seemed a natural step to make her a milliner. And indeed, it is hats that change her life as she rises from nowhere to become the world's greatest milliner. It also allowed me to create my perfect wardrobe of hats within the pages of the book.

To help my research, a friend sneaked me into the workshop of a couture milliner. The smell of glue, the massive rolls of feather and sequin trims, and lines and lines of polished wooden hat blocks were all just how I'd imagined, and made me yearn for a new bit of frivolous headgear. Sadly, my bank balance didn't allow anything approaching a luxury buy. I went out and bought a Halloween hat from Claire's Accessories, complete with floating bats, to satisfy my desires.

Now, in my temporary home, I am almost entirely hatless. I brought my beloved black trilby and a new one – a trio of silky butterflies that hover above a tiny woven disc, trembling when you move. I feel somewhat bereft.

But I'm on a mission to drag hat-wearing out from the back of the closet where it has been relegated to ladies' days at the races and weddings, and into everyday life. I'm urging my friends – and, I hope, you – to discover the life-enhancing, confidence-boosting sheer fun of wearing hats. Of course, that may mean adding to my own collection, but it's all research, I tell my accountant, and so entirely justifiable. Which reminds me, how about that novel set in a diamond mine?

***Jessica's novel* To Touch The Stars *(Headline, £6.99) is out now.* w&h**

PHOTOGRAPH ANGELA SPAIN HAIR & MAKE-UP LAURENCE CLOSE STYLING RACHEL FANCONI JESSICA WEARS HAT, GABRIELA LIGENZA. DRESS, NOCTURNE. SHOES, LK BENNETT HATS PINK ROSE HAT, PHILIP TREACY. ALL OTHERS, GABRIELA LIGENZA

Figure 13.5 A feature spread in a women's magazine: *Woman & Home*, April 2011, page 47.

The heading is short and uses a stylised serif font that, in line with the rest of the magazine, is light, clean and fresh. This page, in common with the remainder of the magazine, tries to maintain a light touch, not forcing itself upon the reader but allowing them to join with it, chatting as you might do with a friend.

The whole makes for a light, delicate read for the reader who has a little more willingness and concentration to stick with a page for long enough to read a few hundred words. This is not for a reader who wants a magazine to compete with their phone, Facebook and the TV. A *Woman & Home* reader has finally managed to get a little peace and quiet, with the youngest doing homework and the eldest out with friends or at uni. A little quiet relaxation while hubby watches TV is what this offers.

Figure 13.6: a tabloid picture page: *Daily Mirror*, 11 October 2002, page 3

Right-hand page, full colour, tabloid

This *Daily Mirror* page breaks from the traditions of newspaper design and that is one of the reasons why I chose it. The whole page is a giant colour picture of model Sam Fox on the Paris catwalk, playing the part of Sally Bowles as played by Liza Minnelli in the film *Cabaret*. Although there is nothing particularly newsworthy about the story, it is topical and the pictures are nice; they were used by a number of newspapers on the same day. The *Mirror* obviously decided that if you've got it, you should flaunt it, and went to town on them. Using the whole picture, they were able to make use of the shaded area down the right to bleed into a black patch. They then overlaid heading, additional pictures and text on the patch. This gives the impression that text and pictures *pierce* the picture. This impression is enhanced by the white border around the pictures. The headings are in the sans serif font that the *Mirror* normally uses for its pages, with the main lead underlined to add emphasis. This emphasis is required because the heading cannot be any larger without reducing the character count, which is already small at about 8½ characters per line over three lines. The sub-editor goes for a label heading, partly because of this lack of space and partly because it fits the copy, which talks about Samantha Fox playing the part 20 years after first appearing on the *Sun*'s page three.

The other pictures used are from Sam Fox's early modelling days, one of Liza Minnelli as Sally and one from the same Paris show of Sam Fox with another model. The main picture fills half the width of the page, leaving just enough room for the heading, text (only about 200 words) and secondary pictures. There's an excellent feel of balance about the page, and the white on

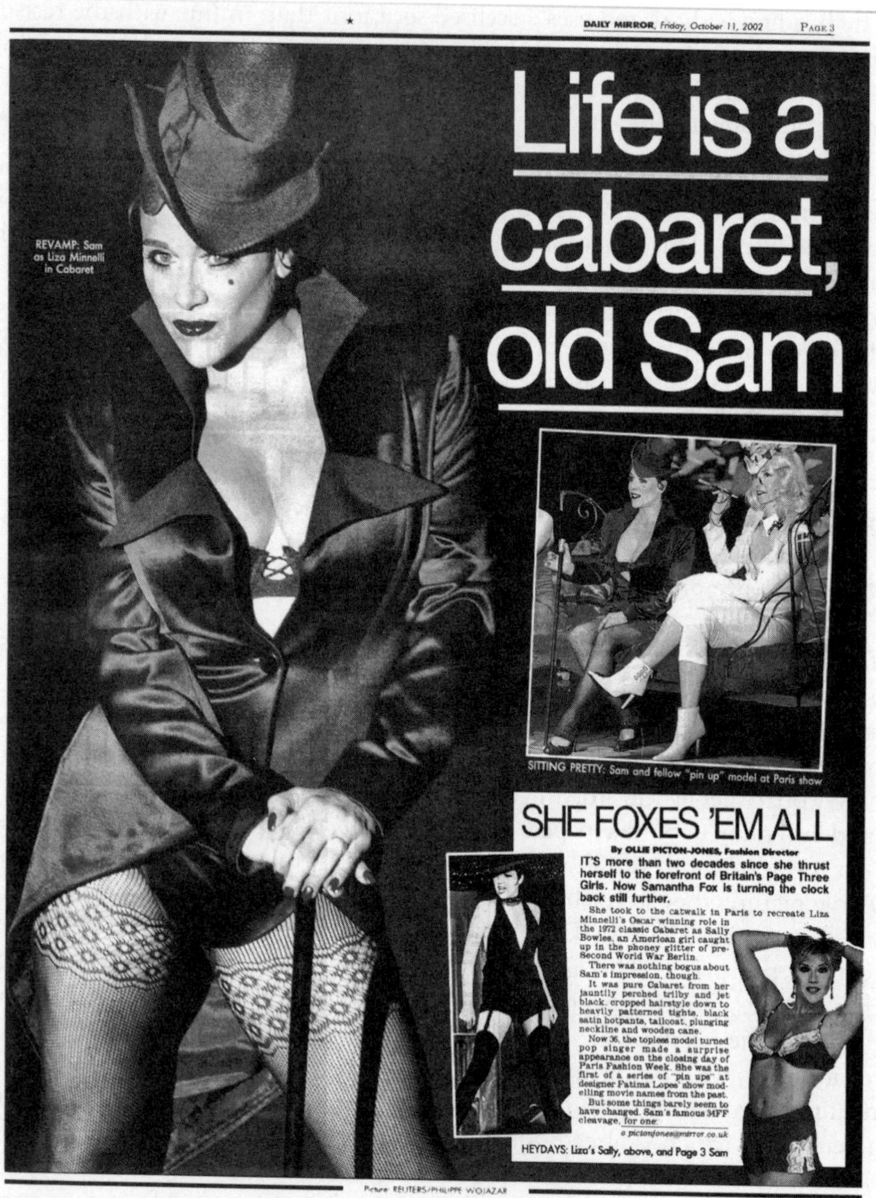

DAILY MIRROR, Friday, October 11, 2002 PAGE 3

Life is a cabaret, old Sam

REVAMP: Sam as Liza Minnelli in Cabaret

SITTING PRETTY: Sam and fellow "pin up" model at Paris show

SHE FOXES 'EM ALL

By OLLIE PICTON-JONES, Fashion Director

IT'S more than two decades since she thrust herself to the forefront of Britain's Page Three Girls. Now Samantha Fox is turning the clock back still further.

She took to the catwalk in Paris to recreate Liza Minnelli's Oscar winning role in the 1972 classic Cabaret as Sally Bowles, an American girl caught up in the phoney glitter of pre-Second World War Berlin.

There was nothing bogus about Sam's impression, though.

It was pure Cabaret from her jauntily perched trilby and jet black, cropped hairstyle down to heavily patterned tights, black satin hotpants, tailcoat, plunging neckline and wooden cane.

Now 36, the topless model turned pop singer made a surprise appearance on the closing day of Paris Fashion Week. She was the first of a series of "pin ups" at designer Fatima Lopes' show modelling movie names from the past.

But some things barely seem to have changed. Sam's famous 34FF cleavage, for one.

o pictonjones@mirror.co.uk

HEYDAYS: Liza's Sally, above, and Page 3 Sam

Picture: REUTERS/PHILIPPE WOJAZAR

Figure 13.6 A tabloid picture page: *Daily Mirror*, 11 October 2002, page 3.

black heading and caption are set against the black on white text to hold up the right-hand side of the page against the strong main picture, which easily holds our attention on the left. The entry point is clearly signalled by the white patch under the text, and the whole page is a lot of fun.

Figure 13.7: magazine news page: *Computer Shopper*, November 2002, pages 186 and 187

Double page, full colour, A4

This is a page from a computer consumer magazine. It runs a number of news pages covering mainly product news. The A4 pages contain stories that are all of about the same strength of interest to the reader. Choosing a lead tends to be almost arbitrary, and therefore none gets a particularly big display. The generic header 'Newsfile 11.02' showing the date in a form that mimics computer software protocols is the largest display font on the page. The same sans serif font is used throughout all the headings except for 'CTX kills dead pixels', which is set in a modern serif font to act as a kicker. This is carefully boxed off with a red border under the heading 'Graphics World'. The body font used throughout is also a sans serif font, but it is different from the heading font and is less stylised, more condensed and easier to read.

Despite the apparently haphazard look to the page, it is laid out in clear blocks of material. The page is prevented from being quartered by the addition of the 'In brief' column placed on a black patch staggered across the two facing pages. The *crossheads* here are in yellow, making them highly visible. The story count, once the nibs are included, is high for a relatively small page: nine on the left-hand page, seven on the right.

This gives a busy feel to the pages that is emphasised by the minimalist use of pictures and graphics. Although there are several pictures and graphics on the page, none of them are large and they are used almost exclusively to break the text rather than act as entry points. None of the stories on this page is designed to grab the reader's attention. It is assumed, with the relatively small page size, that the reader is likely to be able to scan the page and quickly zoom in on the displayed headings even though they are not dominant. Colour is used sparingly, although it is available, with the advert for the publication's own website being the most colourful item on the page, apart from the 'Graphics World' story.

The text is arranged ragged right and most of the headings are single line. This allows for plenty of white space, so the overall effect is of a clean, tidy and easy-to-access page, but one that is also busy and packed full of interest.

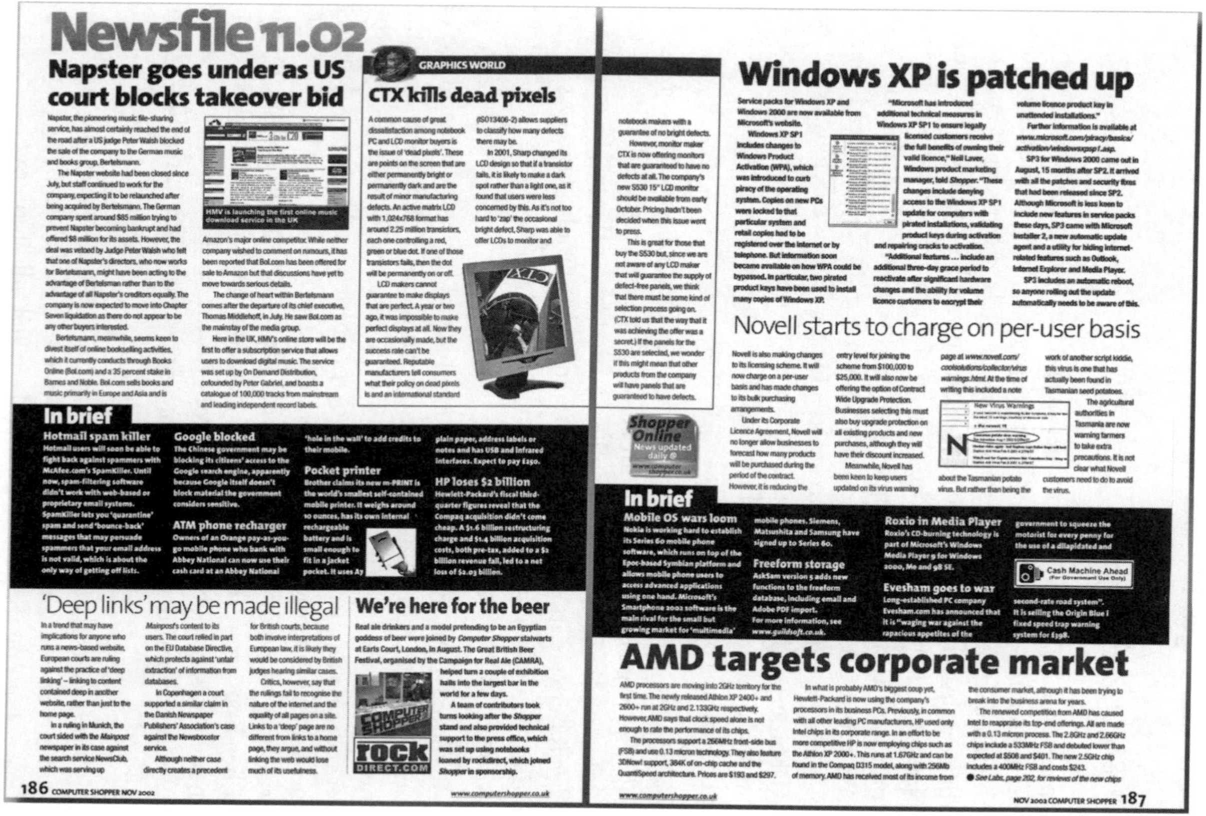

Newsfile 11.02

Napster goes under as US court blocks takeover bid

Napster, the pioneering music file-sharing service, has almost certainly reached the end of the road after a US judge Peter Walsh blocked the sale of the company to the German music and books group, Bertelsmann.

The Napster website had been closed since July, but staff continued to work for the company, expecting it to be relaunched after being acquired by Bertelsmann. The German company spent around $85 million trying to prevent Napster becoming bankrupt and had offered $8 million for its assets. However, the deal was vetoed by Judge Peter Walsh who felt that one of Napster's directors, who now works for Bertelsmann, might have been acting to the advantage of Bertelsman rather than to the advantage of all Napster's creditors equally. The company is now expected to move into Chapter Seven liquidation as there do not appear to be any other buyers interested.

Bertelsmann, meanwhile, seems keen to divest itself of online bookselling activities, which it currently conducts through Books Online (Bol.com) and a 35 percent stake in Barnes and Noble. Bol.com sells books and music primarily in Europe and Asia and is Amazon's major online competitor. While neither company wished to comment on rumours, it has been reported that Bol.com has been offered for sale to Amazon but that discussions have yet to move towards serious details.

HMV is launching the first online music download service in the UK

The change of heart within Bertelsmann comes after the departure of its chief executive, Thomas Middlehoff, in July. He saw Bol.com as the mainstay of the media group.

Here in the UK, HMV's online store will be the first to offer a subscription service that allows users to download digital music. The service was set up by On Demand Distribution, cofounded by Peter Gabriel, and boasts a catalogue of 100,000 tracks from mainstream and leading independent record labels.

GRAPHICS WORLD

CTX kills dead pixels

A common cause of great dissatisfaction among notebook PC and LCD monitor buyers is the issue of 'dead pixels'. These are points on the screen that are either permanently bright or permanently dark and are the result of minor manufacturing defects. An active matrix LCD with 1,024x768 format has around 2.25 million transistors, each one controlling a red, green or blue dot. If one of those transistors fails, then the dot will be permanently on or off.

LCD makers cannot guarantee to make displays that are perfect. A year or two ago, it was impossible to make perfect displays at all. Now they are occasionally made, but the success rate can't be guaranteed. Reputable manufacturers tell consumers what their policy on dead pixels is and an international standard (ISO13406-2) allows suppliers to classify how many defects there may be.

In 2001, Sharp changed its LCD design so that if a transistor fails, it is likely to make a dark spot rather than a light one, as it found that users were less concerned by this. As it's not too hard to 'zap' the occasional bright defect, Sharp was able to offer LCDs to monitor and notebook makers with a guarantee of no bright defects.

However, monitor maker CTX is now offering monitors that are guaranteed to have no defects at all. The company's new S530 15" LCD monitor should be available from early October. Pricing hadn't been decided when this issue went to press.

This is great for those that buy the S530 but, since we are not aware of any LCD maker that will guarantee the supply of defect-free panels, we think that there must be some kind of selection process going on. (CTX told us that the way that it was achieving the offer was a secret.) If the panels for the S530 are selected, we wonder if this might mean that other products from the company will have panels that are guaranteed to have defects.

In brief

Hotmail spam killer
Hotmail users will soon be able to fight back against spammers with McAfee.com's SpamKiller. Until now, spam-filtering software didn't work with web-based or proprietary email systems. SpamKiller lets you 'quarantine' spam and send 'bounce-back' messages that may persuade spammers that your email address is not valid, which is about the only way of getting off lists.

Google blocked
The Chinese government may be blocking its citizens' access to the Google search engine, apparently because Google itself doesn't block material the government considers sensitive.

ATM phone recharger
Owners of an Orange pay-as-you-go mobile phone who bank with Abbey National can now use their cash card at an Abbey National 'hole in the wall' to add credits to their mobile.

Pocket printer
Brother claims its new m-PRINT is the world's smallest self-contained mobile printer. It weighs around 10 ounces, has its own internal rechargeable battery and is small enough to fit in a jacket pocket. It uses A7 plain paper, address labels or notes and has USB and Infrared interfaces. Expect to pay £250.

HP loses $2 billion
Hewlett-Packard's fiscal third-quarter figures reveal that the Compaq acquisition didn't come cheap. A $1.6 billion restructuring charge and $1.4 billion acquisition costs, both pre-tax, added to a $2 billion revenue fall, led to a net loss of $2.03 billion.

'Deep links' may be made illegal

In a trend that may have implications for anyone who runs a news-based website, European courts are ruling against the practice of 'deep linking' – linking to content contained deep in another website, rather than just to the home page.

In a ruling in Munich, the court sided with the *Mainpost* newspaper in its case against the search service NewsClub, which was serving up *Mainpost's* content to its users. The court relied in part on the EU Database Directive, which protects against 'unfair extraction' of information from databases.

In Copenhagen a court supported a similar claim in the Danish Newspaper Publishers' Association's case against the Newsbooster service.

Although neither case directly creates a precedent for British courts, because both involve interpretations of European law, it is likely they would be considered by British judges hearing similar cases.

Critics, however, say that the rulings fail to recognise the nature of the internet and the equality of all pages on a site. Links to a 'deep' page are no different from links to a home page, they argue, and without linking the web would lose much of its usefulness.

We're here for the beer

Real ale drinkers and a model pretending to be an Egyptian goddess of beer were joined by *Computer Shopper* stalwarts at Earls Court, London, in August. The Great British Beer Festival, organised by the Campaign for Real Ale (CAMRA), helped turn a couple of exhibition halls into the largest bar in the world for a few days.

A team of contributors took turns looking after the *Shopper* stand and also provided technical support to the press office, which was set up using notebooks loaned by rockdirect, which joined *Shopper* in sponsorship.

COMPUTER SHOPPER

rock DIRECT.COM

186 COMPUTER SHOPPER NOV 2002 www.computershopper.co.uk

Windows XP is patched up

Service packs for Windows XP and Windows 2000 are now available from Microsoft's website.

Windows XP SP1 includes changes to Windows Product Activation (WPA), which was introduced to curb piracy of the operating system. Copies on new PCs were locked to that particular system and retail copies had to be registered over the internet or by telephone. But information soon became available on how WPA could be bypassed. In particular, two pirated product keys have been used to install many copies of Windows XP.

"Microsoft has introduced additional technical measures in Windows XP SP1 to ensure legally licensed customers receive the full benefits of owning their valid licence," Neil Laver, Windows product marketing manager, told *Shopper*. "These changes include denying access to the Windows XP SP1 update for computers with pirated installations, validating product keys during activation and repairing cracks to activation.

"Additional features … include an additional three-day grace period to reactivate after significant hardware changes and the ability for volume licence customers to encrypt their volume licence product key in unattended installations."

Further information is available at *www.microsoft.com/piracy/basics/activation/windowsxpsp1.asp*.

SP3 for Windows 2000 came out in August, 15 months after SP2. It arrived with all the patches and security fixes that had been released since SP2. Although Microsoft is less keen to include new features in service packs these days, SP3 came with Microsoft Installer 2, a new automatic update agent and a utility for hiding internet-related features such as Outlook, Internet Explorer and Media Player.

SP3 includes an automatic reboot, so anyone rolling out the update automatically needs to be aware of this.

Novell starts to charge on per-user basis

Novell is also making changes to its licensing scheme. It will now charge on a per-user basis and has made changes to its bulk purchasing arrangements.

Under its Corporate Licence Agreement, Novell will no longer allow businesses to forecast how many products will be purchased during the period of the contract. However, it is reducing the entry level for joining the scheme from $100,000 to $25,000. It will also now be offering the option of Contract Wide Upgrade Protection. Businesses selecting this must also buy upgrade protection on all existing products and new purchases, although they will have their discount increased.

Meanwhile, Novell has been keen to keep users updated on its virus warning page at *www.novell.com/coolsolutions/collector/viruswarnings.html*. At the time of writing this included a note about the Tasmanian potato virus. But rather than being the work of another script kiddie, this virus is one that has actually been found in Tasmanian seed potatoes.

New Virus Warnings

The agricultural authorities in Tasmania are now warning farmers to take extra precautions. It is not clear what Novell customers need to do to avoid the virus.

Shopper Online
News updated daily @
www.computershopper.co.uk

In brief

Mobile OS wars loom
Nokia is working hard to establish its Series 60 mobile phone software, which runs on top of the Epoc-based Symbian platform and allows mobile phone users to access advanced applications using one hand. Microsoft's Smartphone 2002 software is the main rival for the small but growing market for 'multimedia' mobile phones. Siemens, Matsushita and Samsung have signed up to Series 60.

Freeform storage
AskSam version 5 adds new functions to the freeform database, including email and Adobe PDF import.
For more information, see *www.guildsoft.co.uk*.

Roxio in Media Player
Roxio's CD-burning technology is part of Microsoft's Windows Media Player 9 for Windows 2000, Me and 98 SE.

Evesham goes to war
Long-established PC company Evesham.com has announced that it is "waging war against the rapacious appetites of the government to squeeze the motorist for every penny for the use of a dilapidated and second-rate road system". It is selling the Origin Blue I fixed speed trap warning system for £398.

Cash Machine Ahead
(For Government Use Only)

AMD targets corporate market

AMD processors are moving into 2GHz territory for the first time. The newly released Athlon XP 2400+ and 2600+ run at 2GHz and 2.133GHz respectively. However, AMD says that clock speed alone is not enough to rate the performance of its chips.

The processors support a 266MHz front-side bus (FSB) and use 0.13 micron technology. They also feature 3DNow! support, 384K of on-chip cache and the QuantiSpeed architecture. Prices are $193 and $297.

In what is probably AMD's biggest coup yet, Hewlett-Packard is now using the company's processors in its business PCs. Previously, in common with all other leading PC manufacturers, HP used only Intel chips in its corporate range. In an effort to be more competitive HP is now employing chips such as the Athlon XP 2000+. This runs at 1.67GHz and can be found in the Compaq D315 model, along with 256Mb of memory. AMD has received most of its income from the consumer market, although it has been trying to break into the business arena for years.

The renewed competition from AMD has caused Intel to reappraise its top-end offerings. All are made with a 0.13 micron process. The 2.8GHz and 2.66GHz chips include a 533MHz FSB and debuted lower than expected at $508 and $401. The new 2.5GHz chip includes a 400MHz FSB and costs $243.

● *See Labs, page 202, for reviews of the new chips*

www.computershopper.co.uk NOV 2002 COMPUTER SHOPPER 187

Figure 13.7
A magazine news page: *Computer Shopper*, November 2002, pages 186 and 187.

Figure 13.8: a large-circulation male-interest magazine: *Stuff*, March 2011, page 33

Left-hand page, full colour, A4

Stuff is a male-oriented gadget magazine and claims to be the best-selling gadget magazine in the world, with 26 licensed overseas editions. Although figures of the reader gender balance were not available, one can assume it is male oriented because of the attractive swimsuit-clad young woman clutching a smartphone on the front cover. Previous editions on the website also feature swimsuited women.

Page 33 is a typical page in the magazine and is beautifully presented, with high-quality bonded paper carrying high-quality artwork. Once we are past the cover, the editorial concentrates almost exclusively on the gadgets, whether a car, camera, smartphone or computer.

A page about new electronic products has two ways to go: a text-dominated page with a picture, or a picture-dominated page with limited text. For a magazine clearly designed for flicking through (as are so many magazines today aimed at a younger audience), pictures are the right way to go. Modern electronic hardware is all about the look; we often can't tell what it can actually do from looking at the outside. The popularity of the Apple iPad is almost completely about its look rather than its capabilities.

A big picture of a shiny, exciting piece of equipment looking new and cool is important, and so *Stuff* places the three key items it is introducing at the top, the bottom and left central. Smaller pics showing optional arcade games that can be loaded onto the iPad relate to the arcade-style housing for iPads pictured centre.

Strict attention to style is important on pages like this to keep them looking clean and attractive. This is especially important when the reader is flicking through. Complicated headings, changes in font and other irritations will spoil the experience.

All the text is sans serif. Each heading is three lines of type at about 16pt, with the middle line in 18pt red identifying the make and model. The first line is a standard heading designed to draw the reader in, and the third line gives price details and a website for further information.

The body text is also sans serif, run fairly small (7–8pt) with very little leading. These are text sizes designed for those with sharp eyes, reinforcing the point that this magazine is aimed at an 18–30 age range. The type is clean to read and leaves plenty of white space because each caption is only about 90 words long,

This year's ears
The early crop of 2011 headphones
tinyurl.com/newcans

S

HOT 03/11
STUFF

It's a tablet, Jim, but not as you know it
Samsung TX100
£tba (due March) | samsung.com/uk

To the youthful gadgeteer, tablet computers may seem a new confection, borne of an unholy matrimony between smartphones and big screens. Not true. Tablet computers have been mainstream since 2004's Windows XP Tablet Edition. While paying mind to this legacy, the TX100 is a thoroughly modern machine. No digitizer pen here: just a strokable Windows 7 interface on a multi-touch, 10.1in, 1366x768 display. And, unlike most mobile OS-powered upstarts, a full-size keyboard that slides neatly away when not needed. It's taken cues from the newbies though, with 32GB or 64GB of solid-state storage fuelling a nine-hour battery life and a start-up that's done quicker than you can say, "ooh, it has USB and HDMI ports".

Is this some sort of joke?
Ion iCade
£tba (due July) | ionaudio.com

The iCade was originally an April Fools' Day prank posted on American gadget shop ThinkGeek, but Ion has taken the gag and run with it, producing a working miniature arcade cabinet dock for old-school iPad gaming. With a retro joystick and eight big buttons, it plugs in via the dock connector and works with any of Atari's iPad games; others are sure to follow. It'll neatly recreate that '80s arcade environment, minus the chewing gum stuck to the side and the pockets full of 20p coins.

TOP 3 RETRO iPAD GAMES

1 **Pac-Man for iPad**
Trundling around a dark room, munching pills to repetitive music; in many ways, it's the ultimate '80s simulator.

2 **Asteroids X**
Souped-up, touchscreen reboot of the relentless, deep-space, rock-blasting classic.

3 **Warheads**
Launch rockets at other rockets in this frantic iPad remake of the 1980 Atari classic *Missile Command*.

Bus, camera, action!
Sony HDR-PJ30VE
£tba (due March) | sony.co.uk

After using the earphones that came with your iPod, greed is one of the deadliest gadget sins. So while the full HD footage shot by the 32GB PJ30VE might look good on its 3in LCD screen, it'll look even better when you use its built-in projector to blast it on to the inside of the bus at up to 60in, kindly sharing it with your fellow passengers. With GPS on board it'll also geotag your flicks, meaning you'll know exactly where on the N48's route you were when you videoed that fare dodger getting busted.

www.stuff.tv / 33

Figure 13.8 A large-circulation male-interest magazine: *Stuff*, March 2011, page 33.

identifying only the unique elements of the gadget: a tablet that plugs into a keyboard to make a laptop, an arcade-style housing for your iPad and a camcorder with a built-in projector.

Headers and footers are standard but fit the same style, with URLs leading to further information – a clear assumption that readers will have their smartphone, iPad or laptop handy.

Overall, this is a page that is clean and dominated by the amount of white space surrounding the objects, emphasising their shiny, attractive nature. *Stuff* presents the latest gadgets in a way that makes them desirable, and it's interesting to note that for that reason, it's often difficult to tell the adverts and the editorial apart.

Glossary

Advertising feature: Editorial copy and pictures that are produced to support an advert or series of adverts.

Ampersand: Special character (&) to represent the word 'and'.

Anchorpiece: Story placed at the bottom of a page to hold the page together.

Anti-aliasing: Smoothing the rough, pixellated edges of pictures produced in a digital process.

Ascender: Top portion of the letters b, d, f, h, k, l.

Bastard setting: Any measure that deviates from the normal.

Beard: The non-printing portion of type which coincides with descenders on characters that have descenders.

Black: Bold-faced text type.

Bleed: To allow a picture to extend beyond the trimmed area of a page.

Block: Engraved or etched plate from which a picture or graphic is printed.

Blurb: A piece of editorial, usually on the front page, advertising a story within.

Bold: Thickened, heavier version of roman type.

Broadsheet: Large-size newspaper, usually considered to be of a more serious quality. The precise size is defined by the press.

Byline: Reporter's name given with a printed story.

Caps: Short for 'capital letters'.

Casting off: An estimation of the set length of a piece of copy in a given type size and measure. Computerised page make-up has made this skill redundant.

Catchline: One-word name used to identify a story set in type – should be removed before publication.

Centre spread: Two facing pages in the middle of a newspaper or magazine.

Chase: The metal frame that formerly held metal type for printing.

Cicero: European measure of type.

CMYK: Short for process colour, representing the four colours used: cyan, magenta, yellow and black.

Condensed: A type that is narrow for the family from which it comes, giving a higher word count per line of text.

Copy approval: Allowing the subject of a story to read the copy and have approval over whether it is published.

Copy taster: Someone on the editorial staff who 'tastes' (selects) copy for publication.

Crop: To select an area of a picture for publication and remove the remainder.

Crosshead: Display-type sub-heading centred within the body of the story allowing the eye to rest and identify where it is. (*See also* **Side-head**.)

Cut-off rule: A line across a column indicating the end of that story.

Cut-out: A picture with the background, or part of the background, removed to allow it to fit over another picture or to allow text to be wrapped close to the subject.

Deck: Separate section of heading – not simply a separate line.

Descender: Bottom portion of a letter such as g, p, q, j, y.

Dots per inch: A way of measuring the resolution of scanners and printers. The more dots per inch, the higher the resolution.

Double-page spread: Facing pages where the type fills both pages, running over the centre gutter.

Drop letter: Initial letter that is large enough to run alongside two or three lines of text. (Also **Drop cap**.)

Dummy: Mock-up of a newspaper showing on which page the adverts are to go and allowing decisions on story placing to be made.

Edition: A version of a publication. Different editions of a publication might be produced daily, weekly or monthly. They might even be produced for different times of the day or different locations such as district, city etc.

Ellipses: Three dots (. . .), indicating a pause or that something is missing.

Em-dash: A dash the size of an em.

Em-quad: The square of the body type. Usually assumed to be a pica-em or a 12pt em. (*See also* **Mutton**.)

En: Half an em.

Entry point: The starting point on a page for a reader.

EPS: Encapsulated PostScript. A digital graphics format.

Face: Short for 'typeface'.

Fair comment: A defence against a defamation suit where it is claimed the comments are fair, based on true facts.

Flong: A cast in papier mâché or plastic of the type set.

Folio: The part of the page that gives the page number.

Font: A complete set of type characters in any size and face.

Footer: The bottom area of the page, sometimes used to insert the publication title, date or page number.

Forme: A page of cast type put together by printers in order to provide an original to make a **stereotype** for loading on the press.

Full out: Set right to the margin without any indent.

Full point: Another name for a full stop.

Gutter: Space between pages on the same form.

Halftone: Picture or printing plate in which shades of colour are represented as smaller or larger dots to enable printing in a single colour of ink (black, cyan, magenta or yellow).

Hanging indent: Where the first line is full out and the rest of the par is indented, usually by 1 em.

Header: Text printed in the area at the top of the page, often the publication title or page number.

Hot metal setting: Printing process where the type that is used to make the printing plate is formed from molten metal.

Imprint: The name and address of the printer and publisher, which are required by law on any publication.

Intro: The starting paragraph of a story.

Justification: Refers to type set with both sides of the text aligned.

Keep down: Use only lower-case letters.

Keep up: Use caps.

Kern: Part of a letter projecting beyond its body.

Kerning: Adjusting the space between letters in computer typesetting to ensure that different kerns do not leave a displeasing visual effect.

Kicker: A headline set in a font that is distinctly different from the rest of the page, to set it apart.

Layout: The page design sent to the printer.

Lead: Pronounces 'leed'. The main story on the page. Also, the starting point of a story, or **intro**.

Lead: Pronounced 'led'. Originally, strips of metal (lead) that spaced out lines of type. Now, the space between lines which is additional to the body size.

Leader: Editorial – article expressing the editor's opinion, or that of another senior member of a newspaper's staff.

Leaders: A line of dots, dashes or other devices to lead the eye across the page, especially in a table.

Leading: Pronounced 'ledding'. The space between lines of type.

Letterpress: A method of printing involving pressing raised, inked type against paper.

Ligature: Special character designed to save space, such as "&".

Literals: A whole range of printer's errors from spelling mistakes to wrong founts.

Lithography: A method of printing involving the separation of ink and water.

Live page: A page produced on the day it is made up.

Make-up: The sheet on which the design of the page is drawn.

Masthead: Often used to refer to the paper's **titlepiece**. However, as Leslie Sellers points out in his excellent book *Doing It in Style* (1968a), although this usage has wide currency, it is a misuse. 'Masthead' should be used to refer to the title and other material above the editorial **leader**.

Measure: The width (always in 12pt ems) to which type is set.

Mutton: A common name for an em.

Negs: Photographic negatives.

Nut: Common name for an **en**.

Offset: A printing system where the plate is separated from the paper by an offset roller, so that there is no direct contact.

Overnights: Pages designed and set up the night before.

Paste-up: The art of putting together a photoset page.

Perfector: A printing machine that allows pages to be printed on both sides.

Photocomposition (also **photosetting**)**:** A method of setting type photographically by exposing photo-sensitive paper to images of set type. The processed paper is then used as artwork on the finished page.

Pica: The old name for 12pt.

Piercing: Cutting into a picture to allow text, or another picture to be inserted.

Platen: The plate that paper is pressed against during printing.

Play up: Instruction to emphasise a particular story or angle of a story. The opposite is 'play down'.

Point: Standard unit of typographical measurement. There are approximately 72 points to the inch, so 1 point measures 0.01383 inches.

Privilege: A protection against a suit of defamation allowing freedom of speech at public meetings.

Process colour: A method of printing in full colour involving printing in four different-coloured inks. Also known as **CMYK**.

Publication: An identifiable journal that is published on a regular basis.

Puff: An advert, often on the front page, telling about material inside the paper or magazine.

Random: The area where type is assembled for proofing and, sometimes, make-up.

Raster dot: A printing term that allows black ink to be produced in dot screen to represent a shade of grey.

Register: The exact positioning of one colour in relation to others. Colour printing requires that all four colour plates are in register, or the image will be blurred.

Replate: A change of page to include urgent news or correct a major mistake. This would be in addition to a normal plate change for an edition change.

Rule: Lines originally produced with strips of metal but more likely to be photographically produced these days.

Run: The number of copies required in any printing operation.

Shoulder: The angle formed by a change in measure of a story.

Sidebar: A story connected to the main story that runs alongside it on the page.

Side-head: A display-type sub-heading placed within the body of text and aligned with either the right or left side of the text.

Slip A special page for a specific area or particular audience.

Smalls: Classified ads, but also another name for shorts (stories of about 20–40 words used to fill small pages on a page).

Solus: A single advert on a page.

Spot colour: An additional colour added to a publication during printing.

Spread: Material spread over more than one page and designed as a whole.

Standfirst: A display device that introduces a story, often containing the reporter's **byline**.

Stereotyping (often abbreviated to **stereo**): A stereotype is a cast copy of the original **forme** which is then loaded onto the press to imprint the paper. First, a **flong** is made of the forme. This is curved and them a stereotype is cast from this, allowing many stereos to be cast without resetting the page.

Stone: In traditional hot-metal setting, newspapers were made from cast metal that was made up on stone tables. Hence, on the stone.

Strapline: A heading placed over another heading.

Streamer: A long heading, usually covering the full width of the page.

Supplement: A one-off magazine or newspaper insert that is a part of, but separate to, the main newspaper.

Tasted: As in 'copy-tasted'. Refers to copy that has been approved or rejected.

Titlepiece: The title of the publication on the front page.

Web-offset: Print technology where the web of newsprint does not press directly onto the printing plate but is offset by a small rubber roller that picks up the ink from the plate and transfers it to the paper.

Widows and orphans: The lonely word or words that fail to fill the last line of a paragraph but have been allowed to move into the next column and sit alone at the top.

Website of interest

www.poynter.org

Bibliography

Ang, T. (1996) *Picture Editing*, Oxford: Focal Press

Burnham, R.W., Hanes, R.M. and Bartleson, J.C. (1963) *Color: A Guide to Basic Facts and Concepts*, New York: John Wiley

Carey, P. (1996) *Media Law*, London: Sweet & Maxwell

Carey, P. (2000) *Media Law* (2nd edn), London: Sweet & Maxwell

Cook, A. and Feury, R. (1989) *Type and Color*, Rockport, MA: Rockport Publishers

Craig, J. (1980) *Designing with Type*, New York: Watson-Guptill Publications

Crone, T. (1995) *Law and the Media* (3rd edn), London: Focal Press

De Grandis, L. (1986) *Theory and Use of Colour*, Poole: Blandford Press

Durrant, W.R. (1989) *Printing*, Oxford: Heinemann Professional Publishing

Evans, H. (1978) *Pictures on a Page*, London: William Heinemann

Evans, H. (1984a) *Newspaper Design*, London: William Heinemann

Evans, H. (1984b) *Handling Newspaper Text*, London: William Heinemann

Favre, J. and November, A. (1979) *Color and Communication*, Zurich: ABC Edition

Frost, C. (2010) *Reporting for Journalists* (2nd edn), London: Routledge

Frost, C. (2011) *Journalism Ethics and Regulation* (3rd edn), London: Pearson

Garcia, M. and Stark, P. (1991) *Eyes on the News*, St Petersburg: Poynter Institute

Giles, V. and Hodgson, F.W. (1996) *Creative Newspaper Design* (2nd edn), Oxford: Focal Press

Greenwood, W. and Welsh, T. (2000) *McNae's Essential Law for Journalists* (16th edn), London: Focal Press

Hodgson, F.W. (1993) *Subediting* (2nd edn), Oxford: Focal Press

Hutt, A. (1967) *Newspaper Design* (2nd edn), London Oxford University Press

Kammermeier, A. and Kammermeier, P. (1992) *Scanning and Printing*, Oxford: Focal Press

Keeble, R. (2001) *Ethics for Journalists*, London: Routledge

Kieran, M. (1998) *Media Ethics*, London: Routledge

Kress, G. and Van Leeuwen, T. (1996) *Reading Images: The Grammar of Visual Design*, London: Routledge

Kress, G. and Van Leeuwen, T. (2000) 'Front Pages: (The Critical) Analysis of Newspaper Layout', in Bell, A. and Garrett, P. (eds) *Approaches to Media Discourse*, Oxford: Blackwell, pp. 186–219

Mason, P. and Smith, D. (1998) *Magazine Law: A Practical Guide*, London: Routledge

Press Complaints Commission (PCC) (1993) Report no. 16 London: PCC

Press Complaints Commission (1997) Report no. 40 London: PCC

Quinn, S. (2001) *Digital Sub-editing and Design*, Oxford: Focal Press

Quinn, T., Lindsay, M., Hewitt, D., Overbury, K. and Ritson, J. (1991) *The Key: A Guide to Best Practices for Thomson Regional Newspapers*, Belfast: TRN

Sassoon, R. (1993) *Computers and Typography*, Oxford: Intellect

Sellers, L. (1968a) *Doing It in Style*, Oxford: Pergamon Press

Sellers, L. (1968b) *The Simple Subs Book*, Oxford: Pergamon Press

Shipcott, G. (1994) *Typography for Desktop Publishers*, London: B.T. Batsford

Smith, A. (ed.) (1974) *The British Press since the War*, Newton Abbot: David & Charles

Steinberg, S.H. (1955) *Five Hundred Years of Printing*, Harmondsworth: Penguin

Tinker, M. (1963) *The Legibility of Print*, Ames: Iowa State University Press

Twyman, M. (1970) *Printing 1770–1970: An Illustrated History of Its Development and Uses in England*, London: Eyre & Spottiswoode

Weinmann, E. (1998) *QuarkXPress 4 for Windows*, Berkeley, CA: Peachpit Press

Williams, R. (1994) *The Non-designer's Design Book*, Berkeley, CA: Peachpit Press

Zelanski, P. and Fisher, M.P. (1989) *Colour for Designers and Artists*, London: Herbert Press

Index

3D picture 23

addresses 159
Adobe InDesign 22, 54, 79, 82
advertising features 156
Aitken, Jonathan 108
Apple Macs 22
Applegath, Augustus 26

Bartholomew, Harry G. 7
bastard setting 8, 19, 178
Berte, Francis 27
Birmingham Daily Gazette 28
Bizarre 155
blob pars 103
blurb 21, 55, 102, 160, 162, 178
Bourgeousi (type) 90
boxed text 68, 71, 76, 101, 102
brand 9, 10, 21, 22, 137, 139, 144
Brevier (type) 90
bribes and corruption 158
broadsheet 2, 7, 9, 15, 18, 21, 34, 36, 49, 70, 80, 92, 178
BskyB 157
bulleted text 77, 103, 104
Bullock, William 26
byline 52, 64, 74, 75, 77, 81, 104, 113, 114, 115, 144, 147, 162, 163, 164, 178

captions 52, 70, 77, 81, 101, 104, 116, 144, 146, 154, 165, 167
casting off 60, 178
catchline 178
chase 331, 178
children 27, 79, 146, 152, 155, 157, 159, 162, 169
Chinese 24
chinese 24
Christiansen, Arthur 7
Church Times 108
Church, William 27
cicero 88, 179
CMYK 42, 141, 179, 182
Coca Cola 144
Code of Practice 146
colour blind 85
colour 3, 4, 8, 9, 16, 20, 22, 31, 34, 37, 39, 41, 61, 86, 137–144; hue 41, 137 ; psychology of 139; saturation 41, 43, 138, 144; subtractive 42, 141; value 41, 42, 138
composition 27, 35
Computer Shopper 173
cones 137
Conservative Party 12, 152
copy approval 156
copy tasting 44, 51
Copyright Designs and Patents Act 147
copyright 4, 146–150
Cosmopolitan 9, 155
cover price 18
Cowper, Edward 26
cropping 125. 131
crossheads 77, 81, 105, 144, 173

Daily Courant 25
Daily Herald 7
Daily Mail 7, 9, 12, 22, 62, 127, 160–161

Daily Mirror 7, 171–172
Daily Sport 155
Daily Star 9
Daily Telegraph 21
decks 6, 71
defamation 158
diagonal 128
Diamond Sutra 24
didot 25, 88
direct entry 8
drop letters 77, 101

em-quad 90, 178
entry point 61, 64, 66, 70, 74, 101, 106, 113, 130, 162, 180
ethics 131, 145,
Evans, Harold 72, 120

facing spread 19
fair comment 158
families, of type 94
FHM 149
focal lengths 143
footers 22
Forme 25
Fourdrinier 25
framing 138
Fust, Johann 25

Gazette 168–9
Glamour 165–6
golden rules of design 77
graphics 1, 3, 10, 21, 33, 49, 133
gravure 34–35
grey scale 37–40
Guardian 3, 19, 104, 145
Guevara, che 148
Gutenberg, Johannes 24, 25
gutter 18

Hague, William 152
halftones 28, 35
hardcopy 8, 131
Hartlepool Mail 152
Hattersley, Robert 27
headers and footers 17, 22, 80, 167, 177
headers 22
headlines 154
Heath, Edward 152
Hill, Rowland 26
house style 20
Hutt, A. 70
hyphenation 81

imprint 22

jargon, journalistic 108
justification 27, 98, 152, 158, 181
juvenile labour 27

Kastenbein, Charles 27
Kennedy, John F. 148
kicker heading 71, 112, 173, 181
Koenig 26
Korea 25

Le Jeune, Fournier 25
leading 966.81, 90, 92, 167, 169, 175, 191
legibility 21
letterpress 28
library clippings 159
linotype 29, 27
lithography 28
Loaded 106, 155
logo 21
London Society of Compositors 27
long primer 90
Ludlow, Washington I. 28

margins 18
master pages 79
Meisenbach 28
Merganthaler, Ottmar 27
Minion (type) 90
Monotype 28
Murdoch, Rupert 21, 29, 157
muttons (ems) 90

National Graphical Association 8, 29, 118, 148,
National Union of Journalists 8, 30, 118, 145, 148
New Scientist 108
New York Tribune 27
Newspaper Society 156
Nonpareil (type) 90

Nottingham Evening Post 29
nut 90, 178

O'Connor, T.P. 70
Observer 108
Odhams-Herald 7
offset printing 28, 30
Old English 21
Oldie, the 9

pagination 17, 165
Pantone 42
Pearl (type) 90
perfector 32, 182
Philadelphia Ledger, The 26
photocomposition 28, 29, 33, 54, 58, 84, 98, 182
photogravure 28
Photoshop 131, 133
pica 90
pica-ems 90
pierce (pictures) 52, 77, 125, 171
pixelate 152, 153 178
plagiarism 149
platen machines 31, 32, 182
Portsmouth News 30
Poynter Institute 19, 47, 61, 71, 130, 143, 184
Press Complaints Commission (PCC) 107, 108, 145, 152, 155
Press Gazette 23, 108, 156
Private Eye 17, 157
privilege 158, 182
process colour 16, 42, 141, 182
puffs 21, 50, 182

Quark XPress 22, 54, 79
Question Time 129

Randall, Mike 7, 62
raster dot 36–41, 143, 182
red tops 41
Robert, Nicolas-Louis 25
rods 137
Romans 24
rotary press 26, 28, 32, 34
ruby 90

sans serif 90
scaling 3, 130
scanners 38–9, 179
Schoffer, Peter 25
secondary colours 42. 141
Sellers, Leslie 7
Senefelder, Aloys 28, 30
separation 42, 88, 140
Shah, Eddie 29
solus position 450, 183
special effects 133
Sport 155
spot colour 9, 16, 22, 31, 41, 183
spreads 49
standfirst 68, 77, 81, 104, 113, 114, 144, 154, 162, 183
Stanhope, Lord 25
Stead, W.T. 70
Steinberg 25
Stereotyping 25
story count 66, 70, 173
strapline 64, 72
streamers 72
Stuff 175
style sheets 3, 79, 81
sub-editors 8, 10, 35, 54, 86, 116, 145, 156
Sun 3, 7, 21, 106, 112, 145, 150, 157, 163–164
Sunday Pictorial 7

tabloid 7, 14, 18, 19, 21, 34, 41, 49, 53, 55, 61, 70, 80, 92, 100, 121,
target audience i, 10, 12, 13, 106, 108, 169
taste and decency 155
template 3, 10, 22, 52, 61, 79
Thatcher, Margaret 152
Time Out 148, 154
Times 26, 157
titlepiece 21
Trades Union Congress 7
Trajan's column 24

Uher, Edward 28
Uhertype 28
unite 27
United States 144

vertical scoring 101, 103
Vietnam 155

Wang Chieh 24
web feed 28, 35
Weston, Simon 120
white space 1, 78, 92, 100, 101, 104, 122, 173, 175, 177
Wing, William 27
Wolverhampton Express & Star 30
Woman and Home 169

xerography 28
X-Factor 107
x-height 87, 92, 100

Yellow Pages 150

zur Laden, Johann Gensfliesch (Gutenberg) 24